How Nonprofits Work

How Nonprofits Work

Case Studies in Nonprofit Organizations

Grace Budrys

ROWMAN & LITTLEFIELD PUBLISHERS, INC.
Lanham • Boulder • New York • Toronto • Plymouth, UK

Published by Rowman & Littlefield Publishers, Inc.
A wholly owned subsidiary of The Rowman & Littlefield Publishing Group, Inc.
4501 Forbes Boulevard, Suite 200, Lanham, Maryland 20706
www.rowman.com

10 Thornbury Road, Plymouth PL6 7PP, United Kingdom

Copyright © 2013 by Rowman & Littlefield Publishers, Inc.

British Library Cataloguing in Publication Information Available

Library of Congress Cataloging-in-Publication Data

Budrys, Grace, 1943-.
How nonprofits work : case studies in nonprofit organizations / Grace Budrys.
p. cm.
Includes bibliographical references and index.
ISBN 978-1-4422-2105-5 (cloth : alk. paper) -- ISBN 978-1-4422-2106-2 (electronic)
1. Charities, Medical--Case studies. 2. Voluntary health agencies--Case studies. 3. Nonprofit organizations--Case studies. I. Title.
HV687.B795 2013
362.1--dc23
2012040038

♾️ The paper used in this publication meets the minimum requirements of American National Standard for Information Sciences Permanence of Paper for Printed Library Materials, ANSI/NISO Z39.48-1992.

Printed in the United States of America

Contents

Acknowledgments

I am indebted to many more people for help in completing this book than was the case with previous books. In the past I relied on data, scholarly interpretation, and commentary that was publicly available. In collecting material for this book, I spent a lot of time talking to people who are engaged in carrying out the tasks that their organizations strive to accomplish. Without the background and reflections on current issues my informants were willing to share with me, the stories would have been very pale imitations of the living and vibrant organizations you will be encountering. I am truly grateful to everyone who agreed to describe the challenges they face and the accomplishments in which they take pride.

Then there are all the others who have been willing to listen to me as I was gathering information and trying out my interpretations. Some of my colleagues were not only willing to listen but were willing to read and comment on what I was writing. I am especially indebted to Woods Bowman, Michael Bennett, and Carl Milofsky for giving me their reactions to early drafts. That proved to be enormously helpful. Howard Rosing introduced me to a variety of organizations that work with nonprofits that were new to me for which I am very grateful. I thank Susan Sanders for her encouragement over many years when I was struggling to determine the shape this discussion would take. I am very glad to have had a chance to hear Mayer Zald's comments on what I was saying about the Chicago YMCA as well as the other organizations presented in the book. I discussed what I was working on with many more people whose ideas I did not immediately integrate into my thinking. When I did incorporate the ideas, I was no longer attributing them to the persons who suggested them. In other words, this book is the product of lots of ideas coming from lots of sources. I regret that I am not able to give due credit to everyone whom I should credit.

Finally, as always, the person who heard most about the organizations I was interested in is my husband, Dan Lortie. He not only listened, he was willing to discuss the theoretical and practical issues that studying nonprofit organizations brought up. I thought this made for some lively conversations, but I am clearly biased on this point.

Chapter One

Introduction

This book is about nonprofit, charitable organizations. You may have noticed that the media have been devoting more time to stories about nonprofit organizations, probably because these organizations have been growing in size and scope—aiding more people, offering a greater range of services, and reporting steadily rising budgets. That is the big story. However, it is difficult to make that kind of information captivating. Therefore, more often than not, media stories feature a person who is being helped by a nonprofit organization to deal with some heartbreaking problem. This is followed by interviews with one or two organizational representatives who talk about what their organizations are doing to assist people who have similar problems. The upshot is that the public may well remember the sad story told by a particular individual, but it is largely unaware of the extent to which the nonprofit sector has expanded in recent years, the numbers of people who seek its services, or the amount of money nonprofit organizations are collecting to support the programs they have established.

Although the nonprofit sector may be receiving more attention these days because the role it plays in our society has been expanding, it would be a mistake to interpret the attention as total approval. Closer examination indicates some observers are very pleased to see the expansion and others are quite unhappy about it. Making things more complicated, those who are unified in their opposition to the role this sector is playing disagree with each other—one faction argues we would be better off if the government assumed greater responsibility for the services nonprofits provide; the other faction argues that for-profit companies should be awarded contracts to carry out those tasks because they would do it far more effectively.

It would be easy to conclude that arguments favoring one alternative or the other are more firmly grounded in fixed attitudes and ideological preferences than much real evidence. But it might also be interesting to see if evidence supports either side of these diametrically opposed positions. We will do that in the following chapter.

My primary objective in writing this book is to offer a more complete picture of the work that a selected number of nonprofit organizations are doing. I aim to present the stories they tell about their origins and growth, the objectives they set for themselves, and the means they use to achieve those objectives. Taking a closer look at what they do and how they do it should provide us with enough information to reflect on whether they are doing a good job or whether we should be paying more attention to the critics' assessments.

HOW THIS RESEARCH PROJECT EVOLVED

We will be treating each organization as the subject of a case analysis. Let me begin by explaining why I chose this approach and say a little more on how the project evolved. The focus of my research has been on health organizations and occupations. Accordingly, I started out with the intention of looking at the workings of nonprofit organizations devoted to health problems. I specifically intended to look into the workings of organizations not involved in the delivery of acute care, meaning that I would not be including acute-care organizations such as hospitals and medical practice groups in the study. Hospitals and medical practice groups provide mainstream medical care and are governed by health-care professionals. Although the medical establishment and policy analysts may be energetically debating the value of indicators of the effectiveness, cost, and quality of those services, the public is generally not welcome to enter into the fray. Furthermore, hospitals and medical practices rely on insurance, both private and government, to provide them with a steady stream of funding; whether or not it is a sufficient stream is part of the debate, but they certainly are receiving a continuous stream of funding through government programs, which nonprofit, charitable organizations generally do not count on. My plan was to take a closer look at organizations that focus on health needs other than those being addressed by medical providers in well-established, respected facilities. Mostly I was interested in investigating how organizations that are not in the business of delivering mainstream medical care function. I wanted to know how they decide which services to provide and how they go about getting the money to provide them. I knew that nonprofit organizations expend a great deal of effort raising money. I wanted to understand what proportion of their funding was coming from public donations and where they obtain the rest of their money.

Once I began looking more closely at these organizations, it did not take long to discover what nonprofit, voluntary organizations devoted to health issues do that is so different from what mainstream medical facilities do— and why what they do is important to the people they serve. It became clear to me that such organizations respond to the needs that people bring to their doors. After concentrating for many years on mainstream health-care delivery organizations, I have to admit I had to readjust my understanding about what nonprofit health-oriented organizations do. I was really not prepared to find that they consider the wishes of the clients to be so central to the activities they pursue and the services they offer. I was far more accustomed to a system in which the professionals assess what services and treatments those who come to their doors need and what services they will receive. It was eye opening to see the functions that nonprofit, charitable organizations perform from a new and better-informed perspective.

In short, I discovered that the nonprofit organizations I was studying have far broader agendas than I had initially imagined. I found that helping people to deal with the one health issue with which they typically identify (e.g., lung disease, vision problems, physical disabilities) is only the beginning. As my research progressed, I found myself moving along a continuum from organizations that deal with specific health problems, to organizations that deal with other basic human needs—food and housing—and even more basic than that, the extent to which all of these organizations focus on people's need to be as self-sufficient as possible. Thus, the selection of organizations spans a far broader range of issues than I had originally planned. Anyone who has been involved in social science research will recognize what happened. The more I learned about my topic, the more I realized my assumptions had to be adjusted to the reality I was encountering. I think the result is a much improved outcome.

RESEARCH METHODS AND THE CASE STUDY APPROACH

A little more background on how I got to the organizations I studied is in order. Almost all of the organizations that we examine in detail are located in Chicago. Similar organizations operate in other cities. Because no nonprofit organization is exactly like any other, even apart from its location, we can treat the organizations discussed here as a sample, obviously a nonrandom sample, of all such organizations across the country. In other words, the organizations we encounter are unique and, at the same time, exhibit characteristics many other nonprofit organizations share. My aim is to strike a balance between discovering what is distinctive about each of the organizations and identifying what we can learn about the role organizations such as these play in society as a whole.

The analysis of each organization I studied began with a phone call. I simply called to explain what I was doing and asked for help in carrying out my project. I should note that a few of the organizations I contacted refused to participate. As far as I could tell, the individuals I spoke with had a lot to do with that decision. They were not necessarily reflecting official organizational policy. In one instance, my phone call put me into contact with the chief financial officer of the organization first, before I had the opportunity to talk with the staff member in charge of organizational programming. The financial officer was very willing to provide me with volumes of budgetary information, took the time to answer all my questions on revenue, expenditures, the reliability of funding sources, and so on. When I contacted a person in charge of programming in the same organization, she refused to talk with me, explaining that she "had been around the block" and knew what could happen. She maintained this position even after I explained that I already had what was probably the most sensitive information on the organization.

Other organizational representatives said they would participate if I would show them what I wrote about their respective organizations before making the information public. I agreed, saying I wanted to make sure I got the information right. In other cases, organizational representatives invited me in, allowed me to interview anyone and everyone I wanted to contact, loaded me down with documents, and never asked to see what I wrote. I could see no pattern and was not really interested in speculating about what explained these differences, as people seemed to be equally cooperative once I got started.

The research methods I employed in gathering the material to develop the organizational case studies include both personal interviews and review of a variety of public and private documents and written materials. The sources I rely on include internal correspondence, annual reports, organizational websites, newspaper articles, and evaluations presented by oversight organizations. I conducted extensive interviews with a range of organizational representatives in each organization. I used the most recent annual reports that organizations have made publicly available. Some of the reports are current; others go back to 2005. (I should note that some organizations say producing expensive annual reports is not how they want to spend scarce funds in the current environment. They must prepare reports to meet government reporting expectations, but they are under no obligation to produce expensive annual reports for the public.)

Additionally, I would like to make the point that these organizations are living entities, meaning that the case studies are capturing a static picture of something that is always changing. The case studies are much like snapshots of people: the organizations will be recognizable in years to come, but they will not look exactly as they do at this moment—or the moment described in their annual reports from year to year.

I present the pictures of the organizations from the perspectives of organizational participants: in some cases members of the board of directors; more often executive directors; and persons with a wide range of administrative responsibilities, such as finance, government relations, program evaluation, and so on. It is their assessments of the organizational goals, successes, and problems that I am reporting. I made no effort to critique those operations, because I am not sure what the basis would be for doing so. As I told the people I interviewed, my approach is academic and analytical, not that of an investigative reporter.

You will generally not find the names of the people I interviewed in gathering the data, only their titles. I do include the names of founders in some instances, because the founders and other early leaders have not been in those positions for some time. I have intentionally avoided using names of persons who are currently involved in order to keep the focus on the organizations themselves rather than particular individuals affiliated with the organizations.

As you will see, nonprofit, charitable organizations engage in a wide variety of activities and interactions in carrying out their work. Recognizing and discussing the variation in organizational operations is important. However, I wish to emphasize that their respective approaches are not necessarily superior or inferior to one another. They are generally merely different. How organizational leaders choose to raise money, for example, varies tremendously. Over the years, each organization has developed methods that work best for it. My purpose was to consider the relationship between organizational operations and the wide range of fund-raising approaches that exist. I make no attempt to evaluate the efficacy of those approaches. That would be a very different research objective than the one I have in mind.

As we will see, each of the organizations we will get to know grew out of the perception on the part of a small number of people that there was a problem they decided to address. What happened next is at the heart of each of their stories. We will examine organizational origins and how they evolved once they were created. We will learn about their goals, their sources of support, and the challenges they have faced.

What becomes a distinctive feature in a number of instances has to do with the particular challenge an organization confronts and how it deals with that challenge. For example, dealing with technological advances related to the services the organization provides; incorporating other nonprofit organizations interested in collaborating; arranging to accept gifts in kind (i.e., gifts other than money). In the chapters to follow, we will document what some of the organizations did in response to these situations, and get back to the steps they took in the conclusion as well. I should add that facing challenges is something that for-profit and government organizations also must do. And each organization, regardless of whether it is nonprofit, for profit, or government, must deal with the challenge in light of a unique set of socioeconomic conditions in time and place. In other words, organizations cannot turn to a set of guidelines to help them. They must identify and respond to all the conditions that play a role in how their organizations operate and the full range of interpretations of those conditions on the part of interested stakeholders.

Before concluding the section on my approach to this research, I want to say something more about what motivated me to carry out this project. As I stated at the beginning of this discussion, I firmly believe people who volunteer their time to work with nonprofit organizations, whether by choice or to fulfill educational requirements (e.g., internships, service-learning, etc.), need to know more about the operations of those organizations. It is not enough, in my opinion, to become engaged in the work of a voluntary, nonprofit organization because one feels sympathetic about the people who have the kinds of problems the organization aims to address. There is nothing wrong with that motivation as a start. However, I am convinced that anyone who becomes involved with nonprofit, voluntary organizations that deal in human services should have a fundamental understanding of such things as where the money comes from that the organization uses to carry out its work. How the organization goes about the process of raising the money, even where the organization is known for a very visible fund-raising event, is worth considering, because there are always additional sources. How much money the organization raises and what it costs to raise that money are valuable pieces of information. How that money is allocated is as important as the question of how the organization knows whether it is doing a good job of what it says it aims to do. Those are the kinds of issues we will be exploring in some detail in the following chapters.

THE ORGANIZATION OF THE MATERIAL

The next chapter of the book, chapter 2, focuses on the role that nonprofit organizations play in society. It tackles the question of how organizations in this sector differ from organizations in either the for-profit or the government sector. Additionally, it considers the extent to which this sector has been expanding in recent years, and why.

The third chapter presents a more detailed description of the nonprofit sector as a whole—the amount of money involved, the number of people associated with it, and the kinds of organizations that have sprung up to represent the interests of the nonprofit sector.

Chapter 4 offers a brief exposition of nonprofit organizational theory. It identifies the questions scholars have addressed regarding the role this sector plays in our society and outlines their assessments of the pros and cons of society's reliance on nonprofit organizations. Although I incorporate the insights offered by scholars from a number of different disciplines, my background and training are in sociology. That means I think like a sociologist, and the presentation of the material you will read reflects that. I hope you find the perspective from which I see the world as illuminating as I do as we examine how these organizations operate.

Chapter 5 introduces the case analysis method. In chapter 6 we review the findings presented in two classic studies carried out decades ago using the case analysis framework. Case analyses of one or more organizations per chapter appear in chapters 7 through 13. The final chapter takes up the question of what we have learned in examining how this wide range of nonprofit, charitable organizations operates both individually and collectively.

Chapter Two

What Makes Nonprofit Organizations Special?

This chapter takes up several questions. First, what is the role of nonprofit organizations in our society? Or, more to the point, how is that role viewed by scholars and members of the public? Second, going back to the critique of nonprofit organizational activities mentioned in the previous chapter, we examine how organizations across the for-profit, government, and nonprofit sectors differ from one another. Third, we examine the extent to which the role nonprofit organizations play in our society has expanded in recent years, and why. Obviously, there is a lot to ponder here.

THE ROLE OF NONPROFIT-SECTOR ORGANIZATIONS IN SOCIETY

Assuming that some people do take seriously arguments regarding the role nonprofit organizations play in our society—with some saying they are doing an outstanding job and not getting nearly enough support, others saying they are getting far too much support—what explains that? What would cause people to develop strong feelings about society's increasing reliance on non-profit organizations? The answer has something to do with the fact that the socioeconomic and political divide has been expanding in this country and people are becoming louder in expressing their reactions to that reality.

As we have already noted, at one end of the ideological divide are those who take the position that relying on the nonprofit sector is a mistake be-cause the corporate sector is far more capable of getting the job done, what-ever the job may be. At the other end are those who argue that government is the only entity that can address social needs that are broad and clearly unlikely to produce a profit. They, too, think society is going in the wrong direction. This faction is quick to point out that the business sector is neither interested in, nor capable of, handling the tasks nonprofits are taking on. The proponents of government intervention go on to say that giving the responsibility to government is the only way to ensure that whatever services we have in mind will be delivered equitably, rather than distributed on the basis of a person's ability to pay, or mere chance depending on where a person lives. Those who favor corporate-sector solutions are opposed to increasing government intervention in any form because, they say, government rules are so stultifying. This does not mean that those who embrace conservative ideological beliefs see no role for nonprofit organizations. They might see value in the role nonprofit organizations play but only under restricted conditions.

Peter Frumkin's assessment of the beliefs held by members of each of these factions goes a long way in explaining what makes them feel so strongly (2002). Finding why those who espouse liberal political views might favor nonprofit organizational activity is likely to be less surprising than finding why those who hold conservative political views do so. According to Frumkin, liberals value the following three features: One, nonprofit organizations provide an ideal setting for supporters of progressive policies to come together to locate and advance their progressive agenda. Two, they serve as untainted partners with government and are therefore well positioned to deliver services to the most disadvantaged populations, giving human services initiatives "a more diverse, pluralistic face." Three, liberals appreciate the ability of nonprofits to mobilize groups who will work to exert pressure for social change and justice.

By contrast, the three features that conservatives find attractive about nonprofits, according to Frumkin, speak to a very different set of prospects: One, nonprofits provide an avenue for transferring functions that have been performed by government over the past half century away from government through "devolution" and "privatization," objectives that are central to the conservative agenda. Two, nonprofits can, and often do, bring a moral and spiritual component to human services that public entitlement, as practiced by government agencies, cannot do. Three, nonprofits offer an avenue for innovation grounded in self-help and local solutions, that is, the potential to take human services programs out of the hands of bureaucrats in Washington and give legitimacy to approaches that allow for regional cultural values.

Whether nonprofit organizations deserve social support tends to revolve around particular functions or activities a particular nonprofit organization engages in rather than debate about the sector as a whole. You don't hear too many people complaining about organizations that focus on cultural events and causes that the corporate sector is pleased to support. Only the nonprofit, charitable organizations that are engaged in providing services that champions of the organizations in the other two sectors have some interest in providing that risk being targeted for criticism.

ARE FOR-PROFIT ORGANIZATIONS REALLY MORE EFFICIENT?

So how much evidence is there to indicate that nonprofit, charitable—or, for that matter, public-sector, government organizations—are less efficient than for-profit organizations? One way to answer this question is to compare the performance of for-profit organizations to that of organizations in the other two sectors that do approximately the same kind of work. Only a few arenas have a sufficient number of organizations to provide much comparison. Let's focus on the evidence on the performance of schools, hospitals, and prisons.

A growing body of research is comparing the success of charter schools, some of which are nonprofit and others are for profit, to the success of public schools (Schemo 2006). Diane Ravitch, who makes clear that she was aligned with conservatives for most of her career, has suddenly determined that the conservatives are wrong in their approach to evaluating school success. She offers an extensive review of what we have learned so far about both private and public schools, and charter schools in particular (2010). One of her basic observations is that private schools, either for profit or nonprofit, can reject or dismiss students; public schools cannot. That, she says, explains much of the reason that some, certainly not all, private schools are more likely to end up with higher performance scores in math and reading. She concludes that nonprofit schools are generally more effective, but that family and neighborhood are the most important variables in determining success, far more important than whether a for-profit or nonprofit entity is operating the school.

A far more damning assessment comes from The Educational Trust, a nonprofit organization that focuses on education at all levels. It summed up its conclusions on the performance of for-profit colleges in a statement introducing findings published in an extensive research report on its web page as follows: ". . . the most vulnerable Americans are being targeted by yet another set of corporations peddling access to the American dream but delivering little more than crippling debt" (Lynch, Engle, and Cruz 2010). In analyzing the performance of for-profit colleges over the 1999 to 2009 decade, the report states that enrollment increased at a very high rate, 236 percent. The report also states that students in such colleges were far more likely to apply for government loans, which, in turn, provided a steady income stream to the for-profit colleges. The University of Phoenix, which is singled out for special condemnation, received "over one billion dollars in Pell Grant funding alone in 2009–2010." At the same time, the report notes that the University of Phoenix not only is the largest for-profit college enterprise but that it has the lowest six-year graduation rate at 9 percent of all for-profit colleges. In support of its initial assessment that for-profit colleges do not deliver what they promise, the report indicates the six-year graduation rate at four-year institutions is 22 percent at for-profit colleges, 55 percent at public colleges, and 65 percent at nonprofit colleges.

Turning to the performance of nonprofit versus for-profit hospitals and nursing homes, we find one of the most convincing accounts in a book by Maggie Mahar in a chapter titled "For-Profit Hospitals: A Flaw in the Business Model?" (2006). The chapter presents detailed case studies of the performance of three for-profit hospital organizations. She tracks the rise and fall of the Hospital Corporation of America (HCA), National Medical Enterprises (which became Tenet), and HealthSouth. The central problem these organizations face has to do with investors' expectations of ever-increasing profit. In the initial stages of development the hospital organizations were able to achieve savings by increasing efficiency; they followed that with growth—buying out competitors; but once they got to that stage, few other options for increasing profit were available except fraud. Therein lies the flaw in the business model according to Mahar—hospital organizations have no legitimate way to increase profit from year to year. That makes it hard to continue to be perceived to be an attractive investment opportunity—without relying on increased fraud.

In their review of literature on the difference between nonprofit and for-profit hospitals and nursing homes, Mark Schlesinger and Bradford Gray find that for-profit hospitals mark up prices more aggressively and employ various methods to reduce costs that invariably have implications for quality (e.g., lower patient-staff ratio [2006]). Furthermore, they find that the public sees nonprofit hospitals as more trustworthy, less likely to make misleading claims, and more willing to treat vulnerable patients. They also determined that nonprofit hospitals are slower to react to change, expanding capacity less quickly when demand rises and dropping services or withdrawing from markets less frequently when profitability declines. The trade-off, they say, is that this may make them less efficient, but that it makes them more effective. They also note that nonprofits are the incubators of innovation (e.g., creating prepaid care systems and hospices). The authors conclude that the comparison "predominantly favors nonprofits."

Some interest has also been shown in the differences between the operations of for-profit and government-run prisons (the following is based on Center for Policy Alternatives 2005; Finn 1998). The number of privately operated prisons is growing because politicians in many states are convinced they cost less to operate. Not everyone agrees. The U.S. Bureau of Justice Assistance argues they may actually be more expensive, because they refuse to accept prisoners who are more expensive to house: namely, violent offenders. That requires government-run prisons to accept a disproportionate share of prisoners whose care requires more resources. Private prisons keep their cost down by offering few benefits and less training to their staff, which is thought to explain why they are more likely to be found beating and gassing inmates. As disturbing as that may be, some critics have charged that the owners of privately run prisons are responding to the incentive of increased profit—trying to drum up more business by lobbying for stiffer sentences, including "three-strikes" terms, sentencing juveniles as adults, and mandatory minimum sentences to ensure a steady supply of inmates.

So what does this brief review tell us? To start with, we find ourselves shifting from a discussion about efficiency to a discussion about performance. That is because it is not possible to measure efficiency if one cannot rely on the instruments employed to conduct a cost/benefit analysis, which is how the efficiency of for-profit organizations is calculated. It quickly becomes obvious that cost is relatively easy to measure. It is, however, very difficult to measure benefit when we are not using profit as the indicator.

Using the conventional definitions of efficiency means we must calculate a number of different kinds of costs (i.e., time, energy, and money required to produce a product or service). Under normal circumstances, for-profit organizations are ready and willing to invest a great deal of time, money, and energy to create markets for products that will produce a profit. Efforts to ensure the success of a product are launched well before it is available (e.g., testing the market effects of several kinds of packaging or symbols that might be used in the marketing campaign). In fact, the advertising campaign may be launched well before the product is released in an effort to build up demand before there is a supply. The objective is to entice as many people as possible to be ready to buy the product when it hits the market. Accordingly, a corporation is considered efficient if the profits produced through this process exceed the costs and inefficient if costs exceed profits. It may even be considered inefficient in cases where the profits are thought to be smaller than investors expect. As we will see, when we look more closely at the various organizations on which the case studies in this volume are based, determining whether the organizations are attaining the goals they have set for themselves poses a challenging question to which those involved devote considerable attention.

STRENGTHS AND WEAKNESSES OF ORGANIZATIONS IN EACH OF THE THREE SECTORS

Although society seems committed to criticizing the workings of each of the three sectors and possibly experimenting with shifting more attention to one approach or the other from time to time, the shifts do not actually cause the sectors to expand or contract to a very great extent or for more than a decade or two. (There have been exceptions; the two twentieth-century world wars, for example, greatly increased the role of government.) In other words, the three sectors have generally operated side by side in this country and will undoubtedly continue to do so. In order to understand what accounts for this arrangement, we are committed to striving for a more complete understanding of what the organizations in each sector do that those in the other sectors do not do, and more importantly, do not do as well. Burton Weisbrod provides us with a fairly comprehensive answer (1988). Indeed, he begins his assessment by telling us society could not operate without arriving at a functional balance across the three sectors because the organizations in each sector have a different set of strengths and weaknesses. His assessment of the strengths and weaknesses of organizations in each sector are as follows.

The for-profit sector

The main strength of the for-profit sector is its ability to meet consumer demand. It is important to remember, however, that the private sector does not respond to society's wants and needs unless they are accompanied by willingness to pay for the goods and services involved. The greatest strength of the for-profit sector lies in the efficiency with which it responds to the profit incentive that comes along with consumer demand. The profit incentive is also responsible for this sector's greatest limitations. For a start, it is not in the interest of the for-profit sector to compensate for the inequality of information available to consumers. Because producers invariably know more than consumers, producers can reduce the quality of products in ways that consumers find difficult to detect. The profit incentive in combination with the inequality of information may lead to the temptation to take further advantage of consumers—through false advertising, corruption, "cream skimming," environment pollution, and so on. In short, the excessive pursuit of individual self-interest leads to adverse effects on others, whether individuals or society at large.

The fact that the success of the proprietary sector is grounded in self-interest explains why it does not do as well in responding to consumer demand for collective goods and services. The sector is poorly equipped to address demand for basic research in any sphere, environmental protection, national defense, equitable distribution of a wide range of socially beneficial services including health and education. In fact, the shortcomings of the private sector can manifest themselves along one of the three dimensions—the choice of goods and services, the production process, and distribution arrangements.

Here is where the potential of socially beneficial overlap across the three institutional sectors comes in—the government can intervene to compensate for these flaws. For example, in the case of a corporation that creates environmental pollution, the government can set standards restricting the level of environmental pollution or penalize organizations by taxing them for it; it can offer to subsidize manufacturers in return for their commitment to spend more on research and/or investment in pollution-control equipment; it can purchase the goods that are the source of pollution, allowing the corporation to shift its production to nonpolluting products. Of course, the government can only succeed in reducing environmental pollution to the extent that it can monitor it. When monitoring is too cumbersome, too costly, or too imprecise, then society must try to develop other mechanisms to achieve desired results. Not so easy.

One mechanism that has been introduced in recent years and seems to be working fairly well is an individually grounded financial incentive. The introduction of "whistle-blower" monetary rewards has proven to be an effective mechanism for attaining information about deceptive and illegal corporate practices that would otherwise be difficult to obtain. This is not to say that whistle-blowers are only, or even primarily, motivated by the financial reward. Indeed, we don't know very much about the individuals who take this route—what motivates them or how they fare after they make their revelations. Although legislation exists aimed at preventing whistle-blowers from being sued, it is not difficult to appreciate the fact that making public the misdeeds of one's employer and fellow workers is not a choice most people make lightly.

The public sector

Turning to the advantages and disadvantages associated with the public sector (i.e., government), we find its basic differentiating characteristic and strength is its ability to provide goods and services to consumers who may not have the resources to pay for them.

Government agencies are invariably established with the expectation that they will provide equal access for all persons who qualify for the benefits offered by the program the agency operates—regardless of ability to pay. The criteria for eligibility are determined through legislative mechanisms that presumably capture societal preferences. In other words, the programs are constituted by politicians, who represent the public will—at least the will of that portion of the population that voted for the party with the majority of seats in Congress. Their charge is to come to consensus on program design and funding. They decide how extensive or restrictive social programs will be. The greater the shift in prevailing political arrangements, the greater the probability a significant degree of consensus will be hard to achieve.

It is also important to note that the social values, preferences, and ideals regarding the need for all the programs our political representatives turn into law are not fixed. This is a major weakness of government programs. There is no assurance that programs will continue to receive the same amount of government support and funding—they may be cut, expanded, or reorganized to reflect shifts in social attitudes and political arrangements. The state of the economy may influence the amount of money society is willing to allocate to various programs. New priorities may come into existence in response to well-organized campaigns by particular groups of activists. The needs of those who were served by existing programs may simply be swept aside in the competition for funds. However, it is also possible that some members of society will turn their attention to the need for goods and services that government agencies are suddenly not providing and have never been provided by for-profit sector organizations. These parties may decide to take steps to compensate for what they see as a sudden abandonment on the part of the government of people with pressing needs. That is where nonprofit sector organizations come into play.

The nonprofit sector

As is true of both for-profit and government organizations, the strength of nonprofit organizations is their commitment to meeting the demands of interested parties. In this case, however, the demands are actually appeals because the so-called demands are likely coming from persons who are able to voice their demands but not able to pay for or otherwise obtain the goods and services they require. It is also true that the people who are most effective in articulating those demands and who play an important role in establishing the organization are very likely not the same people who benefit from the services the organization provides.

The commonly recognized weakness of nonprofit organizations is that they are not constituted to provide the required and/or desired goods and services for all those who might benefit. There are limitations on the number of clients they are able to serve. Therefore, their efforts in the end look like and perform like a patchwork of organizations that vary in how successful they are in addressing the needs of clients from one geographic area to another.

Many claims are made regarding the performance of nonprofit organizations, as is true of organizations in the other two sectors. The attributions are often highly laudatory. For example, nonprofits are generally described as altruistic, therefore trusted to provide particular kinds of services that for-profits cannot be trusted to deliver. And, of course, at the other end of the spectrum, critics claim that nonprofits have no incentive to perform in an efficient manner, so they cannot be anything other than inefficient and ineffective. If nothing else, the claims nonprofits make regarding their accomplishments identify the issues that energize the opposition in building its counterargument.

A claim that the nonprofit sector could make but is not making deserves attention. According to a series of bulletins issued by the Center for Civil Society Studies, the nonprofit sector has continued to add jobs over the past few years (i.e., during the recession), while the for-profit and government sectors were eliminating jobs. Curiously, representatives of the nonprofit sector, who could legitimately boast about this accomplishment, have not chosen to do so.

GOODS VERSUS SERVICES

For a variety of reasons, it is generally difficult to sort out the accuracy of the claims by any one of the three sectors. In fact, we are far better equipped to evaluate the performance of organizations that provide a product, as opposed to a service. This is especially true in the case of products that a significant number of people are interested in purchasing, most notably those that exhibit clearly identifiable improvements in quality accompanied by a steady reduction—at least no great increase—in price and bring a significant profit in doing so.

The market for handheld calculators serves as an excellent illustration. Cell phones are apparently following this pattern as well. Calculators became more reliable, smaller, and cheaper over a relatively short period of time. Once one could see which calculators were the most dependable and attractive, it was easy to determine which companies would be showing a steady increase in profit—a clear indicator of organizational success. The market—the meeting place of buyers and sellers—was clearly able to provide a highly efficient mechanism to accomplish this.

The improvements in handheld calculators offers yet another lesson worth attending to. That is how two of the three sectors interacted to benefit both. The basic research on miniaturization of components used in handheld calculators was done, not by the companies that manufactured them, but by the government in support of missile programs. The results of the research became a public good the corporate sector could employ to improve the quality of the products it produces. As we will see in the chapters to follow, this development is not unique. The government and nonprofit sector organizations can be seen, on occasion, to be actively and, according to many, successfully working out cooperative arrangements on a number of fronts.

Getting back to evaluating products as opposed to services, without putting too fine a point on it, products are typically easier than services to see, compare, and evaluate. Nonprofit organizations are more likely to be dealing in services than in producing tangible goods (i.e., products of some kind). We will return to the issue of evaluating programs that provide services because there is obviously much more that can be said about program evaluation.

ORGANIZATIONAL SIZE MATTERS

Across the three sectors, one characteristic of organizations that does not seem to receive as much attention as it deserves is organizational size. Undoubtedly that is because size is such an obvious characteristic that it does not seem to require further elaboration. The reason I bring it up at this point is my impression that small businesses, small nonprofits, and local government entities have more in common with each other than they have with big, successful organizations in each of their respective sectors.

Some small community organizations are clearly successful whereas others continue to operate even though they are struggling. The parallel is that some small businesses are profitable and others struggle. Some small government units are well run and effective, others are not. In short, making blanket statements about all organizations in any one sector is likely to lead to a long list of examples that contradict both positive and negative assessments. Yes, there are examples of government agencies that are inefficient, just as there are examples of for-profit companies that are so inefficient that they must appeal to the government to give them special tax considerations, even bail them out. It is worth noting that nonprofit organizations that have financial troubles are not candidates for government bailouts. If we can conclude little else, we can point to clear examples of organizational inefficiency and ineffectiveness in each of the sectors.

It is true that some observers have a far more blunt interpretation of the differences between and among the organizations in the three sectors. They say society has accepted the idea that the private sector is more efficient, but that it is less trustworthy; that the nonprofit is less efficient but more trustworthy; and finally, that society is willing to accept the downside in these trade-offs rather than placing its trust in the government.

In actuality, as we have been arguing, determining which sector is most efficient is not easy to do and is, therefore, not a question many researchers have addressed very systematically. We can also see that cooperation across sectors can produce very satisfying results, but it does not necessarily happen with regularity. Commenting on how to achieve greater cooperation across sectors is, however, not the purpose of this book. The main outcome I hope to attain, in light of the comparisons across the three sectors, is a better understanding of how to interpret how well nonprofit organizations are doing when they work toward the objectives they set forth for themselves.

NONPROFIT-SECTOR EXPANSION IN RECENT YEARS

As we have already stated, nonprofit organizations have been growing over the past few years. They report seeing more people come to their doors seeking assistance. Their budgets have been growing as well but not always as consistently. One big factor that explains why nonprofit organizations have been doing more is that the need for the services they provide increased once the effects of the economic downturn that started at the end of 2007 started to register. If one realizes that this is the most severe recession the country has experienced since the Great Depression of the 1930s, it is easier to understand why the effects of the downturn have become so troubling and continually turn up as material for news stories. It also explains why some people are calling what we have been experiencing the Great Recession. Let us take a closer look at how the Great Recession is affecting the performance of nonprofit organizations.

While the recession is causing a dramatic rise in the number of people who need the kinds of help nonprofit organizations provide, it is also responsible for two other trends that make it more difficult for nonprofits to provide the services they are committed to providing. First, it is causing those who usually support the efforts of nonprofits to cut back on how much money they contribute to charitable causes; and, two, it is causing local and state government agencies to cut back on the services they provide because persons who have lost their jobs during the recession are not contributing as much to the tax coffers, which means that some people must look for alternative sources for the services they require. We will look at the data on these trends shortly.

Nonprofit organizations are reporting that the number of people seeking their assistance has been growing. Government statistics indicate that the number of people living in poverty increased by 27 percent since the Great Recession began, and that number continues to increase even after the official end of the recession. In 2006, the year before it began, 36.5 million Americans were poor; as of 2010, 46.2 million Americans had fallen into poverty according to government statistics (Seefeldt et al. 2012). The poverty cutoff in 2012 for a single individual is $11,170; for a family of four, $22,113.

It is also worth noting that while some people were becoming poorer, others were steadily becoming richer; and, that the rate at which this was happening has been accelerating. Indeed, the difference between the income of the poor and the income of the rich has not been this wide since 1929 (i.e., since the Great Depression [Picketty and Saez 2010]). Robert Reich, former U.S. secretary of labor and currently professor of public policy at the University of California, gives us a sense of how the variation in the income of the rich and poor has changed over the past half century (2010). He tells us that corporate executives took home about twenty-five to thirty times the pay of the average worker during the 1950s and 1960s. By 1980, the executives were taking home about forty times the average worker's wages; by 2007, just as the Great Recession was beginning, they were taking home about 350 times what the average worker was earning.

If the economists are right and the recession ended in June 2009, why are all the indicators telling us the economy has not recovered? The fact of the matter is that it takes quite a while to recover fully from a recession, especially one as severe as the one we have just experienced. To get some insight on how long it takes, let's look at how long it took for the economy to recover from the Great Depression. There was little evidence of recovery over the entire decade of the 1930s. Only entry into World War II assured the country of recovery. It was like this: Wartime production meant that consumer goods were not being manufactured. The war also meant that young people were waiting to get married and start families. Once the war ended, Americans were eager to indulge their pent-up demand for goods. They bought new houses and everything required to make them livable. That was happening because they were now getting married and having babies, producing the baby boom generation. The arrival of so many babies at the same time is credited with creating a huge new market—for baby products at first. But baby boomers went on to generate demand for all the other things that people want and need as they go through each stage of life. Actually, they had a major impact on all the social institutions they encountered along the way—schools, the entertainment industry, the automobile industry, and so on. The fact that the baby boomers are reaching retirement age is a current cause for concern. How will society arrange to provide the goods and services they will need in their old age, when they are no longer working and receiving a steady income?

Getting back to the recovery from the Great Depression and the financial progress achieved after World War II, once it became clear the economy was growing at a much greater rate during the 1950s than it had been for the previous two decades, a few observers pointed out that people in some parts of the country were not enjoying the benefits of the economic recovery. These commentators exerted enough pressure to force the government to find a way to identify who these people were. That is when the federal government established the poverty line and counted the number of people who fell below that line. That happened in 1959. The results were so disturbing that the country set about the task of addressing poverty through a variety of social programs including Medicare, Medicaid and educational and community development funding during the decade of the 1960s.

It is interesting to look at how the distribution of government-sponsored programs dealing with the problems being experienced by poor people has changed over time. According to the Congressional Budget Office (CBO), the share of government benefits going to the least-affluent households fell from 54 percent to 35 percent between 1979 and 2007 (2011).

However, it is not only desperately poor people who need assistance. The Great Recession has caused enormous destabilization in the labor market. Middle-class people who lose their jobs may not need assistance right away. Things are very different for those who remain unemployed for twelve months or more. They are very likely running out of savings and have already cashed in whatever they could to support themselves over that period. Currently, more than four million Americans have been unemployed for twelve months or more (Seefeldt et al. 2012). These people are being defined as the "new poor." Furthermore, according to some the expectation is that their ranks will continue to swell until 2017.

As you can see, we are witnessing two opposing streams gaining momentum—while the number of people who need assistance because they are not receiving a steady income is increasing, the amount of money states are collecting in taxes is declining, because the number of people who are contributing has been dropping. Thus the population boom and all the programs created in the wake of World War II responsible for the economic boom of the 1950s are not being replicated at the present time. The recovery from the Great Recession is proceeding, but proceeding slowly.

It is important to understand that states, rather than the federal government, are primarily responsible for providing human services. The federal government may contribute to these efforts, but the states determine who is eligible to receive aid and are responsible for providing the full range of human services. The decline in state revenues due to unemployment and underemployment is causing states to cut back on services at exactly the time more people require such services.

When members of the public are asked whether they would be willing to address these problems by paying more in taxes, they respond negatively. The majority of Americans (55 percent) are convinced they will be paying more in taxes than they will get back in benefits (Applebaum and Gebeloff 2012). They say they have no interest in paying more to support people who are not working and supporting themselves. Organizations in the for-profit sector are certainly not about to step in to address the need for services for poor people who cannot pay for them.

The only other option is turning to organizations in the nonprofit sector. Whether they can rise to meet the increased demand for services depends on whether they can raise the funds to support their work. That brings us to the record on charitable giving. People are seeking out the services nonprofit organizations provide because needed services are not available anywhere else. Indeed, the fact that types of services nonprofit organizations provide are not being offered by organizations in the other two sectors is exactly why the nonprofit organizations came into existence in the first place.

According to the Giving USA Foundation, the rate of charitable giving between 1973 and 1996 was about 1.8 percent of GDP (gross domestic product) (Rosenberg et al. 2011). It increased to 2.2 percent from the late 1990s through about 2007. The year the recession hit, 2008, it declined by 7 percent; by 6.2 percent in 2009. The researchers doing the study estimated that giving would be around 2.1 percent of GDP as of 2010. Taking a closer look, we find that households with an income of less than $200,000 lowered their level of contribution by 5 percent between 2007 and 2009. However, the contributions on the part of households with incomes above $200,000 dropped by 37 percent over the same period.

The increase in contributions that occurred in 2010 benefited some non-profit organizations more than others. About 43 percent of nonprofits saw an increase, while one-third reported continuing decline in level of contributions. Larger organizations with budgets of $3 million or more were more likely to see an increase than smaller organizations.

Keeping in mind the information about the level of need for services combined with the shortage of funds, let us now take a closer look at the nonprofit sector as a whole—its size and its scope—so we may appreciate the larger context in which the organizations we will be examining in greater detail are operating.

Chapter Three

The Size and Scope of the Nonprofit Sector

Many of us hear about the activities of nonprofit organizations only intermittently, in the wake of major natural disasters such as tornadoes and hurricanes. We are likely to hear more regularly about runs, walks, and bike rides of varying lengths and perhaps something about the cause embraced by the organizations that rely on such events to raise money. Even if we don't participate in these events, although increasing numbers of people are doing so, we are certain to know others who do participate because they ask everyone they know to sponsor them to raise money for their cause. Some other familiar fund-raising practices include sending us personalized address labels and a return envelope suggesting a donation. Some organizations request a contribution in a phone call or letter explaining their cause. Unless we become more closely involved with these organizations, we tend to know more about their fund-raising activities than we know about what they do with the money they raise.

In this chapter we will focus on the nonprofit sector as a whole rather than the workings of any one particular organization. We will discuss how much money is involved, how many people are involved, who is legally responsible for seeing that the money is used appropriately, and so on. In short, we will now consider the size and scope of the nonprofit, charitable sector.

It would be easy to assume that fund-raising activities, such as those mentioned above, are sporadic, that only a small number of people need be involved on a regular basis, and that the organizations do raise money but that the amount of money involved is not all that remarkable. A closer look at the range of nonprofit activities and size of the nonprofit sector presents a picture that might surprise those who have had little reason to give it much thought.

THE NUMBER OF ORGANIZATIONS

Statistics on the size of the nonprofit sector are tracked by a number of different organizations. (I will provide citations for authors and organizations that release information. If there is no specific citation, then the information, which is continually updated, comes from the website of the organization to which I refer.) The National Center for Charitable Statistics at the Urban Institute (NCCS) 2011 report indicates there were 1.4 million nonprofit organizations in the United States in 2009. This is an increase of 19 percent between 1999 and 2009. This report focuses on organizations that report their revenue to the IRS. Only those that have receipts of $5,000 or more are required to file an annual income tax statement.

TYPES OF ORGANIZATIONS

The following list of nonprofit "industries" was developed by Burton Weisbrod (1988) based on the Internal Review Code (table A.15), which captures the range of activities nonprofit organizations are involved in:

Education
Health
Culture
Welfare
Mutuals
Inner-city and community development
Scientific research
Advocacy
Business and professions
Legislative and political action
Employee or membership benefit
Sports, athletic, and social clubs
Conservation and environment
Civil rights
Youth
Housing
Litigation and legal aid

When you think about it, it is very likely that we are involved with some of the organizations on this list more regularly than we might have first thought. Now that we have some sense of the types of organizations that constitute the nonprofit sector, let's move on to another measure of size and scope of the sector—money.

HOW MUCH MONEY ARE WE TALKING ABOUT, AND WHO IS DOING THE GIVING?

The NCCS indicates that nonprofit organizations reported $4.3 trillion in total assets in 2009. The total amount in contributions reported by Giving USA for 2010 was $290.89 billion, up from $289.30 billion in 2009. Prior to this time, Giving USA indicates that charitable giving was stable at 1.8 percent of the gross domestic product (GDP) between 1973 and 1996 (Rosenberg et al. 2011). However, as we noted in the previous chapter, the rate of giving declined during the 2007–2009 recession.

It is interesting to look back at the years shortly before the recession, when some in the philanthropy community were expressing concern that Americans would be spent out after the stream of disasters the country faced during the early years of the twenty-first century and would not have much interest in contributing to causes that were not spectacular.

According to the Tax Policy Center (which is a joint venture of the Urban Institute and Brookings Institution), individual giving hovered around 8 to 12 percent of charitable gross receipts over the 1996–2003 period. In fact, if donations for disaster relief are excluded, giving rose only slightly between 2005 and 2006, and gifts to human services organizations dropped by 12 percent over this period. So those connected to the human services sector were not entirely wrong to think that Americans might feel spent out.

This is a matter of concern because individual giving continues to be the largest source of nonprofit funding. Foundations serve as the most stable source at 14 percent of total funding. Corporate giving provides 5 percent. Finally, government grants make up the remainder.

Closer examination of individual giving indicates it is more complex than the single giving figure can reveal. "Noncash contributions—such as corporate stock, real estate, cars, and clothing—have grown more rapidly than cash contributions since 1988, but have also been more volatile and fallen more during the most recent recession" (Rosenberg et al. 2011, 2). Cash contributions hit a peak at $156 billion in 2006, while noncash contributions peaked at $62 billion in 2007. Both types of contributions fell during the recession; cash contributions fell at 13 percent between 2007 and 2009; and, noncash contributions fell by 47 percent.

The information on who has been doing the giving is mixed. According to one report, the profile of individual donors has been changing (Johnston 2006). The richest Americans, those earning more than $1 million, decreased the percentage that they donate to charity from 4.1 percent in 1995 to 3.6 percent in 2003. At the same time, those earning less than $1 million increased their giving from 2.8 percent to 3.5 percent. Of those with estates worth $1 million or more, 73.8 percent gave nothing to charity in 1995 and 78.1 percent gave nothing in 2004. The latter also spent $500 million lobbying to repeal the estate tax. Although the percentage differences may be small, the amount of money involved is huge and is a matter of some concern to the charities that depend on the generosity of those who can afford to contribute.

Some other reports indicate that wealthy Americans have been giving more than ever before, at least during the middle years of the first decade of the twenty-first century. According to a report in the *Chronicle of Philanthropy*, those with assets of at least $10 million increased their giving in 2006 over what they gave in 2005 by 20 percent (Lewis 2007). Another report in the same publication indicated that wealthy Americans committed $7 billion to charity in 2006, a substantial increase over the $4.3 billion they contributed in 2005 (DiMento and Lewis 2007).

According to the most recent assessment of individual giving by Rosenberg and his colleagues at the Urban Institute, contributions as of 2009 by households with income of less than $200,000 fell by 5 percent (2011, 3). Those with incomes over $200,000 contributed 37 percent less, 20 percent less in cash and 61 percent less in noncash donations. It is important to note, however, that cash contributions as share of income actually increased for both groups (2011, 4).

HOW FUND-RAISING GETS DONE

One of the most basic challenges nonprofit organizations face as we will repeatedly find throughout this discussion is raising enough money to pursue the objectives that they have set forth for themselves. Nonprofit, charitable organizations offer goods and services for which they do not expect to recoup their costs, let alone make a profit. This is in sharp contrast to corporations, which produce only those products or services that will bring in a steady—and, ideally, a growing—stream of revenue. Nonprofits may require clients to pay a nominal fee for some of the services they receive, but that is invariably far from the full value of those services. How organizations choose to obtain the funds they require creates major dilemmas because fund-raising activities invariably involve trade-offs. To start with, fund-raising is costly. The amount of money that is raised must be sufficient to justify the cost and the effort that must be expended in order to raise it.

This is more than a question of organizational efficiency: it is a matter of social expectations and values. Years ago nonprofits were far more likely to host charity balls, which did raise a great deal of money. However, hosting fabulous balls—ballroom rental, dance band, cost of special food and drink, waitstaff, plus the costs associated with publicizing the event—took a big chunk of the money taken in. So the amount of money remaining after ball expenses was considerably less than the total amount of money received.

Then, when you add how much the women, and some men, spent getting decked out to attend the ball—you can see that the money going to the charity could be a lot higher if people gave the money directly to the charity rather than spending it on all the related expenses—not that people would actually do that. Nevertheless, social values have changed, and fund-raising no longer depends nearly to the same extent on expensive balls as it did in the past. As we noted earlier, fund-raising through runs, walks, and climbs (up many stories of tall buildings) has become very popular—not that the costs of paying for security, availability of emergency medical services, and so forth can be disregarded. It is also true that an organization may wish to hold a gala event in spite of the cost because it wishes to celebrate a landmark, anniversary year.

There are alternative funding possibilities that are much like the celebrated free lunch (i.e., there is no such thing). Government grants, as well as gifts from private donors, often come with strings attached. Either might require the addition of new services or attention to a new, somewhat different client group, which would require a shift in allocation of funds. Whether making such accommodation is consistent with the organization's basic purpose is not necessarily immediately apparent, nor is it always easy to predict how the accommodation will affect the organization in the future. We will focus on who makes those determinations shortly. How they make them and how well those accommodations work out is the subject of the remainder of this book.

Let's stop here to consider the opposition on the part of some members of the public to the amount of money that is being channeled to nonprofit organizations by government agencies. FamiliesUSA, which is itself a nonprofit organization, analyzed the social impact of the funds distributed in 2007 by one government agency, the National Institutes of Health (NIH). It turns out that for each dollar of NIH funding, communities benefited more than twice as much in state economic output.

The overall investment of $22,846 billion from NIH generated $50.37 billion in new state business activity in the form of increased output of goods and services. This happened because the NIH grants created "more than 350,000 jobs that generated wages in excess of $18 billion." The average wage of all the jobs created by NIH funding nationwide was $52,112. That is nearly 25 percent higher than the average wage in the country at that time. FamiliesUSA calculated that a 6.6 percent increase in funding would offset past flat funding and compensate for current inflation. That would add up to $3.1 billion in new business activity, 9,185 additional jobs, and $1.1 billion in new wages.

The FamiliesUSA analysis is meant to show that most of the money the government distributes comes back into the economy and benefits the community. When the money is poorly distributed and ends up in the pockets of a few, including a few scam artists, then it is far less beneficial to the economy and society as a whole. The money may even leave the country to be invested offshore in an untraceable account. In short, the lesson is that distributing money well results in socioeconomic benefit whereas distributing it poorly gives rise to a range of new social and economic costs, starting with the loss of tax income, and goes on to include the cost of identifying culprits, collecting information to prosecute them, and so on. As an aside, this suggests it is wiser to spend more to evaluate the credentials of those who are applying for government funds to begin with (i.e., paying a cadre of bureaucrats to do it initially), rather than investing in law enforcement agencies and paying agents to chase after the perpetrators of malfeasance after the fact.

FOUNDATIONS

Foundations are nonprofit organizations. The difference between foundations and charitable, nonprofit organizations is that foundations do not offer products or services directly to those who need them. Instead, they use their funds to support the activities of other nonprofit organizations. The Foundation Center, which is affiliated with the National Center for Charitable Statistics, states that 109,952 private foundations were registered with the IRS in 2006. The Foundation Center also tells us that nearly half of the larger foundations were formed after 1989. According to the Foundation Center, they held $682.2 billion in total assets in 2007. This constitutes a 379 percent increase in assets since 1990. They distributed $44.4 billion in 2007. It is worth noting that all foundations, regardless of size (unlike charitable organizations, which must file only if they have more than $5,000 in revenue), are required to file what is known as a 990 form reporting their finances; however, they are not closely monitored, so they may miss some years.

Newspaper stories sometimes report what a particular foundation contributed for this or that, but we usually don't hear how much any one foundation distributes over the whole year. The foundation that has gotten most attention from the public media over the past decade, particularly in 2006, is also the largest—the Bill and Melinda Gates Foundation. The news media informed us that it distributed $14 billion in 2003 (Thomas 2006). We may not have heard this if it were not for the fact that Bill Gates announced he would be retiring from Microsoft, the corporation he founded, in order to spend more time managing his foundation. Shortly after that announcement, Bill Gates's close friend Warren Buffett, the founder of Berkshire Hathaway holding company and reputedly the second-richest man in the world after Bill Gates, at the time announced he would be giving $37 billion to the Gates Foundation ("Buffett Still Has More . . . ," 2006). His explanation was that giving away money and doing it right is a very difficult task, and, in his opinion, the Gates foundation does it very well. Just in case you wondered, Buffett's decision has not left his three children without an inheritance. He has allocated considerable amounts of money to his children, who have used the funds to create their own foundations. He explains his decision to give the bulk of his fortune to the Gates Foundation by saying that he does not believe in "dynastic wealth" being passed on to the "members of the lucky sperm club" (Thomas 2006).

The Bill and Melinda Gates Foundation was already the largest, with $29.8 billion in assets before the Buffett transfer of funds. With the Buffett gift, the foundation would have roughly $66 billion in assets, which it would not have all at one time. The Foundation Center report of March 2012 indicates the Bill and Melinda Gates Foundation had $37.4 billion in assets at its disposal. One of the conditions of the gift is the requirement that the foundation give away what Buffett contributes on an annual basis for tax purposes. This means the Gates Foundation had to agree to give away about $3 billion per year over the next few years, or about twice as much as it was giving away in 2005. The evidence that giving away that much money is not so easy to do is confirmed by the plans to expand the Gates Foundation's workforce. Gates announced that the foundation would have to double its staff to about six hundred and build a new complex.

According to the 2012 Foundation Center report, the next four biggest foundations in terms of assets were: the Ford Foundation with $10.3 billion; the J. Paul Getty Trust with $9.5 billion in assets; the Robert Wood Johnson Foundation with $9.1 billion; and the W. K. Kellogg Foundation with $7.6 billion. The list of foundations at the top and the assets they hold vary somewhat from year to year, reflecting the current value of their investments.

Foundations are required by law to pay out a minimum of 5 percent of their assets in grants on an annual basis. When you consider that foundations paid out a total of $4 billion in grants during 2004, the last year for which data are available, you can see they are distributing a great deal of money. The amount of money involved means that the activities of foundations have been attracting the attention of observers who had not expressed much interest in the past. For example, they have been characterized as "elite institutions" with self-perpetuating boards, too heavily influenced by family members who "may or may not have 'the common good' as part of their portfolio" (Capek and Mead 2006, 3). Indeed, a growing number of critics are demanding greater accountability and increased monitoring (Eisenberg 2005).

That the volume of criticism was great enough to reach policy makers in Washington, D.C., is reflected in the fact that Congress considered passing legislation some years ago requiring foundations to distribute a larger share of their holdings (Lipman and Wilhelm 2003). This led to consideration of how much foundations spend on administrative expenses, which at least one congressman argued should be better controlled. Others have wondered what the political effect might be of foundations providing more money than the government for particular causes—as in the case of the Gates Foundation's funding aimed at eliminating AIDS in Africa. Consider for a moment the possible political implications of individuals being in a position to outspend governments for causes they wish to support. That is not a question we will try to answer, but it is an intriguing one.

Foundations can use their resources to engage in activities other than distribution of funds to other organizations. They generally create separate organizations if they wish to collect and analyze statistics. One organization that has become highly influential in the health policy arena over the past couple of decades, the Kaiser Family Foundation, has determined that the public has not been exposed to nearly enough of this kind of information. In one of the studies in which it collaborated, it found that only 1 percent of stories covered by news media focus on health policy. Accordingly, the president of the foundation announced in late 2008 that it was starting a news service that would provide in-depth coverage of policy and politics of health care (Sack 2008, B4).

THE PEOPLE INVOLVED IN THE NONPROFIT SECTOR

It is difficult to get an accurate count of the number of persons nonprofit organizations employ. The Independent Sector's 2011 estimate is that about 13.5 million persons or 10 percent of the nation's workforce was employed by nonprofit sector organizations. This is far higher than previous estimates. The Bureau of Labor Statistics (BLS) reported that 8.7 million persons were employed by nonprofit organizations in 2007, which is about 5.9 percent of the American work force (Butler 2009).

Interest has been growing in finding out why people choose to work for nonprofit organizations given that "everyone knows" they don't pay as well. It seems that nonprofit sector employees differ from their counterparts in the for-profit sector (Schwinn 2003). According to a survey of social services workers associated with private, government, and nonprofit agencies, conducted on behalf of the Brookings Institution in 2002, nonprofit workers are more likely to say they took their jobs for the chance to help people (Light 2002). Only 5 percent of human services workers in nonprofit organizations said they were working mostly for the paycheck, in contrast to 41 percent of federal employees and 47 percent of for-profit employees. On the downside, 81 percent said it is easy to burn out in the work they do; 75 percent said they always have too much work to do; 67 percent said their pay was low (so there is some evidence for what "everybody knows" about nonprofit employment); and, slightly more than half said they felt unappreciated. The author of the survey conducted in 2001, Paul Light, concludes: "The nonprofit sector has the most motivated workforce—its 11 million employees have a greater sense of mission, a deeper desire to make a difference, and a greater love of their work than any other workforce in America today" (Russo 2002). He warns that society should not take this devotion for granted. "It's like the nonprofit field is in some kind of parallel universe, where labor is plentiful and no one minds that they don't have benefits and resources and don't get paid well" (Joslyn 2002).

Nonprofit employees may differ from employees in other sectors because they report different motivations for working than their counterparts in other kinds of organizations. But what "everyone knows" about earnings may be the result of some misunderstandings (Butler 2009). Based on BLS data, nonprofit workers earned slightly more per hour ($21.68) than workers in the for-profit sector in 2007 ($20.46). Government workers earned more than both for-profit and nonprofit workers, more at the local level ($25.16) than at the state level ($23.77). The explanation the BLS offered is that the occupational composition of the workforce may account, at least in part, for the difference. In other words, the for-profit sector may employ a greater number of people who have less education or are less skilled.

VOLUNTEERING

The number of persons who are not paid but contribute their time working for nonprofit organizations is tracked by the Department of Labor. The Department of Labor is primarily interested in tracking employment and unemployment statistics, which it collects through the Current Population Survey of sixty thousand households of the nation's civilian noninstitutional population age sixteen and over. In carrying out this survey, the Department of Labor asks about volunteering. The Corporation for National and Community Service (CNCS) issued its first report on volunteering based on that survey in 2006 and has followed up with an annual report since then. The CNCS expressed concern in finding there had been a 6 percent decline in the number of people who volunteered between 2005 and 2006. That trend continued in 2007 when an estimated 22 million volunteers dropped out. More recently, the number of volunteers has increased slightly, from 61.8 million in 2008 to 62.7 million in 2010. This amounts to 8.1 billion hours of work contributed, which by Independent Sector calculations is worth $173 billion in 2011 dollars.

The 2006 report prompted the CNCS to compile a Civic Life Index using twelve indicators to gauge state levels of community and civic engagement. It turns out that the states that have a higher rate of volunteering also have higher civic index scores, meaning that people in those states live in communities that exhibit greater levels of social well-being. The CNCS conducted a first-ever analysis of the differences between volunteers and non-volunteers on how they spend time. It seems that the largest difference is in the time allotted to television viewing. In a typical week, volunteers report approximately fifteen hours of television viewing compared to twenty-three hours for non-volunteers. The eight-hour difference adds up, according to the CNCS, to more than four hundred hours over the course of a year.

The Independent Sector, an umbrella organization whose purpose is to collect and disseminate data on voluntary organizations, also tracks the number of Americans who are volunteering and issues its own estimate of the monetary value of those efforts. Its estimates of the numbers of people who volunteer are higher than the numbers reported by the Department of Labor. It estimated the monetary value of the work volunteers performed in 2010 to be $21.36 per hour. (The hourly value estimate is based on Bureau of Labor Statistics reports of average hourly earnings by production and nonsupervisory workers on private nonfarm payrolls plus 12 percent for fringe benefits.) The rate varies considerably by state from a low of $14.89 in Montana to a high of $32.74 in the District of Columbia.

IRS TAX CODE DESIGNATION

Nonprofit organizations must incorporate (i.e., establish a legal identity) under the laws of the state in which they are located. States have the power to exempt organizations from state income tax whether or not the organization is exempt from paying federal income taxes. In order to have income exempt from being taxed by the federal government, the organization must apply to the IRS for recognition as a public charity.

The rules set up by the IRS are designed to make sure that the organizations that solicit funds from the public are actually engaged in the activities they claim to be engaged in and to ensure that those activities are really charitable rather than being operated for the benefit of private interests. Americans enjoy a reputation for generosity, as the figures above clearly indicate. Unfortunately, there is another less attractive characteristic. Con artists appear out of nowhere, create elaborate scams seemingly overnight, and proceed to take advantage of the generosity of fellow Americans. Such efforts are usually short lived, and many of the perpetrators are caught. Legitimate nonprofits are, of course, interested in making sure that Americans know that they can rely on them to do what they say they will do with the funds.

The IRS has developed a sizable list of different categories of tax-exempt organizations—nine major groups, twenty categories, and more than six hundred subcategories—each with its own designation that includes such disparate entities as credit unions, benevolent insurance companies, labor organizations, and cemetery companies, among others. The IRS uses the National Taxonomy of Exempt Entities developed by the National Center for Charitable Statistics at the Urban Institute. Among the most common categories are the following:

1. 501(c)(3) organizations that are charitable, religious, scientific, educational, literary, aim to prevent of cruelty to children and animals, foster national or international amateur sports competitions, and carry out tests for the benefit of public safety.
2. 501(c)(4) mutual benefit organizations (i.e., civic associations, local associations of employees, some volunteer fire departments, and some types of veterans' organizations).
3. 501(c)(6) chambers of commerce, trade associations, real estate boards (such as condominium associations).
4. 501(c)(8) fraternal organizations such as the Shriners of North America.

The focus of this volume is limited to 501(c)(3) organizations. The significance of the designation is such that nonprofit, charitable organizations are often referred to as 501(c)(3) organizations. Nonprofit organizations that operate outside of the United States are known by a different label. They are generally referred to as NGOs (nongovernmental organizations).

Organizations granted 501(c)(3) status are characterized by two special privileges. First, they are tax exempt, as is true of other 501(c) organizations, meaning they are not required to pay federal income taxes. Second, and this is unique to the 501(c)(3) category, they are allowed to accept contributions that donors are permitted to deduct from their taxes (i.e., the contributions are tax deductible).

As a condition of receiving this designation and in order to maintain this status, 501(c)(3) organizations must observe the following set of guidelines:

- They must develop articles of incorporation stating the organization's purpose. The articles must be accompanied by a set of bylaws stating operating procedures.
- The organizers must apply for an Employer Identification Number, even if they have no employees.
- They must ensure that the organization is permanently dedicated to the purpose set forth in its charter and provide for the distribution of assets in case of dissolution.
- Organizations with $25,000 or more in assets must report on their finances to the IRS in order to ensure their 501(c)(3) status. This means that they must file what is known as the 990 Form, complete with balance sheet accounting for funds taken in and funds expended; and, they must make

such reports available to anyone who wishes to examine them. The form requires organizations to report the percentage of money spent on fund-raising and for administration. This is done to provide potential contributors and volunteers the opportunity to determine how well the organization is functioning. Although there is a fair amount of concern about the accuracy of information on fund-raising practices, these reports stand as the primary source of information on fund-raising expenses. Furthermore, every scholar who has written on the subject argues against creating a single standard for evaluating fund-raising practices.

- Finally, no one associated with the organization may engage in "more than an insubstantial" amount of lobbying designed to influence legislation or participate in campaign activities—as a representative of that organization. The IRS moved to define "insubstantial" by passing the Lobby Law in 1976 and issued clear rules on how much an organization can spend on lobbying known as the "section 501(h) expenditure test." Organizations must report lobbying expenditures to the IRS. They may choose to file a formal statement under this rule using a one-page form to report expenditures related to activities that could be considered lobbying. Obviously the IRS provides a more detailed statement on the kinds of public activities that are excluded and the kinds that it considers to be lobbying.

The IRS may revoke the 501(c)(3) designation if the organization is found to be violating any of these conditions. That this does happen is confirmed by the fact that the IRS regularly publishes a list of the names of the organizations whose 501(c)(3) designations it has revoked.

OBTAINING INFORMATION ABOUT NONPROFIT, CHARITABLE ORGANIZATIONS

A number of organizations have come into existence to advise potential donors on what to look for when they are considering making a contribution. This is in addition to government or quasi-government organizations that collect data and make it publicly available. The statements nonprofit, charitable organizations submit to the government as a condition of maintaining nonprofit status are considered to be public documents. However, the information is easier to understand after it has been interpreted by analysts and published by the organizations that have developed with that purpose in mind.

One source is GuideStar, which maintains a website that provides financial information on nonprofits. According to its mission statement, it aims to make such information available to anyone who wishes to use it and do so free of charge. It says of itself: "GuideStar's mission is to revolutionize philanthropy and nonprofit practice by providing information that advances transparency, enables users to make better decisions, and encourages charitable giving."

Another organization that aims to help donors determine which organizations they should support is the BBB Wise Giving Alliance. This organization was established in 2001 through a merger between the Better Business Bureaus Foundation and the National Charities Information Bureau for the purpose of helping donors "make informed giving decisions." The Alliance recommends contributing to organizations that spend at least 65 percent on program service activities and no more than 35 percent on fund-raising expenses.

The Charity Navigator, established in 2001, states that it has become the nation's largest and most used evaluator of charities. Since it was formed, it has created reports on more than five thousand charities. The Charity Navigator says it is primarily concerned with two areas of organizational financial health: how responsibly the organization functions and how well positioned it is to sustain its programs over time. We will refer to the reports provided by one or more of these organizations, when they are available, on the organizations we will be examining in later chapters.

BOARD MEMBERS AND 501(C)(3) ORGANIZATIONAL OPERATIONS

As you can see, the nonprofit sector is a major player in our society, in terms of the amount of money and number of people involved in addition to the problems it has chosen to take on. According to the Urban Institute, nonprofits contributed $779 billion to the economy and accounted for 5.4 percent of gross domestic product (GDP) in 2010. This is why getting the facts about nonprofit organizations right is important.

A huge number of books have been written on running nonprofit organizations. There are books offering advice on such matters as financial management, marketing, fund-raising, grantsmanship, organizational culture, and leadership, to name a few of the most commonly addressed topics. The explanation behind this is that there is no formal educational program that trains people to serve as "board members," as opposed to managers, of a nonprofit organization. Managers can get their training in business schools just like managers of for-profit organizations. There are also programs that offer degrees in nonprofit management. The difference is that managers are paid to carry out the board's directives whereas board members carry out their responsibilities without pay, as volunteers. Board members are not expected to have nonprofit management degrees or other degrees, for that matter. Ideally they are asked to serve because they can bring some kind of experience and expertise that will benefit the nonprofit organization.

Nonprofit organization boards are sometimes referred to as: boards of trustees, boards of governors (as in the case of the Red Cross), as well as boards of directors. Publicly held, for-profit organizations (i.e., corporations) also have boards responsible for their operations. Those who serve as board members of for-profit corporations, unlike those who serve on nonprofit boards, typically receive a fee for doing so.

Nonprofit organization board members play a crucial role. They decide on the direction the organization will take—whether it will expand its activities, shift its emphasis, introduce new goods and services, and so forth. The board's most important fiduciary, legal responsibility is making sure the organization maintains its tax-exempt status (back to this point shortly). Board members do so by setting policy, overseeing the production of financial reports, recruiting new board members when necessary, supervising fund-raising, and so on. As is true of for-profit boards, the members of a nonprofit board delegate the day-to-day running of the organization to the staff, but they are ultimately legally responsible for everything the organization does.

After conducting a two-year study and taking hundreds of comments into account, the National Charities Information Bureau issued a set of standards in 1992 outlining board member responsibilities. The Bureau states that board members are not only responsible for policy setting, fiscal guidance, and ongoing governance; they must regularly review those policies, programs, and operations. They are to be guided by the following standards: the board should be independent; have a minimum of five voting members; have an attendance policy; have specific terms of office for its officers and members; hold in-person, face-to-face meetings at least twice a year; pay no fees to members for board service (payments may be made for costs incurred as a result of board participation, such as travel); employ no more than one paid staff person, who shall not serve as chair or treasurer; have no material conflicts of interest involving board or staff; and have a policy promoting pluralism and diversity. As of 2002, the Sarbanes-Oxley Act codified much of this into law reinforcing the fact that board members, in both for-profit and nonprofit organizations, have legal responsibility for the activities of the organization on whose board they serve and outlining the punishment for failure to take this responsibility seriously. What was new in this legislation is that the law clarified who can be sued. It made clear that individual board members could be sued for oversight failure. Scholars who have examined the implications of the Sarbanes-Oxley Act for nonprofit organizations have concluded that nonprofits were already following all these practices, so the law required little change in their operations.

The fiduciary responsibilities of the board are handled by selected members who make up the finance committee. A high-functioning board is also likely to have a high-functioning finance committee that conducts periodic "internal audits" (i.e., reviews of policies related to financial affairs) in order to ensure that appropriate accounting methods are being used, documents required by the state and federal government are being filed on a timely basis, payroll taxes are being paid, and so forth. The committee generally also oversees the organization's investments and reviews operating expenses in order to make sure that the organization is using its resources in an efficient manner. In short, the finance committee bears primary responsibility for ensuring that the organization is using its monies wisely and using its funds to accomplish what the organization says it aims to accomplish.

CONCLUSIONS

One well-respected observer of the workings of this sector sums up the essence of the situation the sector finds itself in currently. His assessment brings together the facts that we reviewed in this chapter and their significance as reflected in the country's response to one of the major disasters that occurred over the past decade, the Katrina hurricane. He puts it this way:

> This sector occupies an increasingly critical and visible position in our political, social, and economic life. Yet despite its size and perceived influence, there is considerable uncertainty and confusion about its boundaries. The lines delimiting the sector have frequently been subject to challenge and revision, as funds and responsibilities have shifted back and forth among business nonprofit and government organizations. Reaching consensus on the very definition of the nonprofit and voluntary sector is difficult because many of the core features and activities of nonprofits increasingly overlap and compete with those of business and government. (Frumkin 2002, 1)

We end this chapter by noting that we focused on the organizational structure of the nonprofit sector. In the following chapter we will take up the discussion from a more academic perspective. We will take a closer look at the kinds of questions that researchers who study the organizations in this sector raise, the answers they offer to those questions, and outline the questions we will be addressing in the remaining chapters.

Chapter Four

Analytical Framework

This chapter outlines the theoretical framework we will use to examine the operations of the organizations we encounter in the following chapters. I am not prepared to argue that there is such a thing as a nonprofit theory. This is not to say that scholars have ignored the topic. Researchers have investigated and discussed how well nonprofit organizations operate, the role nonprofits play in society, and the value of their contribution. However, scholars have typically addressed specific questions rather than attempting to present a single, totally integrated explanation. Accordingly, it is more accurate to say that we will now consider the theoretical foundation underlying the case presentation framework we will be using.

The number of researchers who focus on nonprofit organizations specifically, as opposed to organizations in general, is relatively small. As a result, scholars from different disciplinary backgrounds tend to be familiar with each other's work. This has resulted in an interdisciplinary approach to the study of "nonprofitness." Although scholars interested in the topic may be familiar with each other's work, presenting a comprehensive review of what academics from various fields of study, including political science, economics, and sociology, plus those who come to this topic from applied fields such as public administration and public policy, have had to say is daunting. When you add it all up, there is quite a bit of literature to review. We will only be skimming the surface of this body of work in the hope that this review will provide some context for better understanding the issues that scholars have addressed. For those who develop greater interest in this topic, I suggest checking out the references that appear throughout this chapter, especially references to edited volumes in which a wide range of topics are considered.

The rationale for presenting an admittedly limited literature review is that my primary objective is to examine the practical side of organizational operations. We employ some of the theoretical concepts presented here in order to advance our understandings of how nonprofit organizations work. We do not aim to advance nonprofit organizational theory. With that said, let us consider what a selected number of observers have to say.

Scholars, regardless of disciplinary affiliation, often start their discussions on nonprofit organizations by noting that Alexis de Tocqueville, the French aristocrat who toured the United States in 1831, was enormously impressed with the number and range of voluntary, nonprofit organizations Americans had established. He documented his impressions in *Democracy in America* (1969). In his view, such organizations provided the foundation for democracy in this country. Those who argue we must do more to ensure the vitality of nonprofit organizations generally proceed from this assessment. In de Tocqueville's view, voluntary organizations stand as an important countervailing force that offsets excessive government intervention in citizens' lives. They offer people with shared interests the opportunity to join together to engage in activities related to their respective interests without necessarily requiring the rest of society to become involved in their activities. At the same time, according to de Tocqueville, membership in such organizations provides people who share particular views with a far more powerful voice than they could possibly have on an individual basis. Indeed, for that reason our society can support both the activist environmental group such as Green Peace and a well-known conservative group such as the National Rifle Association without forcing the rest of us choose between the two.

Many scholars also note that Robert Putnam, president of the American Political Science Association at the time his book *Bowling Alone* was published, gained a great deal of attention by stating that what de Tocqueville admired about the United States was rapidly disappearing (2000). Putnam argued that Americans were no longer actively participating in voluntary associations. He documented this assessment by showing the steady decline in membership in a wide range of voluntary organizations. Extending de Tocqueville's observations, Putnam took the position that the decline is worrisome because of what is being lost. His interpretation is that it indicates a loss of "social capital." He explained the value of social capital this way: "[It] is the principle of generalized reciprocity—I'll do this for you now, without expecting anything immediately in return and perhaps without even knowing you, confident that down the road you or someone else will return the favor" (2000, 134).

The declining rate of participation in voluntary organizations, according to Putnam, has had a spiraling negative effect. The commensurate decline in social capital has led to a decline in trust in others, which is, in turn, allowing people to justify acting in a self-interested manner, and ironically, in the end, tolerating an increasing level of dishonesty in society. That explains why we so often hear the idea expressed, that if others are "getting away with it," why shouldn't I do it, too?

Putnam made special reference to how his observations apply to charitable, nonprofit organizations by noting that Americans are far more willing to send a check than they are to contribute time to help carry out the work being done by such organizations. His point is that the act of giving money can be done at a distance, is quick, and requires no personal contact with either those helping or those being helped. It is an indicator of personal generosity but does not do much to build social capital, which arises out of personal contact and social interaction that form the basis for trust and confidence in the other person. It is the decline in trust that Putnam is particularly concerned about, and a major factor in what others see as the decline of "civil society."

THE SOCIOECONOMIC PERSPECTIVE

Scholars have had a good deal to say about the reasons behind the growth of the nonprofit sector before and after Putnam observed that participation in nonprofits was declining. One of the basic questions they address focuses on which side of the following observation is more convincing in explaining the existence and subsequent shifting composition of nonprofit, voluntary organizations, especially charitable organizations that focus on health and human services issues. The basic idea, known as the "failure of performance approach," holds that the existence of nonprofits is a response to either a) market failure (i.e., on the part of the for-profit sector) or to b) state failure (i.e., on the part of government). European scholars tend to see the growth of nonprofits or NGOs as a "legitimation crisis" of the "welfare state" (DiMaggio and Anheier 1990). In other words, Europeans tend to take the position that the existence of and increase in the number of nonprofit organizations is the result of the government's failure to deliver essential services, especially to those who cannot afford the services. American scholars are divided on this issue, but they may lean a little more toward the failure of the market side of the debate as opposed to failure of the government side.

Lester Salamon says it is even more complicated than that. He argues that contract failure of the state and of the for-profit sectors has a counterpart in "voluntary failure" that occurs in the nonprofit sector (1987).

He identifies four factors related to "voluntary" failure that characterize malfunction in the nonprofit sector.

1. *Philanthropic insufficiency.* This occurs when nonprofits cannot meet the demand for the services they aim to provide, which sometimes happens during periods of recession when donors give less or give only to causes they can enjoy and benefit from, or too many applicants act as "free riders."
2. *Philanthropic particularism.* This is the result of the decision by nonprofits to focus on particular ethnic, religious, or ideological categories.
3. *Philanthropic paternalism.* This happens when the organizational leaders insist on addressing problems as they see them, not in the way that clients see them.
4. *Philanthropic amateurism.* This is associated with nonprofit reliance on less-qualified workers.

He wants to make sure that we do not become complacent and assume that the performance of nonprofit organizations will always be superior. In other words, with the addition of Salamon's analysis of "voluntary failure," we end up with what is now referred to as the "three failures" theory, which captures the potential for failure on the part of all three organizational forms or sectors—government or public sector, market or for-profit sector, and voluntary or nonprofit sector (Steinberg 2006).

Although Salamon may express serious concerns about the risk of nonprofit organizations' failure to perform as expected, his assessment of the positive functions they perform is far more extensive (2003, 12–14). He defines nonprofit organizations:

- First and foremost, they are major service providers. They deliver hospital care, employment and training, low-income housing, community development, and emergency aid services.
- Second, they contribute to national life by identifying unaddressed problems and bringing them to public attention. He notes that most of the social movements that have animated American life over the past century operated in and through the nonprofit sector. He says that organizations in this sector have served as critical social safety values, permitting aggrieved groups to bring their concerns to broader public attention and rally support aimed at improving their circumstances. He mentions such movements as antislavery, women's suffrage, civil rights, environment, antiwar, gay rights, as well as a number of conservative causes.
- The third function is related to their expressive role. He says they are "the vehicles through which a variety of sentiments and impulses—artistic, religious, cultural, ethnic, social, recreational" find expression. He men-

tions symphonies, soccer clubs, fraternal societies, and book clubs, which he says enrich human existence and contribute to social and cultural vitality.

- Fourth, they help build social trust by establishing connections among individuals. This is their community-building role. He points out that social trust is crucial "for a democratic polity and a market economy to function effectively." This helps us continue to have confidence in our social institutions even if the wrong people are in charge for a time. He claims that valuable new products the nonprofit sector generates are sure to become available at an affordable price because the market operates very well at that level.
- Fifth, they perform a "value guardian" role. They give expression to two principles that are important to the American national character—the principle of individualism, which reflects the idea that people should have the freedom to act in their own interest; and, the principle of solidarity, the notion that people have responsibilities to other members of their community. We see these two principles operating in combination as people contribute time and money to a highly diverse array of purposes that nonprofit organizations embody.

Burton Weisbrod, whose views we encountered previously when we discussed his comparison of the strengths and weaknesses of the three sectors, has found much to criticize in reviewing the performance of nonprofits. However, he concludes that we cannot get along without them because both of the other two sectors have "serious limitations" (1988). He argues, and many others agree with him, that the concept of "transaction costs" goes a long way in explaining the existence of nonprofits. The basic idea here is that under conditions of mismatched information between suppliers and clients, clients prefer organizations that are characterized by greater "trustworthiness."

In a relatively recent turn of events, an increasing number of observers, especially economists, have begun to question whether our government is delegating away far too many functions over which it has ultimate responsibility. Returning to the discussion on the three sectors in chapter 2, we are finding that delegating to the for-profit sector, or "privatizing," has been enthusiastically embraced by the corporate sector and a large proportion of the public based on the presumption that for-profit organizations are more efficient. Representatives of the corporate sector argue that for-profit organizations are naturally more efficient because they have a powerful incentive to be efficient, namely profit. Nonprofits and public-sector organizations, they say, obviously do not have this highly motivating incentive. Given this assessment, why, they ask, would government agencies delegate any functions to nonprofit-sector organizations rather than for-profit corporations?

In answer to this question, a number of economists, who are more critical of market solutions, say there are good reasons to delegate to nonprofits in spite of the absence of a profit motive. They point out that government agencies do so because:

- shifting responsibility to nonprofits lowers the total cost to the government;
- private sector organizations can charge fees in instances where government cannot, which is not something that all observers consider to be a positive feature;
- private organizations cost less to operate because they do not have to observe civil service wage rates, so they pay lower wages; and,
- services can be differentiated by language, religion, or culture (which some observers consider desirable and others consider to be destructive to social cohesion) (James 1990).

The disciplinary interest economists have in "utility functions" has them addressing a number of more targeted questions about the larger social impact of nonprofits. For instance, they debate the impact of user fees (i.e., fees organizations charge their clients) on voluntary organizational structures and goals. They have also considered the extent to which nonprofit commercial activity (i.e., producing or selling products as a means of increasing income) might have a negative impact on philanthropic donations, which by extension would cause a decline in the services they would otherwise be able to provide. The debates continue because the answers to these questions are not so clear (Tuckman and Chang 2006).

Where and how nonprofits get their funding is undoubtedly the most commonly addressed topic across disciplines and is a topic to which we will devote much more attention in the following chapters. Regarding the question of how accepting funding from the government affects nonprofits, two political scientists, Smith and Lipsky, make some intriguing observations (1993). On the question of whether nonprofits benefit by accepting government funding, they say government contracting makes nonprofits both more powerful and more vulnerable—more powerful because government is becoming more dependent on nonprofits; and more vulnerable because the government sets the rules, thereby reducing nonprofits' level of control over their own operations.

An apt illustration of this observation can be found in the relationship the government has with nonprofit health and human services organizations (Cho and Gillespie 2006). Government has become their primary source of funding. At the same time, the level of funding is the subject of continuing antagonistic debate, as are charges of government failure to monitor organizational performance.

Smith and Lipsky make one other particularly controversial observation related to funding. They charge that the government disposes of public-sector administrative and service delivery failures (i.e., cases of "state failure") to nonprofit organizations. This allows the government to escape blame for handling problems that require more comprehensive solutions than it is willing to work out. Nonprofits carry the burden in such cases without much chance of real success.

Perhaps those who say the government has simply not developed effective contracting and monitoring mechanisms, and is not doing so because society is not exerting sufficient pressure, are right. Committees organized to investigate wasteful practices might be stricter in handing out penalties if enough people indicated they care about it. Or Putnam may be right, and we all simply assume everyone will be dishonest if they think they can get away with it—and the majority of Americans are willing to leave it at that. In the end, there are no definitive answers to such questions and no clear indicators that things are about to change, so we are all left to reach our own conclusions.

Finally, one of the most contentious questions economists continue to debate revolves around tax policy. They wonder whether nonprofits differ from for-profits enough to justify exempting them from paying income taxes. Burton Weisbrod makes the point that whether they deserve this advantage depends on how society sees their benefit to society, which, in turn, depends on how that benefit is measured (Weisbrod 2001). He makes the point that flawed attempts to measure the social contribution nonprofits are making results in systematic underestimation. This, in turn, allows for-profit enterprises to critique the work of the nonprofit sector and to argue that it does not deserve the privileges it receives.

Most categories of nonprofit organizations—nonprofit hospitals, for example—must allocate a certain portion of their funds, at least 5 percent, to caring for the underserved in order to retain nonprofit status. Although the debate starts by questioning how much is enough, it can quickly mushroom into a range of related questions. In the case of hospitals, it raises such questions as: Should the fact that a nonprofit hospital is located in an area that brings in poor patients, who are unable to pay for the services they receive, count as charity? Economists call that "bad debt," which is not the same thing as charity care (for which the hospital is required to outline criteria in advance). Then there are questions of what we mean by charity care: Does providing a health fair count as community education, or is it really a marketing mechanism intended to attract more patients?

According to Bradford Gray, the problem is that monitoring performance often involves measuring the kinds of indicators that are relatively easy to measure such as number of beds, number of patient visits, number of people employed by hospitals, and so on. However, a count of such things does not get at the basic issue, which is outcome (i.e., the effect on the patient of the care being provided [2001]). Furthermore, such measures may be misleading, because more is not necessarily better. Gray ends up saying that the most important thing to capture is difference between the outcomes that nonprofit and for-profit organizations achieve. Doing that right is sure to show the extent to which input affects output—in other words, it is much harder to produce good results when you are dealing with patients who have more serious problems and/or more complications to begin with. As a matter of fact, a review of the research on the quality of care provided by for-profit compared to nonprofit organizations indicates that nonprofits do a better job, according to Gray.

SOCIOLOGICAL OBSERVATIONS AND THE PROBLEM OF COMPLEX GOALS

Sociologists have a long tradition of studying how organizations work (Handel 2003). However, most have not been particularly interested in what distinguishes nonprofit organizations from those operating in the other two sectors. The small number of sociologists who are interested in nonprofit organizations devote considerable attention to examining their findings in light of general sociological organizational theory (Galaskiewicz and Bielefeld 1998; Froelich 1999). The exercise has introduced concepts that have led to valuable insights rather than consensus regarding the superiority of one theoretical perspective over any other in explaining the workings of nonprofits. Some of the best work specifically devoted to the nonprofit sector has been complied in handbooks that address a wide range of issues (Powell 1987; Powell and Clemens 1998; Powell and Steinberg 2006).

It is fair to say that sociologists are especially interested in the fact that nonprofits espouse goals that are complex, amorphous, and sometimes contradictory. They point out this means that nonprofit organizations generally operate under conditions of uncertainty, especially financial uncertainty. Given that nonprofits generally operate under comparable constraints, sociologists are interested in identifying factors that help to explain why some nonprofit organizations are very successful and others are not. They do this by investigating how the goals nonprofit organizations embrace become translated into the operating structures they create. They examine the relationship between organizational structures or frameworks and the processes that govern organizational activities. They are particularly interested in determining the extent to which the rules and procedures organizations create over time promote adaptations, and possibly promote far more extensive changes, in organizational objectives. We can easily see that nonprofit organizational mission statements tend to be very broad, often basically unattainable. Sociologists say the upshot is that the people who are charged with attaining the vague goals expressed in mission statements end up interpreting, possibly altering them, in an effort to identify more attainable goals, which typically translate into short-term objectives. That, in turn, poses the risk of "goal displacement" or "mission drift." In short, the idea is that the complex, difficult to define, original goals are at high risk of being replaced by clearly defined and more easily measured short-term goals that may not be consistent with the organizations' primary or original goals.

Another question sociologists raised is whether the structures and processes organizations employ are rational (i.e., whether they "make sense"). This question focuses directly on the idea that nonprofit organizations espouse goals that are complex and difficult to measure. A couple of particularly perceptive sociologists have argued that organizations deal with this by mimicking the approved "organizational form" comparable, visibly successful organizations use and replicating notable rituals in an effort to establish their "legitimacy." They do so in order to be viewed as outwardly successful when objective measures of performance are not available (Meyer and Rowan 1977). Schools, particularly grade schools, provide an effective illustration.

Traditionally, if an elementary school displayed all the right symbols (flag, pictures of national heroes, posters appropriate to the seasonal holiday, etc.), the children played nicely, the school was clean, the playground was well maintained—parents and the community tended to be satisfied that the children were getting a good education. If all this was working well, there was no need to focus on education per se because that is too hard to do. It is also true that the No Child Left Behind legislation has put in place a new set of presumably much more concrete measures of school performance. So, does that mean most people agree that test results constitute a far better indicator of school performance than the vague symbols that served this purpose in the past? Not at all, critics abound. Critics argue that teachers are now teaching to the test, which is not the goal that the broader definition of educational institutions should strive for. Another way of looking at the impact of the legislation is that it very effectively triggered goal displacement by causing teachers to devote themselves to attaining the short-term goal of raising test scores rather than keeping the focus on the complex and amorphous long-term goal of providing children with a comprehensive education and all other manner of personal development.

Because nonprofit organizations embrace a multiplicity of goals that are highly ambiguous, making the matter of measuring organizational performance much more difficult, sociologists among others (Flynn and Hodgkinson 2001) have devoted a great deal of attention to the matter of performance measures (Kanter and Summers 1987). Sociologists are also interested in the fact that nonprofit organizations have many constituencies, all with their own reasons for participating in any particular organization together with differing notions about what that organization should be accomplishing. That makes the specification of goals problematic, which, of course, makes measuring achievement of those goals all the more complicated and challenging. The solution that social scientists have turned to is measurement of "effectiveness," which is generally understood to mean attainment of a multiplicity of goals. Thus, the ideal performance assessment tools, which someone must create, have to incorporate measures of short-term objectives as well as long-term goals.

To sum up, sociological research on nonprofit organizations can be said to reveal agreement on the following points:

- organizations have multiple and, in some cases, competing goals, which is far more likely when the organization is a nonprofit
- organizations must be concerned with and responsive to the expectations, constraints, and potential rewards presented by the interactional fields in which they operate (i.e., to multiple constituencies)
- because no organization can generate all the resources it needs, organizational leaders must make difficult, strategic choices, paying special attention to environmental considerations, (i.e., the interests of the other organizations in the environment in which they operate)

When asked to explain why sociologists devote so much effort to evaluation, a task that is so difficult, Paul DiMaggio explains that the effort itself is rewarding (2001). Bringing people together to discuss outcome measurement forces all those involved to focus on objectives, which provides an arena for different parts of the organization to bring their respective organizational aspirations to the table and, with any luck, an opportunity for all those disparate parts to coalesce.

INTERDISCIPLINARY ASSESSMENT AND POLICY IMPLICATIONS

The fact that the nonprofit sector serves the needs of multiple constituencies makes it "at once a visible and compelling force in society and an elusive mass of contradictions," according to Peter Frumkin (2002, 1). This, he argues, makes it "the contested arena between the state and the market where public and private concerns meet and where individual and social efforts are united." He identifies four functions of nonprofit activity that grow out of the sector's interstitial position.

1. First, service delivery, which is a response to government and market failure.
2. Second, civic and political engagement, which provides a venue for mobilizing citizens to become politically active, which, in turn, builds social capital within the community.
3. Third, social entrepreneurship, which offers an innovative vehicle for creating social enterprises that achieve charitable goals through the creation of successful commercial ventures.
4. Finally, values and faith, which allow volunteers, staff, and donors to express their own values, commitments, and faith through nonprofit activities.

Dennis Young has made a number of observations that reinforce Frumkin's observations but challenge a number of traditional assumptions about the nonprofit sector. His basic message is that the lines between sectors are becoming less distinct. He says the blurring of boundaries between nonprofit and for-profit organizations over the past two decades has occurred in response to five clearly identifiable trends (2001).

1. First, declining government support together with increasing charitable giving has given rise to greater dependence on income generated through the offer of services that carry a fee.
2. Second, the greater reliance on earned income is responsible for the growth of "social purpose enterprises," which Young defines as "revenue-generating businesses that are owned and operated by nonprofit organizations with the express purpose of employing at-risk clients."
3. Third, nonprofits have been more ready to get involved in for-profit business ventures. Examples of collaborative efforts include event sponsorship, cause-related marketing, royalty and licensing arrangements, joint ventures, and so on.
4. Fourth, because nonprofits must compete for societal resources in an environment that places so much emphasis on market solutions, nonprofits are being asked to measure up to business standards. They are expected to demonstrate their impact on society, their cost-effectiveness, and justify the special public policy benefits they receive.
5. Fifth, all of this is having an effect on the internal workings of nonprofit organizations. Nonprofits are becoming different kinds of organizations than they were in the past as evidenced by the fact that they are now using such terms as entrepreneurship, marketing, and management expertise. Paralleling these developments is the growth in the number of businesses that have become socially conscious and active.

There is some good news and some worrisome news regarding the direction the nonprofit sector has taken in recent years. When Pablo Eisenberg looks at the nonprofit sector, he sees steady expansion that he says is worth celebrating. However, he also sees serious unforeseen effects in the wake of expansion, most notably fragmentation. He notes that this is making the sector less capable of uniting to take collective action (2005, 5). In his view, organizations that have been most successful in coalescing to take a united stand, most notably the Heritage Foundation and the American Enterprise Institute, are the highly politically conservative ones. To the extent that other nonprofit organizations have been successful, they have largely been those devoted to middle-class issues such as the environment, government reform, and Medicare. Eisenberg charges representatives of nonprofit-sector organizations with lacking the courage to demand that the most pressing social problems (i.e., those linked to poverty) receive the attention they deserve.

The observations Jerome Himmelstein made are related to concerns that Eisenberg expresses. Himmelstein focuses on the role the corporate sector plays in American society and the pragmatic stance it takes in deciding how it will use the power it wields, and how that affects its relations with nonprofit organizations. Himmelstein points out that corporate philanthropy has become an increasingly important factor in the life of the nonprofit sector. However, in his somewhat caustic view, what lies behind corporate generosity is a large measure of self-interest. He argues that the basic reason behind corporate giving is promotion of corporate interests, but that the ultimate goal is protection of corporate capitalism itself (1997, 29). Himmelstein goes on to call our attention to the "discursive presence" of "nonstop policymaking" that takes place in this society in which the corporate sector plays a significant role. In other words, he says, big business feels it must be vigilant in wielding the power it has at its disposal to ensure the existence of a favorable operating environment for private enterprise in any form, including private charity. This is not meant to interfere with the government's role in funding safety net services because corporate donors are only interested in supporting services that will benefit them in some way (1997, 147). He puts it this way:

> The key to preserving free, competitive enterprise lay in protecting the principle of "voluntary association" and the various "private sectors" of society. That is, corporations had to protect not only the private for-profit sector but also the private nonprofit sector from state encroachments, because the fate of the two were closely tied. (1997, 21–22)

POPULAR LITERATURE

Were one to restrict one's review of the literature to scholarly works produced by academics, one might conclude that it is all being produced by a small coterie of researchers. However, even the briefest of glances at the shelves in major bookstores or bookseller websites reveals that the nonprofit sector has attracted an enormous amount of public attention, which has, in turn, generated a huge number of volumes. The titles indicate that a wide range of topics are being addressed including organizational culture, leadership, managerial style, legal considerations, fund-raising, board member responsibility, and on and on. The advice is sometimes offered in a format reminiscent of an elaborate cookbook recipe. The fact that so many authors have come up with so many different recipes suggests that the surefire, best recipe is yet to be discovered.

On the other hand, there is no denying that a great deal of truth and thought-provoking commentary is to be found in some of these volumes. The problem is implementation. Yes, it is best if the executive director or CEO is energetic, truly committed to the organizational goals, knows how to motivate the staff, stays long enough to get to know and respond to the full range of stakeholders, and so on. The supply of books on leadership and management is endless. Authors are less clear about how effective leadership or management is to be realized.

To the extent that one wants to consult a fairly complete reference book that outlines the basic steps and possible pitfalls involved in creating, managing, and observing legal requirements, a handful of easy-to-understand presentations are available. These include: *Financial & Strategic Management for Nonprofit Organizations*, 2nd ed. (Bryce 1992); *Strategic Management for Nonprofit Organizations: Theory and Cases* (Oster 1995); *Starting and Managing a Nonprofit Organization: A Legal Guide*, 4th ed. (Hopkins 2005); *Nonprofit Kit for Dummies*, 2nd ed. (Hutton and Phillips 2005); and *Nonprofit Law and Governance for Dummies* (Welytok and Welytok 2007). The latter two books include up-to-date lists of resources and websites. The author of *Donor-Centered Fundraising* may have captured the secret to successful fund-raising that all those complicated treatises have not been able to do (Burk 2003). This wise observer tells us that success in fund-raising amounts to something we all should have learned from our mothers—say thank you, and it's even better if you do so in a nice, personalized letter. This is obviously an extremely limited selection out of literally hundreds of titles.

Summing it all up, there are those who are ready to conclude with a blunt assessment of the situation on why all three sectors need to be scrutinized because, in their view, none is totally free of problems. They say society has accepted the idea that the private sector is more efficient, but that it is less trustworthy. The corollary is that nonprofit organizations may be less efficient but that they are more trustworthy than for-profit organizations. Finally, a considerable amount of evidence indicates that society is willing to accept the downside in these trade-offs rather than place its trust in the government to deliver the services that people require. Indeed, there is reason to believe that the level of distrust in government has been increasing. According to the Pew Research Center, 80 percent of Americans said they don't trust government in 2010. The Pew Research Center assessment is that three major factors are involved: the deep recession, high unemployment, and a polarized Congress (Pew Research Center 2010).

Chapter Five

The Case Presentation Framework

The framework we will be using to examine the operations of specific organizations in the chapters to follow grows out of the theoretical insights found in the research that gave shape to the previous chapter. In this chapter, we outline the case study method of analysis that we will be applying. We will be using five organizational characteristics in exploring each case.

- the organization's **mission**—what it says it aims to accomplish
- the organization's **history**—the circumstances that led to its creation and subsequent development
- the organization's **structure**—its size, number and types of programs, number of branches, people served, and so on
- the organization's **funding** arrangements—how it obtains the funds it uses in its operations
- the organization's **evaluation** procedures—how it gauges how closely it is coming to accomplishing the mission it has set out for itself

It is important to recognize that the pictures of the organizations we study are much like snapshots. That is to say, we are looking at those snapshots in the effort to understand what the organizations are doing and how they are going about doing those things at a specific point in time. Much of what we will be discussing comes from annual reports and other publications that are publicly available. It is worth noting that some charitable organizations have been directing the money they would normally devote to producing an annual report to other more pressing needs. As a result, the financial information we are looking at may not be based on the same year across organizations. We will review revenue and expenditure information presented by the organizations based on the last year being reported.

ORGANIZATIONAL MISSION

A mission statement articulates the organization's purpose. Unless one realizes the significance of the mission statement's instrumental function, one might conclude that such statements are merely expressions of idealistic aims. In actuality, the mission statement serves as both the goal and the standard against which a nonprofit organization measures its performance. It keeps the organization focused on its basic purpose.

Let us look at a sample of mission statements in each respective organization's self-description of its purpose on its web page to consider the challenge involved in achieving the goals expressed in the mission statement. I have arbitrarily selected a handful of nonprofit organizations to see what they say about the goals they have set for themselves. All the organizations mentioned below are committed to socially beneficial goals. Our purpose here is not to comment on the value of the goals that the organizations have embraced. It is to examine the goals in order to think about how clearly what they say they aim to achieve translates into organizational programs and activities.

Oprah's Angel Network:

Oprah's Angel Network is dedicated to inspiring people to make a difference in the lives of others. It grants awards to organizations and operates projects in underserved communities that provide educational initiatives as well as assisting people in fulfilling basic human needs and regaining dignity.

American Diabetes Association:

The mission of the association is to prevent and cure diabetes and to improve the lives of all people affected by the disease.

AIDS Research Institute at the University of California, San Francisco:

The AIDS Research Institute at UCSF is committed to fostering innovative and integrated science—basic, clinical, prevention, and policy research—to prevent, understand, treat, and someday cure HIV infection; rapid dissemination of our findings; and training new scientists to continue working toward our ultimate goal of ending the HIV/AIDS epidemic.

Alzheimer's Association:

To eliminate Alzheimer's disease through the advancement of research; to provide and enhance care and support for all affected; and to reduce the risk of dementia through the promotion of brain health.

Alzheimer's Disease Center at Rush University Medical School in Chicago:

Dedicated to reducing disability due to Alzheimer's disease and other age-related conditions through research on the treatment and prevention of disease for this and future generations.

Cognitive Neurology and Alzheimer's Disease Center at Northwestern University Medical School in Chicago:

The mission of the CNADC is to investigate the neurological basis of cognitive function, to elucidate causes of dementia, and to ensure that the patients and their families are the beneficiaries of resultant discoveries.

Although the differences may appear to be subtle when you first look at them, you can also see that some organizations have far broader aims than others. Looking at the first three statements we can see that the American Diabetes Association's statement is the shortest and most direct. However, that does not necessarily mean it is the clearest in defining what activities the organization intends to promote in order to achieve its primary objective. Oprah's Angel Network's mission statement says considerably more about the organization's aims, but that does not mean it is stipulating how it will attain those goals. The AIDS Research Institute at the University of California, San Francisco, is far more specific in outlining its objectives as well as the means it will use to achieve those objectives.

The mission statements of the three organizations dedicated to elimination of Alzheimer's disease make the differences in how clearly the "ends and means" are spelled out more obvious. The two university centers indicate that their purpose is Alzheimer's research leading to a cure. The mission of the Alzheimer's Association includes research, but that is one of three objectives. The other two objectives focus on enhancing care and support for all who are affected by the disease and promoting brain health.

Research aimed at finding a cure provides a more concrete objective than the goal of helping people deal with problems—whether problems associated with a particular disease or problems experienced by people in underserved communities, as is the case in Oprah's Angel Network organization. This is not to argue that the broader aims expressed in mission statements should be made more concrete. It is to say that it is far more difficult to know how to attain broader aims and even more difficult to know how well the organization is doing in meeting its objectives.

ORGANIZATIONAL STRUCTURE

Organizations vary in the way they are configured—in size, number of branches or sites, number of employees, number of programs, and so on. Size is something over which organizations have a fair amount of control. Let's consider universities for a moment. Universities may not set exact limits on the number of students they will admit, but they have a clear range in mind. The vast majority of universities are either private, nonprofit organizations or government sponsored and supported organizations. Only a small number of universities are operated on a for-profit basis, as we noted as part of an earlier discussion. The enrollment issue might well raise the following question—if a university does not make a profit by increasing enrollment, then why would it want to do so; and what, if any, are the consequences of increasing enrollment?

Here are some possible interpretations: A university that severely limits the number of students it will admit is doing so to maintain exclusivity. A university that is allowing enrollment numbers to increase may be doing so to include students who might not otherwise have the opportunity to attend college. There are implications associated with the latter choice. For example, it may mean the university must then create special services and programs to help those students who would not have been admitted to a more selective university. More exclusive universities expect students to be well prepared upon entry to deal with the challenges involved in earning a college degree. Introducing new programs needed to assist students who are not well prepared for the rigor of college requires an increase in the size of the administrative staff to coordinate activities that fall outside of the realm handled by well-established academic departments.

Clearly, the difference in student body size and composition as well as staff and faculty size is directly related to the difference in the missions universities set forth for themselves. Universities that are prepared to admit everyone who applies and do not add programs to help students overcome inadequate preparation for college risk being perceived as "diploma mills" to which only those students not admitted anywhere else would apply—not an identity most universities would find desirable.

Another dimension of structure is centralization. A highly centralized organization generally has a great deal more control over the units that are associated with it than an organization that operates as a loose federation of independent units. To illustrate—the American Cancer Society has a centralized organizational structure. It develops fund-raising campaign materials as well as the programs the organization aims to deliver at its headquarters in Atlanta, Georgia, and distributes these to 3,400 local offices. By contrast, the American Heart Association has 297 local offices, which create their own programs and mount their own campaigns. The American Heart Association operates as a federation of largely independent local offices. One approach is not better than the other; they are simply different, largely because of how the organizations evolved. The core difference has to do with the direction from which ideas and plans flow—from the bottom up (i.e., upward from the branches to the headquarters) or from the top down (i.e., downward from the headquarters to the branches).

Size can also be measured in terms of budget, clients served, number of employees, and number of volunteers. Let us consider the issue of volunteers. Organizations vary greatly in the number of volunteers they depend on. That is entirely up to the organization. Volunteers provide valuable services, but coordinating volunteer activities is not without its costs. Their activities must be planned and scheduled. They must be oriented and trained. When they cannot come in, they have to be replaced by someone else, which the staff member in charge of volunteers must see to. Organizations that do not have the funds to hire staff or choose not to do so depend on volunteers to do a great deal. That gives volunteers considerably more influence within the organization.

In the end, whether or not programs are expanded must be determined in light of the organization's mission and the resources any new program will require. Finding the right balance is the task of the organization's board of trustees and administrative staff. This requires careful calculation, as non-profits generally do not have discretionary funds (i.e., funds that are not already allocated). Every decision that involves structural change is likely to have an impact on other organizational aspects (e.g., finding space for the new activities, possibly increasing staff, creating a dedicated fund to support this activity, and so on).

ORGANIZATIONAL FUNDING

Fund-raising is crucial to nonprofit organizational survival. According to two scholars who reviewed the literature on the fate of a large number of non-profit organizations, it is the single most important defining characteristic of nonprofits. They say:

> We suspect that the fundamental difference between nonprofit and for-profit
> organizations does not turn so much on intrinsic differences in organizational
> form or capability, or even on legal criteria that distinguish nonprofits from
> for-profits, as on differences in the availability of resources and the constraints
> associated with their acquisition. (Powell and Freidkin 1987, 191)

Being certain of a stable, predictable source of funding constitutes a major operating advantage. Relying on individual contributors is considered by some commentators to be the most unpredictable and unstable source of funds. According to one observer, establishing a relationship of mutual dependency with a particular funding agency that "may only reluctantly attempt to escape" is the reason behind the success of many agencies (Gronbjerg 1991). In other words, the decision to rely on one major source of funding brings greater predictability than opting to count on the generosity of individual contributors even in large numbers. Other researchers say their findings do not support the idea that dependence on a narrower range of funding sources increases the chances of success (Galaskiewicz and Bielefeld 1998). In short, deciding to rely on multiple funders or on a few dedicated funders does not make fund-raising easier. On the other hand, most organizations are not in a position to make this choice and simply attempt to obtain funding whatever way they can.

Why an organization would need to think about accepting, or not accepting, a substantial amount of money from an individual is worth considering. The decision to return a gift comes only after a great deal of careful thought. The nonprofit organization may determine that the gift is not acceptable if it requires introduction of new programs that are inconsistent with the organization's mission. Nonprofits are regularly faced with such dilemmas; for example, what would be the benefit versus the cost to a hospital of creating an "alternative and complementary medicine" unit requiring hiring new staff, allocating space, buying different types of equipment, and so on even if it received a major contribution to do so? Would there be a net benefit to a university in creating a new visual arts program requiring a major investment in new technology and facilities? Would the benefits produced by a major bequest outweigh the costs to a community health organization if it started a substance abuse program to which its neighbors in the community were opposed? In each case, the programs may very well benefit a selected group of clients. The main question is not so much whether familiar funding sources would dry up, which is certainly an important consideration, but whether the introduction of the new program would be consistent with the organizational mission or would require the organization to shift its resources, possibly decreasing its support for existing programs in order to create the new program even with the significant contribution being offered by the donor. Even the appearance of a shift in priorities could have a negative effect.

An excellent illustration of the problems a generous donation can present has unfolded in recent years after Joan Kroc, wife of McDonald's Corporation founder Ray Kroc, gave the Salvation Army $87 million to build a center in San Diego with three swimming pools, an indoor ice skateboard rink, a sports playing field, and a 600-seat theater. Upon her death in 2003, she bequeathed $1.5 billion to build another thirty to forty Kroc Centers in low-income communities (Strom 2006). They did not have to be exactly the same as the San Diego Center, but they were to have many of the same features.

According to Commander Israel Gaither, who assumed national leadership of the Salvation Army in 2006:

> We are at a crossroads, and the challenge for us is to remain true to our mission. . . . The whole idea is to build on what has been accomplished, not to build something completely different. (Strom 2006, 1)

Here's the problem. Mrs. Kroc left enough money to cover half of the funds needed to operate the centers. That means the Salvation Army would have to raise as much as $70 million a year to cover the other half of the cost of operating the centers. Some of the money could be raised through fees. Of course, requiring people in poor neighborhoods to pay fees creates its own problems, even if the charge is not more than individual users can afford. The leadership of the Salvation Army had good reason to worry that the centers would change the public's perception of the organization, which had built its reputation as a frugal church devoted to serving the needy. More worrisome to the leadership was the fact that the money and the grand new facilities it was creating could change the way the organization saw itself.

As it turns out, the leadership was right to be worried. As of the middle of June 2009, of the thirty centers that were projected, four had been completed; two others were scheduled to open later in the year, plus five others next year; two were abandoned in the planning stages. The problem is that the Salvation Army was able to raise only 34 percent of the $214 million that it needed to operate the centers (Strom 2009, 13).

TALES ABOUT LENDING THE ORGANIZATIONAL LOGO TO RAISE FUNDS

Another source of problems comes when a nonprofit agrees to accept funds from a corporate partner in exchange for lending its name and logo. Economists call this commercialization. Nonprofit representatives see it as one way of obtaining "earned income." A couple of examples illustrate how this can work. In the case of the American Cancer Society (ACS), it permitted the Florida Citrus Commission to use its logo to market orange juice and SmithKline Beecham to use its logo on its antismoking patch in 1996. ACS did so in the expectation of receiving at least $4 million to help meet a $427 million annual budget. Then there is the case of the Arthritis Foundation, which agreed to enter into a $1 million deal with the makers of Tylenol in 1995.

What critics found problematic about the ACS and Arthritis Foundation contracts had to do with the exclusivity feature. In other words, is the ACS saying that Florida oranges are better than California oranges? Or is the Arthritis Foundation saying that Tylenol is better than similar drugs made by other pharmaceutical companies? Economists point out that donations might decline if the public were to decide the nonprofit was getting more than enough money in such a deal or, worse yet, selling its reputation.

The deal the American Medical Association (AMA) made with the Sunbeam Corporation resulted in an even more complicated and embarrassing saga, which illustrates very nicely how the thinking of high-level administrative staff and the board of trustees might differ. On August 12, 1997, the AMA executive vice president, Dr. John Seward, entered into an agreement with Sunbeam Corporation that would allow it to use the AMA logo on Sunbeam "Health at Home" products such as humidifiers and heating pads. The membership was not consulted. When the deal was made public, the membership registered strong opposition. The board of trustees agreed to call an emergency meeting to take place within the next few weeks to consider the situation. The board met on September 6 and voted to withdraw from the deal. Two days later, Sunbeam filed a $20-million suit charging breach of contract.

On September 18 the AMA board initiated an investigation of the process leading to the Sunbeam deal. On October 23, the board announced it had appointed a task force to set standards on association-corporation relations. The upshot was that three top AMA executives were forced to resign the same week. The AMA general counsel quit on October 31 and Dr. Seward handed in his resignation on December 4. The documents associated with the settlement of the lawsuit were sealed. However, the weekly newsletter to the membership revealed that the suit was settled for $9.9 million. Associated costs amounted to $3.3 million. This includes $670,000 in legal fees; $638,000 in executive search fees to replace key AMA executives; $771,000 in costs associated with the two special committees that investigated the Sunbeam affair; plus, $1.2 million in lost profits from eliminating products that were not in compliance with interim guidelines the special committee constituted to guide corporate relationships. Because none of these expenses had been planned, the AMA was forced to raise the money needed to meet these unanticipated expenses by selling some real estate, which brought in

$18.4 million. In order to reassure the membership and other observers, the association reported that it enjoyed a good year in terms of investments, revenues from sales of various professional products including books and data-based licensing, plus revenue from such sources as parking fees for the lots it owns. In the end, the AMA had an operating surplus for the year. What was not discussed in connection with these favorable reports was the fact that membership was continuing to decline; and that the fiasco may have contributed to an even lower rate of membership renewal and, of course, the corresponding drop in funds coming from dues.

The negative publicity such reports generate does not mean that nonprofit organizations have stopped lending their logos. Corporate executives continue to try to persuade nonprofit organizational leaders that the benefits outweigh the risks. They say their surveys indicate people will switch brands to purchase the products made by companies that advocate causes they believe in and that the funds this produces for the nonprofit organization are clearly well thought of. Many ethicists take a dim view of this process. They say nonprofits are undoubtedly hurting their credibility. Many nonprofits share this concern. In some cases, nonprofit organizations have chosen to provide endorsements without requiring compensation; for instance, the American Dental Association puts its logo on some brands of toothpaste, and the American Heart Association endorses low-fat, low-cholesterol foods.

ON THE DILEMMAS THAT ACCOMPANY ACCEPTING FUNDS FROM OTHER SOURCES

We have already touched on the question of whether nonprofits can succeed when they enter into contracts with the government and accept funds to deal with specific challenges that turn out to be truly intractable problems. There are also circumstances that leave nonprofits little choice but to reject funds, including government funds that are readily available to them, because organizational leaders have determined the funds come at too high a cost. To illustrate, many U.S. organizations that provide health-care services and supplies to people in developing countries have not accepted U.S. government monies because government grants have prohibited the distribution of contraceptives. Organizations that aim to reduce the spread of AIDS have certainly been taking this position. President Obama quietly dropped this restriction during the first months of his administration.

The question of whether charities have the right to use funds contributed for a specific cause to support the work of the other programs they offer focuses our attention on another aspect of the difficulties related to funding. The Red Cross's decision to reallocate some of the contributions it received in the aftermath of September 11 provides a vivid illustration. Senator Chuck

Grassley, chairman of the Senate Finance Committee, demanded that the Red Cross present a full account of its allocation decisions. The attorney general of New York, Eliot Spitzer, threatened to sue the Red Cross. In the end, the executive director was forced to resign. No one explicitly said that shifting funds contributed for a specific purpose to other legitimate purposes is, on the face of it, illegal. It was just upsetting to the people who wanted their money to go to September 11 victims. Does that make the decision to shift the money unethical? The answer is not clear—it is one of those things people can disagree about, so it is up to you to decide whether contributions must be used for the purpose that contributors indicated even if other needs to which the organization attends are underfunded and, in the eyes of the executive staff, more pressing.

The relief group called Doctors without Borders made a very different decision when it found it had collected enough money to address the particular cause for which it had solicited funds. The leadership of the organization decided to stop raising money when they determined they had collected enough to deal with the 2004 tsunami. The decision attracted the attention of regulators in Britain and France, who lauded the organization's resolution. The attention the organization received on its decision to stop fund-raising had the effect of revealing more about its fund-raising practices. It became clear that the organizational leadership was also declining contributions from corporations it believes are acting in ways that are in conflict with the organization's mission and principles. The public attention the Doctors without Borders revelations received has led to a considerable amount of soul-searching within the nonprofit community (Strom 2007).

The soul-searching has been further fueled by a series that ran in the *Los Angeles Times* in January 2007 reporting on Gates Foundation investment practices. The articles revealed that the Gates Foundation has major investments in:

- mortgage companies that were accused in lawsuits or by government officials of making it easier for thousands of people to lose their homes;
- a health-care firm that has agreed to pay more than $1.5 billion to settle lawsuits accusing it of medical lapses and fraud going back a decade; and
- chocolate companies said by the U.S. government to be profiting from the slave labor of children (Pillar 2007).

All of this is forcing nonprofits to confront whether some funds are simply too tainted. The question of whether to accept funds from corporations that have been involved in scandals, such as Enron, illustrates the dilemma. (The following is from Strom 2007). According to Diana Aviv, president and chief executive officer of the Independent Sector, the number of charities is increasing at a faster pace than the rate of giving. As she puts it: "Where do you draw the line? Some of [the] largest foundations were created by individuals who many regard as robber barons. Should charities look askance at that money?"

On this note, one of my colleagues, Woods Bowman, tells an anecdote about General William Booth, who as you may recall founded the Salvation Army about 150 years ago. It seems that when people criticized General Booth for accepting the "devil's money" from liquor interests, his purported retort was, "The devil's had it long enough." Others attribute the quip to Billy Sunday (the American evangelist who preached against the evils of liquor during the early years of the twentieth century). In any case, the point is that questions about the advisability of accepting tainted money are not new.

Clearly charitable fund-raising is a tough assignment. The decision to reject funds for any reason is not easy. However, it is one that also cannot be ignored.

ORGANIZATIONAL EVALUATION

Evaluators employed by nonprofit organizations continuously struggle with measurement issues. For-profit organizations don't have to worry about this kind of thing, because their purpose is to make a profit—how they make that profit is something to which only small numbers of very dedicated souls devote a lot of attention. As to the for-profit company, if one of its products or services fails to make a profit, the company may alter the product in an effort to increase its chances of profitability, but if that does not increase profits sufficiently, it simply drops that product or service from its offerings. For-profit organizations sometimes purchase other companies that make entirely different product lines in order to increase corporate profits. It is hard to see this as anything other than evidence of the idea that the company's product is not as important to its identity and purpose as the assurance of making a profit. An excellent example of this, one that received a great deal of attention in the media at the time, was the formation of one of the first really big conglomerates, in 1985, when RJR, the maker of Philip Morris cigarettes, merged with Nabisco, the maker of Oreo cookies and Ritz crackers. Now, of course, many other conglomerates offer similarly incongruous product lines.

Performance measurement is challenging even when the indicator of success (i.e., profit), would seem to be perfectly obvious. However, as we discovered in light of revelations connected to corporate debacles, from Enron through Bear Stearns, Lehman Brothers, AIG, and many others, even the measure of profit, which comes with its own clear-cut indicator, may not be completely transparent. Exactly how does a company with several different units do the accounting? Is it fair to calculate losses against a unit that is doing well to make units that are losing money look profitable? After all, the total profit or loss reflects the performance of the company as a whole, or is blending all financial accounts a fraudulent distortion meant to mislead investors? The banks that found themselves in financial trouble in 2008 and 2009 because they had embraced various "creative" performance indicators have been told they should expect far more government oversight in the future and reporting standards designed to achieve transparency.

How one measures attainment of objectives that come in something other than numerical form is even more complicated than anything that accounting firms dealing with profit statements encounter. Social scientists talk about "operational measures" of "nominal variables."

Think of it this way—age, years of education, income—all come in the form of a number, whereas religion or race/ethnicity are nominal, meaning that it is a name with no number attached. In order to determine whether such nominal variables make a difference to the outcome being assessed, social scientists must find a way to "operationalize" or quantify these variables. Sex is easy to quantify because we have traditionally been given only two choices. Marital status gets a little more complicated, but the options can be assigned an arbitrary number without any meaning attached to it. You can do the same thing with religion if you simply want to know the number of people who report particular religious affiliations. However, if you wanted to study whether being more religious has an effect on, say, life expectancy, you would have to figure out a way to measure differences in "religiosity." How would you measure that? How often the person attends religious services? How many times the person prays? Whether the person observes the teachings of his or her religion? As you can see, how many times a person attends services per month is easy to count. Whether the person observes the teachings of the religion is extremely difficult to quantify. You may think the measure of religiosity that researchers report using is far from perfect, but unless you can come up with a better one, you don't have many alternatives to accepting it if you want to know anything about whether a person's religiosity affects his or her attitudes and behavior as it relates to a whole range of issues, including life expectancy.

In short, in many cases there is no objective indicator of how good a measure is. Your reaction indicates how good it is. The more people who agree that the measure is a good one, the more people will accept findings using that measure. Some measures become conventional because they are commonly used or depend on a measure that is calculated by the government and has been used for a long time. The poverty threshold (i.e., how much money a person has to make to fall above or below the poverty line for that year) provides a particularly good example. Almost no one thinks the poverty threshold is a good measure. The list of criticisms is long. However, there is absolutely no agreement on how it could be improved, so it continues to be calculated the same way it has been calculated since the early 1960s when it first came into use in policy debates regarding the need for passage of groundbreaking health and welfare programs.

That brings us back to the central question of how nonprofit organizations assess their performance. What would you consider to be a good measure of success that nonprofits should employ?

Economists generally advocate using some version of a cost-benefit analysis approach. The cost part is relatively easy to calculate—but how do you measure benefit? Therein lies the problem. How much benefit or what degree of benefit are we talking about? How long is the benefit expected to last—for a week, a month, a lifetime? Is client satisfaction a good measure? What criteria do clients use? Is their evaluation of the benefits they are receiving a good measure? Is using measures developed by professionals a better approach? How would such information be collected? As you can see, the questions just multiply once you start thinking about it. It is also true that some organizations do a better job of evaluating performance than others. Of course, it helps to have a very clear objective—like finding a cure for a particular disease. That goes back to the organizational mission. Helping people who are afflicted with a particular disease is certainly a very worthy cause. Figuring out whether you are doing a good job of helping them is, however, enormously complicated.

Organizations that accept funds from the government or other granting agencies generally do not have a choice about evaluating their performance. Grant funds typically come with the stipulation that evaluation reports must be provided to the granting agency. In many cases, the agency requires that the organization receiving the funds hire an independent evaluator. In other instances, organizations have evaluators on staff. In either case, evaluation involves a lot of time and effort. The funding agency usually adds funds to cover evaluation expenses. That amount has been increasing. Performance evaluation has also been receiving a steadily increasing amount of attention from those who say that nonprofits are not being held accountable enough; and from evaluation experts who say too much emphasis is being placed on following administrative guidelines rather than measuring program outcomes (Cho and Gillespie 2006).

Other researchers raise questions about the accuracy of evaluation of organizational performance because they find a disconnect between the priorities of those being served and administrators of nonprofit organizations (Kissane and Gingerich 2004). They say administrators tend to focus on long-term objectives whereas clients tend to focus on immediate needs; not only that, but administrators have more in common with fellow administrators across agencies than they do with their own constituents.

Reactions from other stakeholders, most notably the donor base, serve as yet another source of feedback on organizational performance. How that is captured is a matter that is constantly being refined using both formal, structured surveys, and informal mechanisms such as bringing people together for a lunch presentation or focus group. Informal evaluation is an on-going process in most nonprofit organizations. The success of each fund-raising event is evaluated. Local branches of large nonprofit organizations are typically presented with information that allows them to compare their performance to that of other branches in terms of new programs, new fund-raising events, newly identified sources of funding, and so on. Stand-alone organizations, of course, cannot take advantage of such standards of comparison.

Organizational leaders are generally eager to get the kind of feedback from evaluation studies that they can use in doing strategic planning (i.e., projecting future programming, identifying potential challenges, and setting specific objectives to be achieved over a specified time period).

THE RELATIONSHIP AMONG FACTORS

The five-part case presentation framework outlined here will be used to discuss each of the organizations we consider in the following chapters. We will be in a position to look more closely at the hurdles each organization confronts and see how it responds. We will reflect on what gives each organization its unique identity. For a start, we will pay special attention to the direction from which it emerged—from the top down or from the bottom up. The influence of stakeholders and others in the organizations' respective interactional fields (i.e., clients, funding sources, and other organizations to which they may be linked) constitutes a more complicated set of factors we will try to untangle. We will devote special attention to the organizations' fund-raising practices and evaluation processes.

Chapter Six

Two Classic Case Studies

In this chapter we will examine the workings of two well-known charitable organizations that are the subjects of what are considered to be classic case studies, namely, The National Foundation for Infantile Paralysis by David Sills (1957) and the Young Men's Christian Association (YMCA) by Mayer Zald (1970). The case studies tell us how these organizations came into existence—their history; what their purpose was—mission; why they took the shape they took—organizational structure; where they got the funds to support their efforts—funding arrangements; and, how they assessed their own performance—evaluation. In short, we will be using the framework outlined in the preceding chapter. We will go on to discuss their current status and activities.

THE NATIONAL FOUNDATION FOR INFANTILE PARALYSIS

The National Foundation for Infantile Paralysis was established in 1927 by Franklin D. Roosevelt, who was a victim of infantile paralysis (i.e., polio). The organization was originally known as the Georgia Warm Springs Foundation. It was created to support a lodge built for the purpose of housing people afflicted with polio who came to take advantage of the natural warm springs in this region of Georgia. The foundation and the facility it operated were wholly supported by Roosevelt and a few of his friends. That lasted until the Great Depression of 1929. The coming of the depression meant that the small group of supporters could no longer fully fund the lodge without additional money coming from outside. The members of the group came up with the idea of holding a President's Birthday Ball to raise money. The first such event was held in 1934 raising more than $1 million after expenses, which was an impressive amount for the time. Between 1934 and 1937, local community organizations, Committees for the Celebration of the President's Birthday, emerged to help with the fund-raising effort.

The structure of the organization changed when President Roosevelt announced that he would create a new foundation, the National Foundation for Infantile Paralysis, to replace the Georgia Warm Springs Foundation. The funds collected by this new foundation would be used to seek a cure for infantile paralysis. The treasurer of the Georgia Warm Springs Foundation, Basil O'Connor, became the chairman of the board of trustees responsible for the National Foundation for Infantile Paralysis in 1938. He and the other trustees, who were all originally associated with the Warm Springs Foundation, determined that the funds from the Birthday Ball would be divided as follows: 30 percent going to the National Foundation for Infantile Paralysis headquarters office and 70 percent going to the local Committees for the Celebration of the President's Birthday, which eventually became local chapters of the National Foundation for Infantile Paralysis. After a few years, the headquarters office of the foundation announced to the local committees it would keep 50 percent of the money raised each year. The additional funds received by the headquarters were to continue to be devoted to research. And, the local chapters would continue to use their half to help the victims of polio in their own communities.

The rules governing the activities of local chapters were delineated by the trustees in a manual. One of the more interesting rules prohibited the chapters from hiring full-time staff. Everyone associated with the chapters was expected to contribute their time and effort on a voluntary, nonpaid basis. Larger chapters were eventually permitted to hire an executive secretary for clerical assistance. Another rule made clear that although doctors and other hospital personnel might have been more knowledgeable about the technical aspects of caring for polio victims, they were specifically prohibited from holding official positions that would give them a major say in the activities of local chapters. The local units were encouraged to establish a medical advisory committee of volunteers to give doctors and hospital administrators a vehicle to express their views. All other chapter functions, including approving medical bills, maintaining records, and so on, were to be carried out by persons in the community who were willing to serve as unpaid volunteers.

The thinking on the part of the trustees was that volunteers, as committed as they were, should not be permitted to make a career of this work. The prohibition against full-time staff was enacted in order to prevent the emergence of a small group of administrators who might become entrenched and in a position to promote a personal agenda. This edict was built on the expectation of a steady stream of new volunteers that would compensate for inevitable resignations. And, that turnover would, in turn, have the beneficial effect of keeping enthusiasm high. It avoided the apathy that can occur when a few people are associated with an organization for too long a period, get too set in their ways, and become more interested in preserving their jobs than being innovative.

What is especially interesting about the way the foundation operated is that it depended on two largely separate sets of volunteers—those connected to the headquarters and those connected to the local chapters. The trustees determined they could raise more money by replacing the annual President's Ball with a nationwide fund-raising event. They settled on a month-long, concerted fund-raising operation. The foundation invited a socially prominent person, usually a successful, well-known businessman (invariably a man), in large cities across the country to assume a once-a-year honorary chairmanship of the annual fund-raising effort in that region. The honorary chairman was given the responsibility for organizing the fund-raising activities in the area. Headquarters provided him with all the materials he would need, posters and such. When the fund-raising period ended, the honorary chairman gladly gave up his position to be replaced by another prominent person the following year.

Serving as a chairperson was a lot of work and provided no occupational ladder for upward mobility within either the foundation or the organization where the executive was employed. Even if the chairperson did not actually do much of the work, because his office staff assumed the burden, office routine would clearly be disrupted. In those days, the chairperson's wife undoubtedly played a major role as well, organizing a variety of related social events aimed at increasing visibility. For example, in later years the windows of the most fashionable stores in Chicago and many other cities displayed very large photographs of the honorary chairman and members of a committee of other successful businessmen that he assembled, and, of course, all of their wives, to promote the fund-raising cause.

The local chapter in Wausau, Wisconsin, came up with a new fund-raising initiative in 1951. The chapter organized a Mothers' March on Polio. The idea was that the march would collect dimes that would be placed in small folders, like greeting cards with slots for the dimes. The innovation quickly spread across the country. The foundation's annual month-long fund-raising effort became known as the March of Dimes.

Discussion

The March of Dimes continued until the foundation's quest to find a cure for polio was realized in 1957 with the development of the Salk vaccine. The National Foundation for Infantile Paralysis fulfilled the mission it set out for itself—finding a cure for polio. Clearly, that is an atypical organizational outcome. At the same time, it is also true that the success of this organization was less a matter of a detailed and fully thought-out long-range plan than a series of fortuitous decisions. Let us examine each of the elements involved.

Organizational mission

It is worth recalling that the National Foundation for Infantile Paralysis, with its mission of finding a cure for polio, grew out of the Georgia Warm Springs Foundation, which was devoted to providing a place for people with polio to receive some comfort. The shift in the organizational identity and goals is central to the ultimate organizational outcome.

The volunteers associated with the local chapters continued to embrace a mission similar to that of the Georgia Warm Springs Foundation. They were interested in aiding friends and neighbors afflicted with polio. They were not willing to forgo attention to the pressing needs of their friends and relatives for the promise of an outcome that would help everyone afflicted with polio at some future date. As laudable as the objective embraced by the local chapters might be, all the funds raised by the organization could easily have been used up in dealing with the immediate needs of victims because there would be no end of people who would contract the disease if there was no cure. The creation of the National Foundation for Infantile Paralysis and the insistence on the part of the trustees that a major portion of the funds raised each year be devoted to research was crucial to attaining the goal they set forth.

Organizational structure and funding

The organizational structure of the national foundation was highly central-ized, but there was no permanent headquarters office. The honorary, but temporary, national local chairpersons already had successful careers, so they were not interested in lobbying to turn the chairmanship into a permanent job. The volunteers responsible for the annual national fund-raising cam-paign were involved in this effort for a short period of time over the course of the year. Requiring the local chapters that operated over the whole year to rely on volunteers rather than professional staff meant that the funds raised by local chapters would also not be used to maintain an actual office that would drain finances and possibly lead to the emergence of new costly pro-grams developed to justify the existence of a full-time administrative staff. Clearly, the controls over organizational structure and operations at both the national and local levels instituted by foundation headquarters were crucial to the organization's ability to attain the goal it set out for itself.

Organizational evaluation

The organization attained its ultimate goal in a relatively short period of time. One of Sills's principal insights is related to this point. The organization was highly successful in avoiding "goal displacement," which happens when a short-term goal—in this case, it would most likely have been the amount of money being raised each year—replaces the long-term goal stated in the organizational mission statement (i.e., finding a cure for polio).

Sills's other major contribution was noting that successful organizations do not shut down very easily. When they achieved their goal, the small number of members of the foundation resigned their positions as trustees and prepared to close down operations. Because there were no other members at that level, there was no one to oppose their decision. However, precisely because it was such a successful organization and had such a well-developed and well-motivated network of local chapters already in place, a new coterie of interested parties stepped up to take over the organization in 1958. Everyone understood that because the foundation's organizational goal had been attained, the organization had to identify a new goal. The organization that emerged under these circumstances embraced the mission of finding cures for all birth defects. The new set of trustees changed the name, dropping the Infantile Paralysis portion. It became known simply as the National Foundation. By 1979, the organization changed its name again to the March of Dimes. It now identifies itself as the March of Dimes, with the tagline of Saving Babies Together.

The broader goal of the newly formed organization ensures a continuing need for it to operate because attaining the goal it has set for itself—a cure for all birth defects—is unlikely. The current mission statement is as follows:

> Our mission is to improve the health of babies by preventing birth defects, premature birth, and infant mortality. We carry out this mission through research, community services, education and advocacy to save babies' lives. March of Dimes researchers, volunteers, educators, outreach workers and advocates work together to give all babies a fighting chance against the threats to their health: prematurity, birth defects, low birthweight.

The newly reconstituted organization's account of its activities in the wake of the discovery of the polio vaccine reveals a very impressive list of accomplishments. For example: in 1968, the organization funded the first successful bone marrow transplant to correct a birth defect; in 1973, it funded the first successful procedure to treat a prenatal birth defect; in 1978, it funded the first prenatal diagnosis of sickle cell anemia; in 1981, it funded the first successful surgery to correct a urinary blockage in a baby before birth. It continued to identify a series of other groundbreaking prenatal surgical interventions during the 1980s. It also became involved in public education, efforts to help secure passage of a national children's health insurance program, and other legislative initiatives that would benefit babies. By the early 1990s, the organization was reporting success in identifying genes responsible for various genetic disorders. In 2002, the organization announced that its grantees had won the Nobel Prize awarded for Medicine and Physiology for their discovery of genetic regulation of organ development and programmed cell death.

The original organizational and fund-raising structure instituted by the National Foundation for Infantile Paralysis remains largely intact. The system for allocating the funds that each local chapter raises is also largely intact; in other words, about half of the funds raised by locals are directed to the research projects that the headquarters staff identifies and for which it awards grant support. The most notable change in structure is that local chapters are no longer expected to rely on volunteers to manage their day-to-day affairs. Accordingly, local chapters are now housed in permanent offices and employ full-time staff.

YMCA

The Young Men's Christian Association (YMCA) was founded in 1844 to provide Christian fellowship to young men in London at the height of the industrial revolution. (The Young Women's Christian Association was founded in 1855, but it has no direct relationship with the YMCA. We will return briefly to its evolution a little later.) Young men, who were moving away from their families from places across the United Kingdom in order to find work in the city of London, were eager for the companionship of others like themselves. A few such young men working in a draper's shop, the forerunner of the department store, began getting together in the evening for Bible reading in an effort to avoid the temptations of the big city. One of their group, George Williams, who was eighteen years old at the time, decided to ask his employer for funds to rent space so that more young men could participate. His employer and fellow employers agreed to provide funds for renting a meeting hall, a tea shop, and reading room. The young men wanted to meet to read the Bible on their own because they believed that clergymen could have little influence over them. They were committed to the idea that association with young men in similar circumstances who were dedicated to maintaining their Christian identity would help the steady stream of young men coming into the city to avoid the lure of sinful pastimes that the big city offered.

The YMCA was introduced to Americans by a college student who visited London. A Boston sea captain, who heard about the organization from that student, was sufficiently impressed with the model that he set up two local associations in 1851. By 1856, there were 56 locals in the United States; by the turn of the century, there were 1,476 locals. As of 2008, there were 2,686 locals.

The YMCA started as an interdenominational Protestant organization that embraced evangelism, meaning that Catholics, Jews, and members of other religions were not permitted to join. However, which Protestant denominations were truly evangelical was not so clear and continued to be debated. Its evangelical nature presented one other problem—it prevented the organization from receiving financial support from any organized church. The result was that it was faced with uncertainty from the beginning in terms of resources and membership—basically its survival. It also meant there was no theological prescription or clergy to provide a ready-made, traditional, and church-approved program for Christian character building. That, in turn, gave the organization license to identify new approaches that would increase (or decrease) its chances of survival.

The YMCA's ultimate success in the United States is attributable to the fact that it began offering two benefits attractive to young men who were strangers to the city. One was a place to live; and the other, the opportunity to engage in healthy activities to occupy their time. In this country, the first of these benefits came in the form of a 42-room dormitory that was built in Chicago in 1867. The second dormitory was built years years later in Milwaukee. By 1940, the YMCA could claim about 100,000 rooms, more than any hotel chain in the country.

The second benefit the YMCA provided to young men was the gymnasium. The Y's influence on sports cannot be overestimated. (The organization officially changed its name to the Y as of July 2010 in recognition of the fact this is what people have called it for many years.) Its long-standing commitment to and fame for teaching swimming started with a swimming bath in Brooklyn in 1885. "Bodybuilding," the term and classes, originated in Boston in 1881. The organization is proud to report that it was responsible for inventing basketball in 1891 and volleyball in 1895. It claims responsibility for the creation of professional football in 1895, when it paid a player $10 plus expenses to replace the injured quarterback on the Y team. It gave softball its name in 1926 in Denver. (Prior to that time the game had often been referred to as kittenball and sissyball.) It reports that racquetball was invented by a YMCA member in 1950 at the Greenwich, Connecticut, Y.

Major events in U.S. history influenced YMCA development as well. A number of trends were related to the Great Depression. Bible class enrollment at local Ys had been falling steadily even before the depression, while enrollment in exercise and educational classes had been gradually increasing. Interest in those activities really took off during the years following the depression. The sharp drop in people's income brought on by the depression prompted the Y to begin providing welfare assistance for the growing number of unemployed persons as of about 1928. Only after the introduction of government assistance in 1933 would the organization again turn its attention to the well-established catalog of activities that it had initiated. Other new initiatives that came with World War II included work with prisoners of war and displaced persons, drop-in centers for service personnel, and entertainment for troops abroad. By the end of the war, the Y was a very different organization. All races and religions were embraced at all levels of the organization; 62 percent of Ys were admitting women.

The Y began shifting its focus away from the needs of young men to the needs of families in the wake of World War II. Group child care was introduced by the general secretary of the Y after he visited the Soviet Union and observed how child care offered by the government benefited both children and their parents. The fees the organization charged for child-care services had become the Y's second largest source of revenue by 1996.

There is a great deal more to say about the YMCA's influence on a number of other social institutions that we cannot cover here. A few notable examples include the colleges that grew out of programs created to train Y staff; the Boy Scout groups that were nurtured by YMCAs; and, the Peace Corps, which was patterned after the Y's World Service Workers branch.

Discussion

Let us consider the development of this organization in light of the five-factor framework on which we will be relying throughout the book.

Organizational mission

Although the YMCA's original mission clearly changed, it was never entirely abandoned. Creating new programs that members were willing to pay for is the way the organization sustained itself from the earliest years of its existence. However, there was a strong focus on religious identity, if not religion per se then, and there is virtually no religious programming now. Is this an example of "goal displacement"? Or would it be more accurate to say the mission continued to evolve over time rather than being displaced? It is also true that the original focus was directed to the needs of working-class young men, more specifically young men with rural origins who found themselves alone, without family in an unfamiliar city. Over time the organization began focusing on the needs and preferences registered by middle-class families in settled urban and suburban communities. More recently, it has been directing attention to the needs of disadvantaged individuals and families in urban areas.

The current national general secretary, James Bunting, makes the following observation about more recent shifts in focus. He says the social turmoil taking place during the late 1960s and early 1970s in this country presented the organization with a choice: whether "to keep learning or to become 20th-century Pharisees clinging to forms and theories that were once valid expressions of the best that was known, but that today are outdated and irrelevant." The decision was made to "refine" the organizational mission. The current mission statement identifies the organization's purpose as aiming "to put Christian principles into practice through programs that build healthy spirit, mind and body for all."

Organizational structure

The YMCA's structure developed as new units emerged across the country. These units formed a loosely organized federation of local associations. The local units could, and did, maintain their independence largely because they generated income on their own and were not dependent on headquarters for resources. Their funding came from people in their respective communities. Programs offered in each community reflected preferences expressed by members of the community rather than programs initiated by a professionalized staff either locally or at the headquarters. The organization does have a centralized headquarters office, the National Council of YMCAs of the USA, located in Chicago, but the locals have always been in a position to ignore headquarters' directives. Admitting women, for example, was initially opposed by the national headquarters, but most local organizations did admit women, and headquarters eventually dropped its opposition.

This may be a good time to take a closer look at the Young Women's Christian Association (YWCA), which certainly sounds like it should be a related unit, but, as we have already noted, it is an entirely separate organization. (We will not be examining its operations beyond this short discussion.) It was established in 1858. Like the YMCA, the YWCA started by building housing for women who were moving into urban areas on their own, initially New York and Boston. However, the YWCA quickly shifted its attention to fighting discrimination against women, with special emphasis on discrimination against nonwhite women. It prefaces its current mission statement with the following assertion: "Eliminating racism, empowering women—it's what we are about and what we intend to do." The YWCA formal mission statement is: "The YWCA is a women's membership movement nourished by its Christian faith and sustained by the richness of many beliefs and values. Strengthened by diversity, the YWCA draws together members who strive to create opportunities for women's growth, leadership, justice, and dignity for all people. The YWCA will thrust its collective power to the elimination of racism, wherever it exists, and by any means necessary."

Organizational funding

For the YMCA, funding its operations was, from the beginning, a matter of offering programs for which people were willing to pay a fee. The organization never developed reliance on contributions and bequests. Whether the organization would accept funds from the Community Trust, which is a secular organization operating in many communities, was a matter of debate for some time. When it became clear that the local units that chose to accept such funds had more money to operate and could therefore provide a wider range of programs, the debate ended as increasing numbers of locals were not only willing, but eager, to accept Community Trust monies.

Organizational evaluation

Each local association monitors its own performance. If programs grow, additional money comes in, and that particular branch can add even more programs and activities the members wish to support. To the extent that growth and longevity can serve as indicators of successful performance, the organization is clearly highly successful. The organization makes clear that it considers growth to be an important indicator of success. According to the national headquarters, the YMCA is "the largest not-for-profit community service organization in America." As of 2008, its most recent public report, it was operating 2,686 YMCAs, had 20.9 million members, and a budget of $5.96 billion.

The Chicago YMCA

Since the Mayer Zald case study, which forms the basis of this discussion, was inspired by the YMCA of Metropolitan Chicago, it is fitting that we say a little more about its history and current status.

Efforts to create a YMCA in Chicago were initiated in 1853 by a minister who invited a number of Protestant laymen to discuss the project. However, the idea was met with opposition, in part because Chicago was dealing with the aftermath of a cholera epidemic that took many lives and left the community in disarray. It took another five years before there was enough interest and support for returning to plans to build a YMCA in Chicago. It was established in 1858. The YMCA soon became a vital force in the city and was able to build its own facility. That facility burned down after one year, but it was replaced the following year. The YMCA continued to grow and expand, adding new programs and building new centers. It is worth noting that it was well-enough established to construct a far more impressive building in 1931—at the height of the Great Depression. It did so with the help of a donation from the publisher of one of Chicago's daily papers, the *Chicago*

Daily News. That year it opened the tallest, most luxurious building built to date in the city—the Lawson YMCA—which boasted two gyms, a swimming pool, barbershop, four restaurants, an auditorium, and a rooftop garden.

It is clear from Mayer Zald's account that the Chicago YMCA was highly responsive to the needs of the citizenry of the community it was in. During the first decades of the twentieth century, it was ready to offer Americanization classes to recent immigrants. Its business education programs were so successful it was able to add other courses and open a college, the Central YMCA College, which later became known as Roosevelt University. It opened the first welcome center for African Americans who were newcomers to the city at the Wabash YMCA located in what is now known as the Bronzeville community. The Wabash YMCA was considered an important enough site to merit the National Preservation Honor Award given by the National Trust for Historic Preservation in 2002.

The 1960s through the 1980s brought a large number of new developments such as child-care programs, senior home-help programs, and the YMCA Youth Justice program, which houses delinquent youth as an alternative to incarceration. By 2005, it had become the largest and longest-serving Single Room Occupancy (SRO) housing provider in the Midwest, supplying 1,500 units at five YMCA residences.

The YMCA-MC (YMCA of Metropolitan Chicago) celebrated its 150th anniversary in 2008. As of that year, it could say the following of itself. It had 100,000 members, 65 separate locations, 100 extension sites, and was the fourth largest charitable organization in Chicago. It was proud to announce that it was also the largest nonprofit employer in the state, one of the largest licensed child-care providers in the state, and one of the region's largest human services organizations. It was managing six human services centers, twenty-three membership and program centers, ten housing operations and four resident camps.

It is worth taking a closer look at the statement by the CEO and chair of the board of managers of the YMCA-MC introducing an earlier report—the 2005 annual report. He made the point that the organization needed to engage in some reflection in recognition of the approaching sesquicentennial in 2008. He stated that the financial turn achieved during 2005 was due to the assessment of the organization's strengths and weaknesses in 2000. The 2005 report also stated that this was the first year since 2001 that income exceeded expenses by a small margin. He concluded his report by saying that the assessment led to the observation that the organization's strength lay in its "rich traditions, its time-tested values and its mission." Accordingly, the organization made "mission sustainability" the priority. In other words, the organization was badly shaken by the recognition of the severity of its fiscal problems and was afraid it would not be able to survive, so sustainability became a major concern.

The 2006 report indicates that it continued to have success in overcoming its financial challenges, noting a surplus of $1.7 million after expenses at the end of the year. The report indicated that the largest portion of funds, at more than $58.7 million, is revenue from the fee-based programs. However, the organization was now relying on public support and contributions as well. It received more than $27.1 million in donations from individuals and organizations that year. Because it owns and operates housing units, its capital assets counting both investments and property were reported to be far larger, more than $113 million.

The 2007 annual report made clear that the YMCA-MC's fortunes had turned around. It was pleased to assert that it had the "strongest balance sheet in its history. A $57 million increase in net assets was recognized thanks primarily to gains from two property sales and investment earnings." The 2008 annual report, the most recent made publicly available, indicated that the YMCA-MC sustained a $20-million loss in assets, largely due to a drop in the value of its investment portfolio. As we know, this year marks the beginning of the Great Recession, meaning that virtually everyone's investments lost value. Its 2010 annual report states that total revenue was more than $86 million and expenses under $86 million, indicating that it managed to achieve an impressive recovery.

WHAT WE CAN LEARN FROM THESE CASES

The discussion presented in this chapter is designed to illustrate the case analysis approach. We began our analyses by focusing on the historical circumstances that shaped the two organizations' goals and organizational structures.

In the case of the National Foundation for Infantile Paralysis, the organization evolved "top-down." Not only was the organization formed by a small number of people, but the same people made all the decisions governing the organization's activities throughout its existence. The volunteers affiliated with the local chapters knew they were part of a much larger effort, which they hoped would succeed at some time in the future; however, waiting for researchers in some far-off lab to come up with a cure for this dread disease was not nearly as rewarding as direct contact with friends and neighbors who would truly appreciate the assistance the volunteers could offer then and there. Accordingly, they were pleased to accept the monies for this purpose coming in as a result of the organization's national profile and very visible national campaign.

By contrast, the volunteers who accepted responsibility for the annual fund-raising campaign did not deal with victims of polio directly, only with handling the money raised during their short term of office. The fact that they were not in a position to see the direct effects of their efforts on victims of the disease or to accept their gratitude was undoubtedly fortuitous. The arrangement meant they had less reason to become interested in holding on to the honorary position.

What is remarkable about the national foundation is how well the founders managed the delicate balance between their priorities and vision of the organization's core mission and the priorities of the two sets of volunteers on whom they were relying to help achieve that mission. They did so by imposing a stern set of restrictions on organizational operations, creating a unique organizational structure that was very effective in promoting goal attainment. It is impossible to know whether the structure would have persisted and for how long if the polio vaccine had not been discovered in the relatively short span of its organizational life.

The YMCA, by contrast, is an enterprise that grew "from the bottom up." Local organizations were created by people who then became actively involved in determining the functions those organizations would serve. Because these ventures emerged in response to local community interests and willingness to pay fees to support the programs that were created, the local chapters were in a good position to tailor the programs and services they were offering to fit local needs. The headquarters organization evolved to serve as a clearinghouse of ideas, not as a source of directives. The headquarters office has never had much power to direct the activities of local units because, unlike the foundation's local chapters, the Y locals did not see their activities as an extension of a single, uniform mission.

Evaluation of each local unit's performance was easily assessed by the leadership of that local and by anyone else observing its operations. But the only assessment that counted was that of the local leadership who would decide which programs would go forward and which would not. The popularity of the programs and activities the local organization offered came with a very concrete measure of success, namely, the number of participants they attracted and, probably more importantly, the amount of money they brought in. Programs that were judged to be unsuccessful could be dropped and replaced with programs that members not only wanted but were willing to support by paying a fee.

There was little need for any other form of program evaluation for most of the Y's existence. That changed as units of the organization in some cities, as is true of the Y operating in the heart of the city of Chicago, began to rely on government and foundation grants to fund programs that address far more complicated problems such as providing housing for low-income mothers and children, programs for juveniles at risk of becoming involved in crime, seniors, persons with disabilities, and so on. An increasing proportion of the costs for the services the Y offers, in many locations, is being covered by such funding sources rather than fees paid by participants.

Whether one sees the YMCA as a vital organization that is flexible enough to adapt and embrace new members, members who cannot vote for the programs they want by paying a fee; or, whether one sees it as an organization that is displacing the original evangelical mission that motivated its founders is something one must determine for oneself. One might also choose to see the Y's more recent emphasis on addressing the needs of the less fortunate as a distinctive and more clearly defined manifestation of the organization's original evangelical mission.

To sum up what we have been discussing thus far, one of the basic lessons we have learned based on the comparative analysis of the foundation and the YMCA cases is that it matters whether the organization is formed from the top down or from the bottom up. However, this is generally not a matter of rational choice, but of historical circumstances. It is also not a matter of one form being superior or inferior to the other, merely different. However, the direction from which the organization arises does have a major impact on organizational development, structure, fund-raising practices, and evaluation procedures.

In the final analysis, our review of the two case studies tells us that the problems identified by the founders of the two organizations provided the grounding for the organizations' missions. This, in turn, shaped the two organizations' respective structures and fund-raising arrangements. How we assess the performance of these organizations is a matter of perspective. Assessment of their respective evolution over time comes close to performance evaluation, which as we noted in the preceding chapter is a very complicated venture—which we will see confirmed as the stories presented by all the other organizations we will be encountering unfold.

Another lesson we can take from examining the workings of these two organizations has to do with the role played by stakeholders, that is, the people who have reason to be interested in the organization's work. Because they come to the organization for different reasons, bring varying expectations, and see the organization's accomplishments from distinctive perspectives, their impact on any organization we encounter is likely to be multifaceted and complex. For purposes of this discussion, let us group the interested parties we encountered in the preceding discussion into five not particularly discrete categories:

1. the beneficiaries of organizational programs;
2. those who provide the resources that allow the organization to deliver those services (i.e., those who fund organizational programs);
3. staff—those employed by the organization and, to a lesser extent, volunteers who work without the expectation of monetary compensation;

4. members of the community—community both in the sense of geographic community and community of interest; and
5. outside interested parties—independent organizations that issue evaluations, regulatory agencies, the media, and so on.

The first two categories of stakeholders could be seen to have more direct contact with the organization in the two cases we analyzed. The third category, the headquarters staff at the National Foundation for Infantile Paralysis, had a very direct voice in the organization's future whereas the staff connected to local branches clearly had much less to say about the future of the organization before and after it achieved its initial objective and was reorganized. In the case of the Y, the staff on-site, at the local level, is directly responsible for monitoring the organization's activities and altering the programs being offered accordingly. The fourth and fifth categories generally exhibit sporadic and unpredictable degrees of interest and involvement, but they have the potential to become major players. In combination, all of these interested parties make up the "interactional field" within which a nonprofit organization operates.

The authors who documented the two cases did not focus on the organizations' efforts to develop a "presentation of self," because this was not something to which analysts had paid attention until recently. More recently organizations have been doing much the same thing individuals do to create a public face to present to the world (i.e., the effort we make to be seen as we would like to be seen). This has become known in nonprofit organizational circles as "branding." The image that results is, therefore, largely purposefully developed, but to some extent it can emerge without the organization particularly intending to shape its image in the way onlookers ultimately perceived it. The role played by those in the organization's interactional field has a lot to do with this. In short, the expectations and values the stakeholders in an organization's interactional field bring to the organization may play a major role in shaping organizations' respective presentations of themselves, whether or not they plan for that.

Organizations generally strive to present an image or "brand" that closely reflects their respective organizational missions. The process requires attention to maintaining a careful balance between the identity the organization aims to present to its external audience at the symbolic level and the demands of internal operating arrangements designed to carry out organizational programs and activities with which the organization is associated at the practical level.

Who has been most influential in determining organizational operations within local YMCAs compared to who was most influential in organizing the operations of the national foundation makes the difference explicit. As we saw, the national foundation initially had two kinds of direct recipients of its programs and services: one, the victims of polio; and two, researchers working on the cure for polio. Because neither of these two sets of participants was in a position to influence how much money the organization could raise, neither had the power to influence organizational structure and programs. They could not influence decisions regarding how organizational funds would be spent. The founders who became the trustees of the national foundation were the only full-time members in a position to decree that half the money would go for research and half would go to the chapters operating in communities across the country. Although volunteers associated with the local chapters were very actively engaged in organizing local services, no one had a sufficient base of support to challenge or alter chapter policy. By prohibiting local chapters from creating full-time staff positions, the founders made certain that local chapters would find it difficult to displace the organization's primary goal.

The national foundation created a single presentation of self but employed a dual operating structure—one operating at the national level, but only appearing on a one month per year schedule, and another operating continuously at the local level. The media played a significant role in furthering the organization's goals by promoting its annual fund-raising campaign and giving a great deal of attention to achievements of local chapters. That happened because leading citizens' activities are always newsworthy, at least to members of their respective communities. Outside persons and agencies had little reason to become involved.

The identity of the YMCA was shaped by the fact that it was, at least initially, completely dependent on participants (i.e., recipients of its services) for its funding. This gave recipients of services a great deal of control over the programs each YMCA would offer, which is what gave each local unit of the YMCA its identity. Thus program success, as indicated by the funds any particular program generated, significantly impacted organizational structure. And as we have already seen, organizational structure has implications for all kinds of things, particularly staffing decisions. Because there was little need to rely on sources other than participants for support, neither the staff nor any outside party was in a position to override the preferences of participants of a particular local Y. As a result, each local's presentation of self was closely aligned to beneficiaries' preferences. The role of other stakeholders, especially any outside forces, was limited. That is far from the usual state of organizational operations affairs in most nonprofit organizations, or any other kinds of organizations for that matter.

As we have seen, both of the organizations we considered in this chapter have undergone major transformations. Both are far more dependent than they were in the past on funds from foundations and government agencies, meaning that outside agencies and stakeholders now have much more influence on organizational operations. Organizational leaders in both organizations must perform outcome evaluations of the programs they offer in response to funders' guidelines. And they are now more likely to employ consultants from a wide range of sectors for guidance on "best practices" being promoted in the sectors they represent and the funders whose preferences they must take into account.

The organizations we will encounter in the following chapters all have their own stories to tell. We will examine their unique histories, distinctive missions, structures, funding arrangements, and evaluation procedures. I hope you find their stories as captivating as I do.

Chapter Seven

Delivering Nursing Care in a Person's Home

This is the story of the Visiting Nurse Association of Chicago. The case study documents its response to being forced to confront a significant change in funding arrangements that had a major impact on its financial profile.

ORGANIZATIONAL MISSION

The mission statement: The Visiting Nurse Association of Chicago (VNA-C) is a not-for-profit, full-service home health-care agency that delivers quality service that is of value to the community and is responsive to client needs. VNA-C provides access to home health services to clients, including the underserved, in the greater metropolitan Chicago area.

ORGANIZATIONAL HISTORY

The Visiting Nurse Association of Chicago story begins in 1889. One of the first of many very similar agencies created across the country, it was established through the efforts of a small number of women who recognized that countless numbers of people were not getting basic health services. This was a special era in Chicago when the problems of poor people, especially immigrants, became a cause that a cadre of high-status members of the community began to identify and address. For example, Jane Addams, who is widely recognized as the primary force behind the creation of Hull House, the first settlement house established in the United States, was also a founding member of the VNA of Chicago. Hull House opened its doors the same year as the

VNA with the aim of providing the community with a wide range of social services, cultural events, and, eventually, training for the persons who would be providing these services (i.e., social workers).

The Visiting Nurse Associations of America (VNAA) was formed as a coalition of independently operated VNAs in 1893. Its formation indicates that there was recognition of the need for the services visiting nurses could provide across the country. Although the agencies were similar in their objectives, each was administered by a voluntary board of local community leaders interested in addressing the issues the members of the board were concerned about in their community.

It is worth considering the significance of the approach to nursing care the VNA of Chicago employed. The VNA was committed to providing health-care services to the underserved very directly—in their homes—rather than requiring them to come to a hospital or clinic to receive the services. Of course, this was not an unusual approach at that time. A more detailed historical overview of health care during those early years makes clear why availability of home health care was crucial.

Health-care services prior to the twentieth century have little resemblance to health-care services being delivered now—in the twenty-first century. To begin with, hospitals were dangerous places that no one entered willingly. Surgery was performed, but at considerable risk. Most people relied on folk remedies and the services of the apothecary or chemist (druggist) for advice, potions, and salves, anything to avoid going into the hospital. Those who could afford it summoned the doctor to visit them in their homes (i.e., to make a "house call"). The fact of the matter is that health-care services were largely a matter of whatever care could be provided in the home. However, the small black bag that doctors brought with them contained little, certainly by current standards, that would have a profound effect. (Antibiotics were not available until the 1950s, meaning that infection was not something medicine could control very effectively.) Looking at it from a current-day perspective, doctors could provide solace but not much efficacious medical care. The most effective treatment anyone could offer was keeping patients clean, comfortable, and comforted. This was a job that any middle-class woman was thought to be able to handle. That is exactly the role visiting nurses played: not the only role, but certainly one of the most important roles, at least initially. Offering this form of care to poor people was especially important because, in many cases, the poor either did not realize the health benefits of careful attention to sanitation or simply could not manage it.

By the middle of the twentieth century, doctors were making fewer house calls. However, visiting nurses continued to visit the sick in their homes even as the number of people entering hospitals and nursing homes where they would receive 24-hour care had vastly increased. Given that most people prefer to stay in their own homes as long as they can, meant that there was a continuing need for visiting nurses. By the latter part of the twentieth century, the model of care the VNA had created had become known as "home health care."

The VNA of Chicago can lay claim to a long list of achievements during the first hundred years of its existence. Its earliest accomplishments were focused on public-health needs of the community. For example, VNA nurses offered their services to area hospitals that were caring for smallpox epidemic victims. They helped to care for maternity patients at the newly established Chicago maternity center. They pioneered the development of industrial nursing at the International Harvester Company. These efforts were highly lauded by Chicago-area physicians at the time.

We should also note the VNA initiated services that inspired the founding of a number of other organizations that became well known and respected in their own right. One of its early accomplishments was to establish the "Baby Tent" at Northwestern University in 1905 to provide milk and other basic needs to infants. This led to the founding of the Infant Welfare Society of Chicago. Its efforts on behalf of tuberculosis patients were instrumental in helping the Tuberculosis Institute of Chicago get started in 1906. That institute evolved into the Respiratory Health Association of Metropolitan Chicago (which is the subject of the following chapter). In 1907, it established the Social Services Department at the Children's Memorial Hospital in Chicago, which became a model for hospital-based social work departments across the country.

The VNA launched its first training program in public-health nursing in 1922. It was so well regarded that the Chicago Department of Public Health adopted it when it accepted responsibility for training school nurses in 1910. The VNA later expanded this program to offer graduate and allied health training.

The organization incorporated any and all technologies that could be delivered to the homebound patient as they were introduced. The transformation in what medical care and nursing services could offer underwent enormous change after World War II. Technological advancement in home health care was rapid and continuous. Accordingly, the VNA incorporated IV therapy, chemotherapy, and AIDS care into the array of services it was offering. When the Medicare and Medicaid programs were legislated in 1965, the agency created a new set of offerings designed to provide continuity of care for patients who were being discharged from hospitals to their own homes after hospital stays that were steadily becoming shorter. It did this through the new Coordinated Home Care Program.

In 1989, the VNA celebrated one hundred years of operation. Six years later, in September of 1995, it ceased delivering health-care services. The board of directors announced that, first, its home health-care operation was being sold to CareMed Chicago, an affiliate of the University of Chicago

Hospitals; and, second, that the VNA would be operating as a philanthropic, grant-making foundation in the future. We will examine more closely the factors that contributed to this outcome. Let us begin by considering two dimensions of VNA operations throughout its 106 years as a direct delivery, home health-care agency—funding for its operations and evaluation of its performance.

ORGANIZATIONAL FUNDING

As is true of most of the charitable endeavors established during the early part of the twentieth century that we will be discussing, the women who launched the Chicago VNA did so with the full expectation that they would be assuming personal responsibility for finding the money to support the organization's activities. Over time they began soliciting funds from others in their social circle who were familiar with the work the VNA was doing.

They did not engage in vigorous fund-raising activities during the first half of the organization's lifetime because the cost of the services the VNA was providing was largely for personnel. The salaries going to nurses and nursing aides were not very high in those days. Although raising a sufficient amount of money was not necessarily easy, funding the organization's activities was not so burdensome that it was viewed as a possible threat to the organization's survival. That changed during the second half of the VNA's lifetime. The rapid development of medical technology brought a swift escalation in costs. The agency needed to raise considerably more money to cover the cost of the equipment and other materials associated with the technologically sophisticated services they were now providing.

The passage of Medicare and Medicaid in 1965 produced a new influx of funds, which the agency welcomed. However, implementation of the two programs introduced a whole new set of unanticipated complications that, as we shall see shortly, turned out to be the beginning of the end.

We can get some idea of the challenges the VNA was confronting by considering the rise in the total cost of providing health care, which started to become increasingly more pressing by the early 1980s. The 1980 annual report indicates the year's revenue came from the following sources: return on investments based on investing the endowment (which is essentially an organizational savings account created by donors), current contributions from individuals and corporations, United Way funding, and patient fees. At the end of the year, the VNA found itself with a $369,563 shortfall. The board members reached into their pockets to cover $300,000 of that amount. That left the VNA with an operating deficit of $69,563. Money to cover the deficit came out of the endowment. The board did not expect this to become a pattern. However, the organization found itself operating at a deficit almost every year after that. The agency covered the annual deficit that occurred in each of those years by dipping into the endowment. That meant the organization was losing the interest on the reduced amount of money in the account in the short run. If the organization continued to do this, it would eventually spend down its endowment to zero.

When the VNA board found itself facing a $1,896,414 deficit in 1989, its hundred-year anniversary, board members realized they could no longer put off confronting their fiscal problems. The board explored every possibility over the next four years before deciding to stop doing what the organization had been doing with great success over the previous century.

ORGANIZATIONAL EVALUATION

The VNA did not carry out systematic formal evaluations of its performance during its early years. The founders knew that what they were doing was being well received and recognized because the organization received so much acclaim from a wide range of stakeholders in its interactional field.

During the second half of the twentieth century, accrediting organizations began to play a more active role and assert greater influence over organizational performance in the health sector. Formal evaluation procedures were initiated during the 1960s in connection with the passage of Medicare and Medicaid legislation mandating accreditation by the Joint Commission on Accreditation of Healthcare Organizations (JCAHO) for all organizations receiving government reimbursements. The work of the VNA was reviewed by the National League for Nursing (NLN), which had by then created a set of standards under its Community Health Accreditation Program. Home health-care organizations now undergo NLN accreditation review every three years. The agency's work was also reviewed by the Illinois Department of Public Health. The state is interested in overseeing the quality, quantity, and cost of care being provided to Medicaid patients because the state is responsible for approximately half of the costs of care expended on the people enrolled in the Medicaid program. (We will return in a moment to the role the two major federal health insurance programs, Medicare and Medicaid, played in determining the VNA's fate.)

The VNA's own record keeping required the organization to conduct ongoing internal evaluations, with particular attention to identifying factors responsible for its increasingly troubling financial picture. The results were generally not kept for future reference, so few are available for us to review. However, the financial picture was becoming so troubling that the agency launched a major organizational self-evaluation in 1981. There were several parts to the evaluation. The agency surveyed all patients over sixty-five in its care. The executive director reported the overwhelming majority were happy with the services they were receiving, adding that the suggestions "for augmented service will be used in forming our plan for future service."

The central focus of the evaluation of organizational performance was directed at the agency's ability to address the VNA's goals. The then-president of the VNA began discussion of this portion of the evaluation results in the 1982 annual report by reaffirming the agency's goals very purposefully. She set out the following list of specific objectives that were to be employed in pursuit of the organization's mission:

- Acutely ill homebound patients requiring skilled services under a physician's plan of treatment will achieve recovery of health or a stable condition and functional skills within their level of capability
- Terminally ill patients wishing to remain at home will die in comfort and with dignity in their home environment if at all possible, and their families will be supported throughout the process
- Families with children at risk of serious health problems and/or developmental delay, who are unable to reach out for community-based services, will demonstrate improved parenting skills, and the risk to their children will be eliminated or reduced
- The chronically ill will be maintained in their homes at their maximum functional level, and institutional placement will be prevented or delayed
- Ambulatory clients will have greater awareness of their health risks and methods to reduce risks
- Individuals providing health services will have an increased understanding of community health needs and methods for meeting those needs

She stated very explicitly that Medicare and Medicaid would not fully cover agency costs in providing such services. Accordingly, additional sources of funding would have to be identified. She said the VNA would be instituting two new programs the following year—a hospice for the care of the terminally ill and a long-term care program specifically designed to address the needs of the chronically ill. This was being done with the expectation that the two new programs would bring additional income from Medicare and Medicaid fees. The statement ended with the declaration that the agency would be devoting $2.3 million to provide free care over the following year.

Over the next couple of years, it became clear that the hospice and long-term care programs succeeded admirably in addressing the organizational mission. They were less successful in adding very much to the agency's revenues. A few years later, finding that it was continuing to face annual deficits, the VNA decided to invite business consultants from the for-profit sector to assess its performance and offer advice on making changes that would lead first to more streamlined operations and, ultimately, cost savings.

In January of 1986, the board of directors retained one of the leading consulting firms in the area, Booz Allen Hamilton. The firm agreed to interview health-care professionals throughout the United States to gain insight on prevailing health-care trends and organizational responses. The consultants analyzed the VNA's financial, marketing, and management activities. They compared the performance of the VNA of Chicago to VNAs across the country as well as other types of community nursing services and profit-making home-care corporations. The final report presented in March of that year advised the VNA to do the following:

- lower costs overall, without sacrificing the quality of care
- strengthen sources of payment
- streamline the organization and corporate structure

The VNA began implementing the recommendations the following month. It reduced its management and supervisory staff. It announced plans to consolidate its six district offices into one central office and one branch office at a suburban community hospital with which it had a service contract to serve as "a provider of choice for home care." The VNA initiated a major overhaul of its information system. Shortly thereafter, it retained the services of Louden & Company, which the VNA described as a leader in home-care marketing, to help formulate a marketing plan.

The VNA board of directors initiated another extensive internal review in 1993. The 1994 annual report stated that the agency had invited the Arthur Andersen Consulting firm to help the agency streamline its operations and increase its income. The chairman of the board of directors and the chief executive officer stated that the agency's leadership considered completion of the review to be a significant accomplishment. However, they said the agency was even more pleased to announce that all the effort that had gone into reorganizing the agency's work resulted in an 18-percent increase in business over the previous year. The number of patient visits rose to 167,000. Fifteen percent of those visits were categorized as services delivered to the underserved and uninsured.

The money generated by growth in patient visits in 1993 was not, however, enough to overcome the dismal funding outlook over the long term. The 1994 annual report turned out to be the final one documenting the workings of the VNA of Chicago. The next report was issued under the auspices of the VNA Foundation.

STRUCTURAL REORGANIZATION AFTER 1994

In order to understand why the Chicago VNA stopped providing direct care and reorganized its structure and operations to become a foundation requires understanding the level of commitment on the part of all involved to the organization's original mission. It is difficult to see how the agency could maintain its commitment to that mission in the face of developments in health-care delivery systems in this country that evolved over the second half of the twentieth century. Let us take a closer look at the implications of those changes for the VNA.

As we have already noted, there is no question that the cost of delivering home health care was not nearly as costly during the first half of the twentieth century as it was during the second half of the century. Just as the doctor's black bag did not provide expensive, sophisticated medical solutions to health problems, the services a visiting nurse provided were similarly neither high priced nor technologically sophisticated during the first half of the century.

There is a considerable amount of consensus on the part of health economists and everyone else who studies health-care delivery arrangements in this country that the sudden explosion of technological advances in medicine is one of the main factors responsible for the rise in health-care costs over the past half century, not only in this country, but across all advanced industrialized societies.

Indeed, health care was steadily becoming unaffordable for the majority of poor people during the years following World War II. Recognition of that reality led to the passage of the Medicare and Medicaid health insurance programs during the mid-1960s. Medicaid was designed to reimburse services provided to two categories of the poor and underserved—first, women and their young dependent children; and second, poor elderly persons. It is important to note that adults with no young dependent children were not covered by this legislation regardless of how poor they were.

The second category of persons eligible for Medicaid coverage included poor Medicare enrollees. The Medicare program allows all Americans who have paid into Social Security to enroll in the Medicare program by virtue of reaching age sixty-five, regardless of their income. Over time another category of persons became eligible for Medicare services, namely, persons who are disabled and/or blind. If they were poor enough, disabled and blind persons could also qualify for Medicaid. Because the state is required to pick up half of the cost of delivering Medicaid services, Medicaid legislation permits the state to determine the level of poverty that makes a person eligible for Medicaid in that state. Illinois set the threshold at 100 percent of poverty at the time Medicaid legislation was passed.

The poverty threshold is set by the federal government and adjusted annually; but some states set far lower levels, as low as 24 percent of poverty in a few states; others set much higher cutoff levels. The 2012 Health and Human Services federal poverty guideline or cutoff that determines who is poor in this country is an annual income of $11,170 for one person and $23,050 for a family of four.

The passage of the Medicare and Medicaid health insurance programs had a positive impact on the VNA's finances initially, because the agency was suddenly being reimbursed for the health-care services it had been providing to patients who were unable to pay for their care. Policy makers who authored the two pieces of legislation did so with the expectation that the demand for services would decline once the needs of so many underserved people had been met. It did not take long to discover that this would not happen.

It is not hard to see how the changes introduced with the passage of the two national health insurance programs would turn out to be disadvantageous to the VNA over the long run. What changed was the sudden awareness on the part of many other parties of the potential for financial gain the steady stream of government funding would provide. Suddenly the number of organizations interested in offering home health-care services began to expand. Prior to the passage of the Medicare and Medicaid legislation, the Chicago VNA had virtually no competition. According to the 1986 annual report, a few new home health agencies had come into existence, reaching a total of ten operating in the city as of 1976; by 1986, there were 150. Even more important is the fact that the majority of new agencies coming into existence were being established to operate on a for-profit basis. The for-profit agencies did provide free care in some instances, which happened when patients could not pay their bills. However, this is a situation that the for-profit agencies made every effort to avoid. In order to assure themselves of profit, the for-profit agencies made every effort to avoid patients with no health-care insurance (i.e., poor people who would produce "bad debt"). Enrolling only those who come fully covered by health insurance is now a well-recognized phenomenon in health-care circles called "cream skimming" or "cherry picking."

This had the effect of increasing the number of people who were calling on the VNA to provide free care. The challenge the VNA board confronted over the last decade of its operations was determining how it would respond to the decline in the number of paying patients, who were being recruited via aggressive advertising campaigns by the for-profit agencies, and the increasing proportion of nonpaying patients it was finding itself caring for. The central question was deciding whether it would or should respond by altering its mission in the face of the new competitive environment. In other words, the question was—should the VNA reduce its commitment to serving non-paying patients in order to survive? It chose to revise its structure, not its mission.

Revised Mission Statement of the VNA Foundation as of 1998

The revised mission statement is: The VNA of Chicago now operates exclusively as a grant-making foundation, giving financial support to nonprofit organizations offering home- and community-based care to the underserved. Our methods have changed, but our mission has not: To provide health services to those who need them most, where they need them most, regardless of their ability to pay.

HISTORY OF THE VNA OF CHICAGO FOUNDATION

The VNA of Chicago Foundation (VNAF) began operations in 1996 as a granting agency with financial assets of $32,987,160. That year it distributed $1,609,050 to eighteen grantees. The following year it funded thirty-seven projects. It has been able to increase steadily the number of grants it distributes over the following years. In 2006, it distributed nearly $2 million to fifty-four grantees. The grants are to be used as start-up funds. They are awarded to established, reputable organizations that submit proposals outlining new initiatives aimed at providing nursing care services to underserved populations.

The VNAF has decided to keep down costs in order to be able to distribute more money to potential grantees. Accordingly, it has not published an annual report since 2008. That year it reported awarding more than $16 million to four hundred nonprofit agencies serving the area's medically underserved population since it came into existence. The organization also reported that it had won the Wilmer Shields Rich Award for Excellence in Communications, which is sponsored by the Council on Foundations, for the fourth time over the past six years. The VNAF has been publishing a financial report and list of the grants awarded over the year rather than the more traditional glossy annual report. The 2009 report indicated that the total amount of awards for the year was $2,257,723 distributed to sixty-two grantees. The 2010 report indicated that $2.1 million was distributed to sixty-two grantees that year as well.

WHAT WE CAN LEARN FROM THE VNA CASE

The VNA of Chicago case offers us a lesson in unanticipated consequences. We see an organization being confronted with hard choices that stem from its decision to remain faithful to its mission. The case also tells us that its historical origins gave rise to its organizational mission, which, in turn, gave shape to its organizational structure and fund-raising arrangements. The VNA-C grew "from the bottom up." It was only loosely tied to the national association of VNAs across the country and took no directives and received no funds from the national association. The VNA-C's mission to provide health-care services to clients regardless of their ability to pay meant that its mission was one that would never be fully realized or fulfilled because it was highly unlikely it would run out of needy clients.

The VNA was clearly a leader in the field of home health care at a time when there was not much interest in providing such a service to people who were poor and could not have afforded to have a doctor visit them at home or to hire a private duty nurse to provide what we now call "long-term care." Private duty nurses were widely available during the first half of the twentieth century, but because doing this work was the way private duty nurses made their living, they could not afford to provide their services for free to those who could not pay for them. It was the need for the full range of health-care services for those who could not afford them that led to the passage of Medicare and Medicaid legislation in 1965. The two pieces of legislation identified enough people, in business terms—a sufficiently large market—whose care would be reimbursed by guaranteed government insurance funding to attract investment in new home health organizations. This is not to say that the newly established for-profit agencies were not interested in providing good health-care services. It is to say that they were not charities. They were not interested in giving away their services. They were interested in treating paying patients whose care was reimbursed and in making a profit doing so.

In the case of the Chicago VNA, the unanticipated devastating consequence of introducing the two highly beneficial health insurance programs for a large number of Americans who could not afford home health services was the growing imbalance between paying and nonpaying patients seeking the VNA's services. For-profit home health organizations could and often did offer services to paying patients at a lower price than the VNA because they were not using the surplus (i.e., the profit in the case of for-profit agencies) to cover the cost of serving nonpaying patients.

This brings up a troubling issue that periodically mushrooms into something the media invariably treat as a tremendous discovery attributable to investigative journalism. In actuality it is probably always there, waiting for a slow news period. The General Accounting Office (GAO) is periodically asked to look into the delivery of services by nursing homes. Its most recent report indicates that for-profit nursing homes continue to have more violations than nonprofit or government-owned nursing homes (2009). The GAO reports a very similar finding each time it conducts research to address this question. The story becomes far more attention grabbing when local media offer photographs and statements made by family members regarding the terrible conditions found at some homes.

Getting back to the problems faced by the VNA, from a business perspective, the solution to its need for funds was obvious. It simply had to find a way to provide services that would bring in more money. Business plans make clear that organizational success depends on making products or services that consumers are willing to pay for. The corporate sector solution advises organizations to be a more aggressive and thereby become more successful competitors. How that would happen in the VNA case is not so clear.

Let us look more closely at this option. Think about it—why are so few entrepreneurs interested in starting up new airplane or automobile companies, but so many are interested in starting up new Internet sites? The reason is a matter of start-up costs. Turning to the health sector, it is pretty clear that a great deal of money is to be made in delivering health care, but you don't see much interest in starting up new full-service hospitals these days. You do see a lot of investors willing to start home health-care agencies because the required investment is far smaller.

In sum, the rapid increase in home health agencies that were created on a for-profit basis made it impossible for the VNA to retain a sufficient number of insured patients or self-pay patients to guarantee it would have enough money left over (*surplus* in nonprofit terms and *profit* in for-profit terms) to treat nonpaying patients. Business plans make explicit the fact that products and services that do not bring in profit and, more to the point, in this case—the people who require those services—must be dropped. From a nonprofit mission-driven perspective, providing products and services to people who would otherwise not be able to afford them is exactly what the VNA set out to do. Changing its mission to bring in more money by rejecting patients who could not afford to pay the full cost of VNA services would have required that the agency abandon its essential identity and purpose.

At the same time, given its steady record of financial deficits over a number of years, the VNA's options were limited. One, it could continue to provide services to what was becoming a steadily growing proportion of nonpaying patients and go bankrupt but keep its mission intact. Two, it could turn itself into a for-profit operation and continue to operate but abandon its original mission. It chose a third alternative, that is, to pursue its original mission and turn to a new and different structure to do so.

Establishing a foundation is the route that case law (the practices followed by other organizations and approved of by the courts) says nonprofit organizations may choose to follow when they decide to sell all or part of their assets. The VNA-C board's decision to cease direct care operations and to use all remaining funds to establish a foundation may have been upsetting to some who were most closely involved with the VNA in previous years. However, the question of whether the VNA name would be sold at the same time inspired the most impassioned debates. In retrospect, the decision to keep the VNA name as the identifier of the newly established foundation turns out to have been the right choice for the succeeding organization, the VNA Foundation. According to the director of the VNA Foundation, he is pleased to find that his office continues to receive calls from people who received VNA services in the past and are now interested in expressing their gratitude by making a contribution.

Once the decision was made to form a foundation, there was no opposition from stakeholders to plans outlining how the remaining funds would be used. The organization stayed as close to its original mission as it could given the decision to change its organizational framework. That has not always been true of other organizations that have undergone a comparable transition. Establishing a foundation is often not nearly as harmonious a process as it was in the VNA's case. Let us turn to the implications of conversion from nonprofit to for-profit status and take a closer look at the many problems that are related to the unremitting burden charitable organizations face in coming up with enough money to fund efforts directed at attaining their respective missions.

THE TRANSITION TO FOUNDATION STATUS

Let's begin with a very basic question—who owns nonprofit organizations? The question has practical implications. This becomes apparent when a nonprofit organization decides to sell its assets, as was true in the VNA's case. The assets may include real estate, office equipment, vehicles, other technical equipment, plus less-tangible assets, such as the list of organizations or agencies that had been referring patients (i.e., "the business"). Who gets the money acquired in the sale of those assets? Who should decide who gets those funds? Think about it: the people who contributed all that money years ago to help a particular nonprofit organization carry out its work cannot be asked what they want done, because they are no longer around. Even if they were around, how would you find out what they would like done with the money—survey all of them? Where would you get their names and addresses?

Then, there is the question of how much of a say different people should have. Depending on how much they contributed? But the value of a $10 contribution years ago is not the same as the value of $10 now. How would you deal with that? As you can see, asking contributors for their input is an impossible task. That leaves the job of deciding what to do with the funds to the people who are currently responsible for the organization—the board of directors or trustees.

This is not to say outside observers cannot or will not express their opinion. Decisions regarding the future of high-profile organizations can get a lot of outside attention from a whole range of stakeholders, including those who may have been casual observers prior to the decision; for instance, members of the local community who may not have used the organization's service but for whom the organization carries symbolic meaning or has nostalgic value. Those most closely involved, both current staff members who are losing their jobs and the representatives of the organizations making offers to purchase the nonprofit's assets, can be expected to have a great deal to say about it. Various government agencies are likely to be interested in the process to make sure that insiders are not taking advantage in some way. The list of interested observers can get lengthy. In the end, what happens to the assets may become a matter of negotiation that is finally settled in the courts.

Let's consider how the process of moving away from nonprofit organizational status works out when the organization decides that the best option to assure itself of a future is to switch to for-profit status.

Noteworthy Cases of Shifting from Nonprofit to For-Profit Status

Two types of nonprofit organizations have been especially active in the process of changing their status from nonprofit to for-profit over the past few decades, namely hospitals and nonprofit health insurance companies. Small hospitals, much like the VNA-C, that could not afford all the costly new technology being acquired by large hospitals became excellent targets for buyouts by the newly developing hospital chain corporations. There have also been many nonprofit hospital mergers. However, they have not attracted nearly as much public scrutiny because such transactions have generally not involved the exchange of money in which the public had a stake. In other words, investors are not losing money when nonprofit organizations choose to join together to form a larger nonprofit entity. Members of local communities have, of course, expressed varying degrees of concern when local hospitals were taken over by larger hospitals outside of the community. In some cases, they saw the shift as a loss of an important and familiar local institution, even if it had been undergoing visible decline. However, the community could do little to prevent the takeover unless it could come up with an alternative plan and the funds to carry out that plan. In many cases, the reason the hospital was in the situation it was in was because the community itself was in the process of changing, so it had less attachment and fewer objections.

The increase in health-care costs brought about by the need for expensive technology and expensive staff who would be proficient in using that technology had the same effect on hospitals as it did on the VNA-C. Accordingly, many nonprofit hospitals were forced to close because they were no longer able to attract either doctors or patients and therefore could not afford to purchase the new technology over the past few decades. The boards of those that have been sold for profit have often used the funds to establish a foundation dedicated to addressing a specific health problem, usually providing research monies focusing on the problem. Precedent-setting cases, documented as case law, established the practice of forming a foundation, whether it was designed to assist people with a certain problem or provide research funds, as an acceptable answer to the question of where the money from the sale of nonprofit hospitals should go. A number of states codified as state law what had become a common practice. When government-run hospitals are forced to close, the monies coming from the closures go back to the government unit, whether city or county, that had been supporting the hospital.

BlueCross BlueShield insurance plans, or Blues, constitute the second category of organizations that exhibited a wave of mergers, conversions, and buyouts over the past couple of decades. As was true of the approach to care taken by the VNA-C, the Blues were established to provide health insurance on a not-for-profit basis. This was very appealing when the first Blues plan came into existence in 1929, because people were having trouble paying their bills during the depression years. New Blues plans quickly emerged all over the country associated with cities and various other geographic entities, in some cases the whole state. In 1990 eighty organizations were in existence. A decade or so later, the BlueCross BlueShield Association was reporting thirty-nine. Previously independent associations were merging to form larger regional associations.

Competition from for-profit health insurance companies over the previous couple of decades had made operating on a nonprofit basis more difficult. For-profit insurance companies could be selective (i.e., "cherry pick" and "cream skim") in choosing the organizations they were interested in entering into agreements with and whose employees they were ready to insure— offering lower rates to employers whose employees were engaged in low-risk jobs or were younger (i.e., employees at a lower risk of costly health problems). The Blues' original charter, and accompanying mission, required them to enroll everyone at the same rate, which meant they could not compete with the for-profit companies by offering lower prices to some employers. That eventually led to declining enrollments. An increasing number of Blues plans argued they were forced to make the shift to for-profit status to obtain release from the restrictions related to their nonprofit status. They also needed to provide themselves with a sudden influx of operating funds, which nonprofit status also made more difficult.

The Blues' conversions to for-profit status got a great deal more attention than local hospital conversions for a number of reasons—a larger number of people were being affected, far more money was generally involved, state government oversight agencies were mandated to review such changes, and, probably most significantly, the question of who would or should get the funds resulting from the sale of assets was far less clear. The fact that the conversion trend took off so suddenly and affected people in so many parts of the country caused state insurance commissioners throughout the country to pay attention to how the issue was being addressed in other states. The primary responsibility of insurance commissioners is the protection of consumers from fraud that might be perpetrated by insurance companies.

A few conversions were especially newsworthy. The three that seem to have attracted most attention were Empire in New York, Anthem-WellPoint in California, and Premera in Washington.

The Empire Case

Empire BlueCross BlueShield of New York concluded its seven-year effort to convert from a nonprofit organization to a for-profit corporation in 2002. Empire initiated plans for the conversion because it was essentially bankrupt. Enrollment had dropped very suddenly—it had 8.1 million enrollees in 1992 and 4.5 million in 1996. It had almost no cash left in its reserves (in savings). Some very vocal observers publicly stated that this was entirely due to the incompetence of Empire's administrators and that, therefore, they were unsympathetic to Empire's distress. Empire's administrators admitted they initiated the shift to for-profit status in order to obtain operating funds. The public reaction was so negative that the spokesmen for the organization quickly abandoned their attempt to argue that Empire should get any private funds to facilitate reorganizing the organization's affairs. Empire management could not defend against accusations of mismanagement. This permitted four sets of stakeholders to lay claim to the funds.

1. Representatives of New York hospitals argued they should receive the funds because they had agreed to accept a discounted rate from Empire throughout its existence because of its nonprofit status. They said they would use the funds to set up programs to care for the underserved, carry out medical research, and support medical education.

2. Workers represented by the Services Employees International Union, Local 1199, who had not been given raises for some time because the state was in financial crisis and was not reimbursing hospitals enough to give workers raises, said they deserved a major share of the windfall.

3. A coalition of community organizations, including groups representing AIDS patients, breast cancer patients, multiple sclerosis patients among others, cited case law indicating that all conversions of this sort must create a foundation to support health-care delivery and research. They held that they were the most obvious legitimate recipients.

4. The state took the position that it originally sponsored the BC-BS organization in 1934 and gave it many privileges it did not extend to competing for-profit insurance companies. It was, therefore, entitled to reap the full return on the conversion, which would help it deal with the serious fiscal problems it was facing.

Over the seven-year period while these debates and related lawsuits were being pursued, Empire managed to reorganize on its own and begin operating on a better financial footing. That had a major impact on the ultimate sale price. In 1992, Wall Street evaluated the organization's worth at zero; by 1997, it estimated that its value had risen to $300 million; by 2001, to $1 billion; and by 2002, to $2 billion. The Initial Public Offering (IPO) of the newly formed for-profit corporation, WellChoice, was for $27 per share.

So the big question is—who should be getting the money the sale of this organization brought in? The IPO, that is, sale, could only go forward if and when the New York State insurance commissioner approved the plans for where the money would go. That is not exactly the same thing as deciding who owns this particular nonprofit entity. However, the approval part of the process does have the effect of settling the question of who gets the money. In the end, New York State, with the cooperation of the state insurance commissioner, appropriated the funds in order to spend the money on health-related programs and wage increases for health workers. It agreed to spend the entire amount over the following three years.

The Anthem-WellPoint Case

Anthem, a health insurance company based in Indianapolis, announced it intended to acquire WellPoint of California, which was a Blues insurance company in earlier years, for $16.5 billion in October 2003. (If the name WellPoint rings any bells, it may be because you heard that WellPoint of California's rate increase announcement in February of 2010 played a role in passage of the health reform legislation in March of 2010; back to that in a moment.)

Anthem converted to for-profit status in 2001. It had been operating non-profit Blues plans in Colorado, Connecticut, Indiana, Kentucky, Maine, Nevada, New Hampshire, and Ohio as nonprofit organizations prior to that time. Anthem purchased the Kansas Blues later that year. In 2002, it purchased Trigon, the for-profit company operating the Blues plan in Virginia. In this case, Trigon stockholders were involved. They voted to approve the sale in return for Anthem stock.

WellPoint Health Networks, Inc., of California, the nonprofit BlueCross BlueShield organization, converted to for-profit status in 1993. In 1996, it acquired Georgia Blues. When the Anthem acquisition plan was announced in 2003, the Georgia insurance commissioner quickly approved the purchase of the Georgia WellPoint plan in return for a $126.5 million package of financial assistance from WellPoint. When WellPoint sought to buy the Maryland Blues plan, the Maryland legislature was not nearly as willing to go along with the sale. The Maryland legislature demanded that WellPoint provide evidence the sale would benefit consumers in Maryland. A consultant hired by Maryland's Insurance Department valued the Maryland Blues Plan at $2.2 billion, but WellPoint had offered only $1.3 billion. The state legislature also found the bonuses the executives expected to receive at the point of sale to be excessive. The chief executive officer of the Maryland Blues plan expected to receive $9 million. The legislature stopped the bonuses from being distributed. Ultimately, WellPoint and the state of Maryland came to an agreement, and the sale went through in 2003.

It took another year for the California insurance commissioner and Anthem to come to an agreement. The California commissioner approved the deal in November of 2004 in return for a commitment from Anthem that it would allocate $250 million to improving health-care services for the poor in California. The commissioners from other states did not raise objections. The new entity came into existence as WellPoint, Inc., by the end of the year.

No one could have doubts regarding WellPoint's interest in being profitable after it announced that it would raise its rates by 25 to 39 percent depending on enrollee characteristics in February 2010 just as the Health Reform Bill was coming to a vote in Congress. The fact that the announcement came at this time angered opponents of the bill but provided support for the bill's proponents' charge that insurance companies' drive to attain ever-increasing levels of profitability needed to be reined in, which is one of the central objectives of the Affordable Care Act of 2010.

The Premera Case

Premera of Washington State is a nonprofit health insurance company that also operates in Alaska and Oregon. It initiated steps to convert to for-profit status in 2002. The Washington State insurance commissioner announced he would hold public hearings on this move. A Seattle newspaper used the Freedom of Information Act to obtain information on the details of the plan. It reported the deal required that the chief executive officer receive $750,000 in stock options that would bring his annual compensation to $2.2 million. Four executive vice presidents would nearly triple their annual compensation when they received planned stock options. The public outcry in response to the newspaper story meant the insurance commissioner had no alternative but to reject the proposal. That happened in 2004. The Alaska commissioner rejected the deal as well. The conversion did not go through. The public was not pleased to find that Premera spent $35 million on a campaign to outline its case on the benefits of converting to for-profit status.

WHAT WE HAVE LEARNED FROM HOSPITAL AND INSURANCE COMPANY CONVERSIONS

The public nature of the conversions we have just examined raises a number of difficult questions—not only questions regarding the impact on the enrollees who were receiving their health insurance coverage from these companies, but questions that arise from revelations that would not have come to the surface otherwise. For example, it raises the question of what is appropriate compensation for chief executive officers of organizations that operate on a nonprofit basis. The CEOs argue that persons in comparable positions in for-profit organizations are compensated at even higher rates. They say they deserve a high level of compensation because of the size of the enterprise they oversee. That may be, but it is also true that the compensation of corporate executives has been coming under a great deal of criticism over the past few years. Even a cursory review of articles on the business pages of newspapers will confirm this. Boards of directors have been accused of being lax in their fiscal responsibility regarding oversight of executive compensation.

Another point of contention is the fact that the health insurance companies created through conversions and mergers were becoming so large that they were no longer responsive to any local set of stakeholders. In theory, the newly converted organizations operating as for-profits are expected to be highly responsive to investors, even more so than to the consumers of the product they offer. However, investors are also widely dispersed, unorganized, and largely ineffective in their stakeholder role, which goes a long way in explaining why CEO compensation packages have become so gigantic.

Enormous salaries going to executives whose companies are not doing well or are doing well due to factors over which they have little influence have received particular scrutiny. Oil company executives, for example, who have little influence over the complexities responsible for the high price of oil and high company profits, have been receiving special condemnation from business writers. Close scrutiny of the operations of oil companies may result in more than public condemnation. The fact that British Petroleum violated a wide range of regulations governing the oil rig in the Gulf of Mexico may result in criminal charges against the company in the future. Some observers have argued for criminal charges against individual members of the board of directors.

Similarly, the revelation about the viability of the three big automobile companies, how they presented their cases, the fact that they flew in on company jets and enjoyed lavish comforts in the process when they were called to testify to Congress in the fall of 2008, served to raise the ire of the public. That, in turn, focused attention on the compensation of CEOs whose organizations were being bailed out by taxpayers. Indeed, the CEO of Chrysler Corporation agreed to accept $1 in salary over the coming year. The Ford Company did not take any public funds and succeeded in producing an impressive financial turnaround. To the extent that the performance of a for-profit corporation is a useful standard for setting executive compensation, how should that inform how much compensation executives of nonprofit organizations should receive, and to what extent can they be held personally responsible for corporate misdeeds?

To sum up the discussion on the problems surrounding conversion from nonprofit to for-profit status—this is a story that continues to evolve. Curiously, scrutiny by analysts interested in gauging the impact of nonprofit to for-profit conversions indicates the new for-profit health insurance companies are not doing any better than they did as nonprofits. That has, of course, come as a surprise to many observers.

Whether we will see more nonprofit health organizations seeking to convert to for-profit status remains to be seen. It is not an option open to most nonprofits. It is likely to be considered only by those that can expect a reliable stream of money to keep coming in to the newly established for-profit version of the organization, preferably guaranteed by well-established government programs, as is true in the case of health insurance companies. The more general question—namely, which nonprofit, charitable organizations will grow and flourish, and which will find themselves struggling to find the funds to carry out their respective missions so they may avoid converting to either for-profit or foundation status—is also not easy to predict. What is certain is that finding the funds to fulfill the organizational mission is a never-ending challenge that confronts most nonprofit organizations.

As we will see in later chapters, nonprofit organizations are making varying choices in how they deal with that challenge. Some nonprofits are opting to merge with other larger, more successful nonprofit organizations. Others are choosing to take the opposite route—to disengage from the national, parent organization in order to focus greater attention on the local community and the preferences and priorities of their local constituencies.

Chapter Eight

Confronting a Highly Contagious Disease

The Respiratory Health Association of Metropolitan Chicago (RHAMC) was known as the American Lung Association of Metropolitan Chicago (ALAMC) until July 1, 2007, just one year after it celebrated its hundred-year anniversary. It came into existence in response to what was a leading cause of death in the United States at the beginning of the twentieth century—tuberculosis or TB. TB is a highly contagious lung disease for which there was no cure at that time except bed rest and fresh air. People living in close quarters in cities were at especially high risk of contracting the disease. Accordingly, the first organizational efforts to deal with the problem were launched in New York and Chicago.

We will be using the designation the organization used (i.e., American Lung Association of Metropolitan Chicago) before the name change occurred through much of the discussion.

ORGANIZATIONAL MISSION

The mission of the Respiratory Health Association of Metropolitan Chicago is to promote healthy lungs and fight lung disease through research, advocacy, and education.

The organizational bylaws, approved in June 2006, offer further elaboration, listing the following organizational purposes:

a. To work with the community to promote health and work toward the understanding, prevention, control, elimination, and/or eradication of respiratory diseases;

b. To assemble, publish, and disseminate facts, statistical data, and medical and nursing knowledge concerning the prevention, treatment, and control of respiratory diseases;

c. To conduct, alone or in cooperation with others, programs designed to detect and treat respiratory diseases;

d. To stimulate and assist, financially, research affecting respiratory diseases;

e. To conduct demonstrations designed to illustrate effective methods for the control, prevention, and treatment of respiratory diseases;

f. To assist in the rehabilitation of persons with respiratory diseases;

g. To evaluate programs, projects, incidence, and deaths relating to respiratory diseases;

h. To cooperate with other agencies, organizations, and societies, official and voluntary, in any of the above programs or work, or any other related project; and

i. To do all other things as may from time to time be deemed necessary to effectuate the purposes set forth above.

ORGANIZATIONAL HISTORY

The history of the RHAMC can be traced to the initial effort to launch a campaign to tackle and ultimately overcome TB, which occurred in Atlantic City in 1904. Fifteen prominent leaders, including two physicians from Chicago, met to create an organization that would be dedicated to fighting the disease. The participants formed the National Association for the Study and Prevention of Tuberculosis. The event is notable for one other reason. This was the first national voluntary health agency to bring together physicians and lay persons to cooperate in dealing with a single disease.

The sense of urgency about the need to address the scourge of TB is apparent in the words of one Chicago doctor. In presenting a scholarly paper to the members of the National Association for the Study and Prevention of Tuberculosis in Washington, D.C., in 1906, Dr. Arnold Klebs had this to say: "We have learned to recognize tuberculosis as a social and economic problem, probably the greatest of all problems, which by a systematic and sustained effort is eminently preventable."

The Chicago Tuberculosis Institute (CTI), the forerunner of what was to become the American Lung Association of Metropolitan Chicago, was established in 1906, two years after the formation of the national association. Miss Harriet Fulmer and Dr. Theodore Sachs, who were both active in the work of the Visiting Nurse Association of Chicago, created the CTI. The stated mission of the organization was "to advance the study, diagnosis, treatment, and prevention of tuberculosis and to coordinate the care of those afflicted with this dread disease."

The Chicago Tuberculosis Institute overcame a devastating tragedy during the early years of its existence brought about by the death of Dr. Sachs. Not only was he a founding member of the CTI, he was president of the National Tuberculosis Association, president of Chicago's Municipal Tuberculosis Sanitarium, and a leading TB researcher. However, he was not strong enough to overcome the attack on his character launched by the new mayor of Chicago, William "Big Bill" Thompson, who accused Dr. Sachs of malfeasance and tried to remove him from his position as director of the Municipal Tuberculosis Sanitarium. Dr. Sachs resigned from that position and committed suicide. The Chicago Tuberculosis Institute managed to regroup and to carry on with the work that he initiated.

One of the Chicago Tuberculosis Institute's earliest programmatic efforts was the Modern Health Crusade, which was directed to schoolchildren. The organization launched a program aimed at reducing the spread of TB through the promotion of good health practices in schools. CTI nurses were employed to teach schoolchildren how to avoid the disease. The program promoted such practices as brushing teeth and bathing regularly, exercise, sufficient sleep, and vitamins. As an aside, it is interesting to see that the same practices are still being recommended and are now thought to help prevent, or at least reduce or delay, the onset of an even wider range of diseases in people of all ages.

In recounting its early accomplishments, the CTI is proud of the fact that it was instrumental in helping to pass legislation requiring tuberculin testing of cows on farms providing milk to people in the Chicago area. That occurred in 1925. The value of testing was captured in a statement by Dr. James Hutton, chairman of the Chicago Medical Society's Tuberculosis Committee at that time, who is quoted as noting that "it is safer to be born a calf than a child" in Chicago.

MORTALITY TRENDS AND THE DISCOVERY OF A CURE

Mortality records had been kept by the Chicago Department of Health since 1867. The death rate from TB that year was approximately 24 per 10,000. It rose to 28 per 10,000 by 1870 but started a slow and somewhat irregular decline after that year. By 1890, it was 17 per 10,000; in 1906, the year the CTI was founded, it was 19 per 10,000; by 1910 it was 18 per 10,000; and by 1918 it was 9 per 10,000. No one knew whether the rate would continue to decline or whether there would be an upsurge at a later time. The only way to overcome this possibility was to identify an effective treatment or preventive intervention.

Doctors practicing in Chicago organized the Robert Koch Society for the Study of Tuberculosis, named after the German scientist who discovered the tubercle bacillus. They met to discuss research aimed at finding a cure and to set standards for TB treatment. The CTI was closely connected to this organization and its efforts. In fact, it organized a research committee in 1940 to evaluate research proposals it had been receiving, which were steadily increasing in number. The research breakthrough occurred in 1943 at Rutgers University when Dr. Selman Waksman discovered that streptomycin, an antibiotic, was effective in treating TB.

It is important to recognize that although discovery of the medicine that would cure TB was an enormous step forward, it did not eliminate the prevalence of TB infection. The antibiotic made it possible to treat people afflicted with the disease and cure them of TB, but those requiring treatment first had to be identified. The reason this was so problematic is that symptoms in the early stages of the disease are not immediately apparent. Thus, the CTI shifted its focus from finding a cure to detecting the presence of the TB bacillus in individuals one at a time. Accordingly, the CTI launched the largest continuous X-ray survey in partnership with the Municipal Tuberculosis Sanatorium. The agency reports that the number of annual X-rays performed in Chicago increased from 323,228 in 1947 to 1 million in 1956. The busiest X-ray screening unit in the world was at Chicago's City Hall.

CHANGES IN NAME AND MISSION

The effort to test as many people as possible for TB had a dramatic effect. Even though the disease would not be completely conquered over the next ten years, it was well on its way to being overcome. (The fact that it has reappeared in recent years makes clear that it has not been overcome.) In light of this, the National Tuberculosis Association voted, in 1956, to broaden its mission to include the full range of respiratory diseases and changed its name to the National TB Institute and Respiratory Disease Association. In 1972 it changed its name to the American Lung Association, and the CTI changed its name to the Chicago Lung Association the same year. It changed its name again in 1993, becoming the American Lung Association of Metropolitan Chicago—ALAMC.

In reviewing its activities over the past half century, we find that one of the vital new objectives the organization embraced was the challenge of dealing with the health risks associated with smoking. This was in response to the Surgeon General's report of 1964, which stated: "Cigarette smoking . . . is the single most avoidable cause of disease in our society and the most important public health issue of our time."

The focus on smoking had the effect of broadening the agency's scope to include the air nonsmokers were breathing. It turned its attention to the impact a range of environmental factors were having on the health of Chicagoans. A director of environmental health was appointed that year. He testified before the City Council and the Illinois Pollution Control Board the same year. The organization went on to create the Clean Air Coordinating Committee to advocate for tighter pollution standards, which challenged the Illinois Environmental Protection Agency (IEPA) in court. The agency is proud to note that it won its case.

The ALAMC continued to work on antismoking and clean air campaigns on a number of fronts. It continued to develop antismoking programs, which included starting a smoking withdrawal clinic that was recognized as among the country's thirty-five best health promotion programs by the U.S. Department of Health and Human Services in 1984. In 1988, it organized a grassroots lobbying campaign to pass Chicago's first clean air ordinance restricting smoking in restaurants, workplaces, and public spaces. That led to the passage of a Chicago City Council amendment in 1992 requiring restaurants to make 30 percent of their dining areas smoke-free. The organization persisted in its efforts. In 2005, it achieved an especially important objective. It takes credit for succeeding in its campaign to have the city of Chicago pass a comprehensive clean indoor air ordinance phasing out smoking in all bars and restaurants. Two years later, it was one of a number of cooperating agencies that could celebrate their success in having legislation passed requiring all buildings to be smoke-free throughout the state as of January 2008.

The organization has a long-standing record of work with asthmatics. It initiated the Camp Action program in 1980 to give children suffering from asthma a week-long summer camp experience where they could learn about asthma management. It devoted special attention to asthmatic children in a number of Chicago neighborhoods that have especially high rates of asthma. Why Chicago has the highest rate of childhood asthma of any city in the country has been the subject of both extensive research and discussion in public health circles. Why some neighborhoods have rates that are twice that of the basic Chicago rate motivated the association to devote special efforts to addressing the problem in those neighborhoods. Recognition of the need for more research motivated the agency to spearhead the development of a nationwide network of Asthma Clinical Research Centers to conduct large-scale studies in 1997.

The Chicago office introduced four new initiatives in 2004: "Catch Your Breath," the first annual women and lung health conference; Chicago's first Asthma Action Plan; a COPD (Chronic Obstructive Pulmonary Disease) Initiative to combat the nation's fourth-leading killer disease; and the READI program providing influenza vaccinations to 25,000 Chicagoans. Getting a flu vaccine is especially important for persons with lung disease for whom the effects of the flu can be far more serious than it is for those not so affected.

The 2006 annual report, its hundred-year anniversary issue, states that the agency commemorated the event with a reception at the Museum of Contemporary Art in Chicago and the unveiling of a historical exhibit celebrating its accomplishments. The annual report also describes the agency's achievements for the year. Highlights include the fact that its antismoking campaign culminated in an increase in the city cigarette tax, making the price of cigarettes in Chicago the highest in the nation at $7 per pack. The report states that the ALAMC Board is pleased to note this helped to stimulate similar campaigns in local suburbs. Its clean air campaign resulted in passage of anti-idling legislation to reduce harmful emissions from diesel trucks and buses. Asthma education and research initiatives gained ground. The report goes on to list the research projects aimed at finding cures for lung cancer, emphysema, and chronic bronchitis to which the agency contributed. It outlines the programs to increase awareness of lung disease through community-based testing and administration of flu shots in conjunction with both the Chicago and Cook County Departments of Public Health that it promoted. It notes that its most recent initiative is bringing to the public's attention the threat of radiation exposure from radon. In effect, the agency can claim success on many fronts connected to the four specific objectives inherent in its mission.

1. To advocate for cleaner air
2. To reduce tobacco use and exposure to secondhand smoke
3. To reverse the asthma epidemic in Chicago
4. To improve treatments and cures for lung disease

The organization reported that it was very gratified to have received recognition for a number of achievements in 2011. It was given special recognition for its efforts to protect employees from secondhand smoke by the American College of Physicians, which gave it the Loveland Award for making a distinguished contribution in the health field. And, it was recognized by the Better Business Wise Giving Alliance for meeting all twenty standards for charity accountability established by the Alliance. The organization was pleased to announce that it had awarded two research grants aimed at exploring causes and treatments of lung diseases to researchers at Northwestern University and Stanford University.

ORGANIZATIONAL STRUCTURE

Before it changed its name and status, the ALAMC was one of seventy-eight local affiliates, or offices, of the American Lung Association (ALA). The ALA is composed of independent local organizations that are loosely connected to the national organization through a contract that outlines expectations of and benefits to the local office.

In 1993 the Chicago office entered into a contract with the national organization, renewable on an annual basis, in the expectation of attracting greater attention to its activities and programs through the linkage to the American Lung Association name and logo, which is owned by the national organization. The connection allowed the Chicago office to take advantage of specific services, materials, and programs produced by the national office. All of these had to be purchased from the headquarters office. The officers in the Chicago office reasoned that this was worth the expense because the programs represented in national campaigns brought greater attention to local efforts.

The nature of the relationship changed in 2005, when the American Lung Association announced that it planned to regionalize the local offices. Over the following year the ALA introduced significant revisions in the content of what had become a more or less standardized annual contract. The changes were designed to give the national organization centralized control over the structure and finances of the local offices. This took the members of the ALAMC board and staff aback. Some members were immediately opposed to entering into the arrangements being proposed by the national office; others wanted some time to consider the implications. Those who wanted more time pointed out that refusal to sign would require a considerable number of adjustments, starting with the fact that the local office would no longer be able to use the national association logo and would have to alter its name, with all the implications such changes would have for the organization's self-presentation and, of course, all the costs involved in replacing office materials. Clearly most people associated with the Chicago office saw this as a very disruptive and troubling situation—a crisis.

The relationship with two affiliated organizations would be altered if the ALAMC were to suddenly become one of a number of agencies operating under the direction of a regional officer. It would have implications for the Chicago Thoracic Society, which functions as the organization's medical section and acts in an advisory capacity to the Chicago office regarding medical affairs; and, the Nursing Assembly, which acts to support various programs, promote optimal nursing education, and care for respiratory patients, and serves as a resource to the Chicago office on matters pertaining to respiratory nursing.

We will get back to this part of the story, which is certainly a core issue in this case study, after we review the fund-raising and evaluation processes.

ORGANIZATIONAL FUNDING

Over its history the organization introduced a wide range of fund-raising mechanisms. It has been highly innovative in how it raises money. Returning to the historical record, in 1907 the National Association for the Study and Prevention of Tuberculosis became the first nonprofit, charitable organization to rely on the sale of Christmas stamps to raise money. The sale of Christmas stamps or "seals" was introduced by Emily Bissell, who came across the idea in Denmark. (Such seals are still being distributed by various charitable organizations around Christmas and Easter. The idea is that people would buy them to use as decorations on envelopes.) She convinced the National Red Cross to offer the seals throughout the United States. The Chicago Tuberculosis Institute served as the local marketing agency offering the seals to other charitable organizations. The sale of the seals during that first year raised $9,032 for the Chicago office. The first seal was then auctioned off for $85 in a charity auction.

Between 1950 and 1967, the Chicago office reports that it sold more Christmas seals than any other charitable organization in the country, topping out at $1 million annually. The fact that the stamps were printed in Chicago, next door to the Chicago office, probably had something to do with that. The Chicago office was creative in how it presented the new stamp to the public each year. One year, its publicity materials featured one of the chimps at Chicago's Lincoln Park Zoo licking the Christmas seal before placing it on an envelope.

In 2007, the agency reported that it raised $258,417 from the sale of the seals. One reason why these stamps produced so much less income in 2007 than they did a few decades ago is that other agencies introduced stamps of their own. Christmas seals were no longer unique. In fact, many of the creative fund-raising mechanisms the Chicago office employed have been adopted by other charities, which forced the staff to come up with a steady stream of new fund-raising approaches.

For example, its distance run was especially popular before an increasing number of other organizations started hosting marathons. However, the organization is proud to be associated with a thirty-person group identifying itself as the Lung Power Team. They run in marathons organized by other organizations. Running in the 2011 Bank of America Marathon, they raised $37,000 plus for the agency.

other creative fund-raising activities that are no longer em-
aerobic dancing during halftime at Chicago Bears games. The
esponsible for obtaining sponsors, with the money raised go-
AMC. Then there was line dancing during quarter breaks of
games, which worked the same way.

:y has been sponsoring a bike tour every August, the CowaLUNGa, since 1996. The bike ride starts at a shopping mall in Gurnee,
Illinois, and moves toward Wisconsin, covering about sixty to seventy miles
per day, or a total of about 190 miles over three days. The event is not a race
but what the organization describes as a leisurely ride through the country-
side on safe, scenic roads. Riders can sign up for one, two, or three days of
biking. Participants are provided with meals; those who ride for more than
one day also get to choose accommodations—tents to be set up on camping
grounds, or hotel rooms—when they register.

There is no question that the most spectacular fund-raising event
ALAMC developed is the Hustle Up the Hancock. Volunteers sign up to run
up the stairs of the landmark Hancock building—all ninety-four flights of
stairs, which amounts to 1,632 steps for the full climb. Signing up for half the
climb is possible, too. The Hustle celebrated its fifteenth year in 2012. The
event attracts considerably more attention than other high-rise climbs, including the climb up the 103 flights of the Willis Tower (which was the Sears
Tower until recently), which raises money for the American Cancer Society.

According to the chief executive officer of ALAMC, the success of the
Hustle is undoubtedly due to the fact that it is so well integrated with the
organizational mission. After all, you need to have very healthy lungs to
climb ninety-four flights of stairs.

The 2007 event was described in some detail in an article in the *Chronicle
of Philanthropy*. The reporter states that registration, which is limited to four
thousand participants, "sold out" within thirty-one minutes after the online
registration opened up (Jensen 2007). The first year the event was held in
1997 brought in $84,000. The 2007 Hustle brought in $1.2 million in
pledges. The official sponsor of the event, OfficeMax, picked up the tab for
related expenses including the fruit and water available at the top.

The climb is competitive for some climbers. Those who have finished
among the top twenty-five climbers at previous Hustles or comparable events
begin the climb at the 7 a.m. start. In 2007, the record setting time was 9
minutes and 30 seconds. The time over the following years has been about 9
minutes and 31 seconds. The average time is 26 minutes. Not all climbers go
for the full length; some register to start halfway up. The names of all participants are published on a dedicated website with the finish times for each
participant. Many participants have created videos and blogs detailing the
experience.

Climbers offer many reasons for signing up. Some do it because the cause has special meaning to them. Usually, it is because someone close to them suffers from lung disease. The event is especially popular among firefighters, who are particularly interested in supporting the lung association. They are at far greater risk of lung disease due to exposure to smoke and other air pollutants than the rest of us. Two hundred firefighters, most from around the greater Chicago region, participated in the 2007 Hustle. They constitute a very visible category of climbers because they wear their trademark helmets and bulky boots. Another highly visible group participating for the second time that year was the group of fifteen female friends and relatives in red shorts and T-shirts that say "Fire Drill." The members of this group gather from all over the country for the event. Identifiable groups are the norm because participants are encouraged to do the climb as members of groups.

The organization introduced a new event in 2010—the Skyline Plunge. The first of these events involved rappelling the seventeen-story exterior façade of the Illini Tower building in Champaign-Urbana. The same year the organization launched a similar event closer to its home. This involves rappelling the 27-story Wit Hotel located in downtown Chicago. In 2010, eighty persons participated; in 2011, there were 130 persons. Many participants in both the Hustle and the rappelling events have recorded the experience and posted their comments and videos on the Internet.

The organization has also been holding a black-tie event with hors d'oeuvres and drinks in conjunction with the auto show over the past few years, which allows guests to get a preview of the auto industry's newest models. Finally, since 2006, it has benefited from Chill, an international wine and culinary event that offers a portion of its proceeds to the agency.

TOTAL REVENUE

According to its most recent annual report, presenting the 2009 financial picture, RHAMC raised $4.3 million, which is less than the $4.7 million it raised in 2008, and substantially less than the $6 million it reported raising two years prior to that. The percentages break down as follows: 48.5 percent from a combination of corporate, foundation, and government grants; 13.5 percent from contributions and donations; about 23 percent from the special events; 13.5 percent from contributions and donations; and about 14.5 percent from other sources including interest, program fees, rental income, and so on.

ALAMC's contract with the national organization required it to pay the national organization an annual fee plus 13 percent of all the unrestricted funds it raises in donations. The 2006 annual report states that it paid the national headquarters organization $290,000 the previous year, a cost that was eliminated as of July 1, 2007.

ORGANIZATIONAL EVALUATION

The RHAMC performs formal evaluations required by granting agencies. For example, the funding it receives from the government to address the excessive rate of asthma in particular neighborhoods requires formal evaluation. The organization also uses standardized evaluation instruments to assess client satisfaction with the programs it presents by surveying attendees.

It is, however, the wide range of less formal performance indicators to which the chief executive officer says he pays special attention. This took a number of forms in the past—for example, conferring with CEOs of other ALA offices during periodic national or regional meetings. Such occasions provided the CEOs with the opportunity to explore and share thoughts about new as well as established programs and fund-raising mechanisms. The meetings gave CEOs the opportunity to discuss their respective financial profiles—how much they contribute to support of the national organization—and to compare thoughts on what they get in return. The Chicago office had been contributing 2 percent, which was higher than the contribution made by many other offices including those that represent an entire state. The CEO noted that his office was allocating 20 percent of its revenue to research, twice the percentage recommended by the national organization. In other words, by all accounts the RHAMC's performance had been comparing very well with that of its counterparts.

There is also one major, far less concrete measure that the RHAMC staff believes is a particularly sensitive indicator of performance, namely, the personal contact the CEO and other agency staff have with donors and other interested parties. The CEO offered an example of this in telling a story about a man who came in to complain that the organization was not giving nearly enough attention or service to people suffering from emphysema. He agreed to give some thought to what the man was saying and suggested meeting again to discuss what could be done. When the man returned for the second meeting, he brought six friends—each accompanied by his own oxygen tank. They outlined the kinds of things they wanted help with. The outcome was a newsletter that discusses practical issues such as the best air cleaner on the market, where to buy supplies, what exercises are beneficial, and so on. The men who wanted more attention to their concerns ended up being very satisfied. The CEO takes great pleasure in saying that he was able to provide something the organization's constituents value.

The CEO takes the position that everyone who contributes money, time, and effort should know that their contribution makes a difference. He personally signs virtually all the thank-you letters the office sends out. He believes it is the personal contact people have with the organization that makes a difference. It is the willingness of people to come back and give more of their money and their effort to support the organization that is the primary indicator of performance he relies on to determine whether the agency is meeting the goals set out in the organization's mission statement and specification of purpose declaration.

STRUCTURAL CRISIS BROUGHT ABOUT BY THE ALA'S REGIONALIZATION PLAN

When the American Lung Association announced its regionalization agenda in 2005, the rationale it offered was that fund-raising effectiveness would be increased by reducing the number of offices and combining them all into eleven regional units by 2010. The directive coming from the national headquarters of the ALA stated that the local offices would be given another year or two to prepare for the shift.

ALAMC board members' initial response was to arrange meetings with board members from other offices to discuss the implications of the shift. At first, there was a fair amount of disagreement among board members regarding the wisdom of such organizational restructuring. Debate and discussion of the proposed move went on during monthly meetings over the following year. The matter took on a greater sense of urgency when the national office told the California offices that the state would be the first to enter into the reorganization phase, and the reorganization would have to be completed by the end of the coming year, 2006. Of the eleven local offices in California, five, all in the northern half of the state, decided to withdraw from the ALA rather than form a single regional or state office. The move captured the attention of local offices throughout the country. The Northern California offices formed their own regional association called Breathe California. The New Hampshire local left around the same time and renamed itself Breathe New Hampshire.

The national ALA office reacted to these moves by stepping up the pressure, issuing a new and revised contract at the beginning of 2007 to all the remaining locals. The new contract not only specified that the local offices must join a regional unit, but that they were expected to sign a forfeiture clause assigning their property and assets to the ALA. That had a reverberating effect. In the case of the Chicago office, it convinced those members of the executive board who had been wavering in their assessment of the wisdom of joining a regional unit that the ALA's demands were excessive. The executive board of the Chicago office met in March and voted unanimously to reject the ALA contract. The full board met in April, voting unanimously to reject the contract as well. The board agreed to terminate the contract with the ALA when it expired on July 1, 2007.

According to the Respiratory Health Association of Metropolitan Chicago's director of development, the staff was enormously pleased by the decision because of what it said about the work being carried out at the local office. The fact that the vote was unanimous was seen as a vote of confidence in the abilities of leadership and staff. It was interpreted as acknowledgment of the work they had been doing and a statement of support in future endeavors, indicating they would be able to manage the affairs of the Chicago office very well without the connection to the national organization.

The Chicago office announced the new name it would be using in May 2007. The new name, Respiratory Health Association of Metropolitan Chicago, became official as of July 1, 2007.

Several factors went into the decision to sever the tie to the ALA in addition to the threat of the sudden loss of title to property and other assets acquired by the Chicago office. One of the main factors was the opposition of virtually everyone associated with the Chicago office to being absorbed into an Upper Midwest regional office. The Chicago office was projected to become part of a unit that would include offices operating in very different social and geographic environments and working under very different conditions. The regional unit would encompass Illinois, Iowa, Wisconsin, Minnesota, and North and South Dakota. Clearly the problems presented by the highly concentrated, urbanized population in Chicago differ from those presented by the populations in less-urbanized areas. The types of lung diseases are different—the prevalence of childhood asthma is a good example. Fundraising events are certainly different—the Hustle Up the Hancock event can only be staged in Chicago. Would a regional office be as interested in sponsoring an event that is so identified with a single city in the region and at such physical and psychological distance from the other offices? As the CEO of the Chicago office sees it, addressing local problems locally makes better sense.

Furthermore, according to the director of development, the staff at the Chicago office was convinced that the donor base, which had been so intimately involved with the Chicago office, would not feel nearly as closely tied to activities originating out of a regional office. They would not be as interested in supporting activities they would not be part of. In short, the development director expected contributions to decline, which would ultimately result in an overall decline in the resources available to meet the objectives the lung association as a whole sought to address.

This is ironic, because the primary reason the national office offered for its decision to "streamline" its operations through regionalization was to achieve a turnaround in the ALA's revenues, which had not been increasing during the past ten to fifteen years. Revenue per se had not declined; it just had not increased at the same rate achieved by the American Cancer Society and the American Heart Association, the two biggest disease-focused charitable organizations in the country. John Kirkwood, the CEO of the ALA, was quoted as saying the decision to regionalize was made in order to produce "larger, more efficient, robust organizations around the country," each of which would have a single board of directors and budget (Storch 2007). He played down the loss of the seven affiliates even though other lung association officials said their departure "will cost the national organization about $1 million in direct annual fees and tens of millions of dollars in total gifts" (Schwinn 2007). News articles made the point that Mr. Kirkwood announced earlier in the year that he would be retiring in June 2007 without further comment on how that might be related to the national association's plan to regionalize.

The second major consideration that played into the decision to dissolve the relationship with the ALA on the part of the Chicago office is that it would no longer have to pay an annual fee and percentage of contributions to the national organization. However, it was getting away from the direct mail solicitations coming from the national office that was especially pleasing to the agency's CEO. He noted that the local office was responsible for paying for the mailings, but it had no input in the design of stickers being sent out or the mailing list of the people to whom they were sent. In fact, as he discovered, getting the national association to take some names off of that list resulted in a significantly higher donation level to his agency. He learned that in a conversation with the CEO of the Arkansas local office, who explained that sending solicitations only twice a year and responding with a personal thank-you letter had brought in 300 percent more money than the solicitations coming out of the national office, which were sent repeatedly throughout the year. The CEO noted that he was surprised to find that when he adopted this approach in the Chicago office, it resulted in exactly the same rate of increase in donations as it had in Arkansas.

Another factor in the decision to sever ties to the national office was the fact that staff members were relieved of the burden of dealing with the recommendations of consultants the national office employed. The consultants recommended instituting a number of new internal evaluation procedures, which they labeled "organizational effectiveness indicators," using a "balanced score card" that was part of a "performance-based management system." The staff at the Chicago office suspected this was simply leading to the need to learn a series of new corporate buzzwords, would certainly add to the work load, and would very likely not result in programmatic advice that would improve on what the local office was doing. The staff was certain they already had a very good understanding of the kinds of activities the members of the local community wanted, and formulaic advice from outsiders would not bring much benefit.

Once the decision to reject the contract took effect, the Chicago office began planning the changes that would have to be made. The staff at the Chicago office prepared for the fact that they would no longer be using the ALA logo in any of the agency's identifying material—from the sign on the building it occupies, to its website, to every piece of literature it publishes. According to the development director, the staff could still choose to offer some ALA trademarked programs (programs owned by the ALA), for example, the smoking cessation program. Such programs carry a fee and are identifiable as ALA programs. Or it might choose to purchase similarly trademarked programs from other well-respected organizations.

The remarks the board chairwoman-elect made at the time the split from the ALA was announced to the press sums up the thinking of those most closely involved in the activities of the Chicago office. She put it this way: "We, as a board, believe such a consolidation to be not in the best interest of our lung mission and might undermine our local effectiveness" (Storch 2007). Her statement brings our discussion full circle, back to the core of the organization's purpose as represented by its mission statement.

WHAT WE CAN LEARN FROM THIS CASE

The historical record of the Respiratory Health Association of Metropolitan Chicago indicates that it started out as a "bottom-up" organization. Although it had an informal relationship with the New York–based national association from the very beginning of its existence, it entered into a formal contract with the ALA nearly nine decades later. That turned the Chicago office into one of a network of seventy-eight local lung association offices operating under the leadership of a single national organization, in a "top-down" arrangement. Fourteen years later, the Chicago office severed that tie and returned to its original status as a stand-alone organization. Let's tally up the Chicago office's assessment of the pros and cons associated with both arrangements.

It is not only the concrete advantages and disadvantages that are at issue; it is the perception of which arrangement is more or less advantageous that may shift over time. In this case, the shift that prompted the decision to disaffiliate from the national organization occurred in response to a change in the contractual arrangements the national organization was introducing. The earlier decision to affiliate with a large, well-known entity had the advantage of clear name recognition and the goodwill the name and logo engendered. The reassessment of the disadvantages reflected concern that the costs associated with using that clearly identifiable logo had become too high: for example, the requirement to use ALA-trademarked programs, which could possibly be purchased at a lower cost from some other well-known and equally reputable organization; the cost of the requirement to send a portion of donations to support the national office; costs associated with producing and mailing solicitations over which the Chicago office had no control; and costs associated with the fees charged by consulting agencies employed by the headquarters office and the managerial advice they offered in which the office had no interest. Clearly the list of disadvantages ultimately was greater than the list of advantages.

The other major lesson we can learn from analyzing the facts of this case requires us to consider how the interests of the agency's interactional field of stakeholders are reflected in the Chicago office's decision to reject the conditions outlined in the national organization's revised contract. The decision represents the belief, on the part of board members and staff, that Chicagoans in general and the individuals who enroll in the programs the agency offers in particular were in total agreement with the agency's decision to disaffiliate.

Responding to the interpretation of the views expressed by these stakeholders regarding programs is central to what the staff sees as its main function. These were, after all, also the individuals who had the most influence on the agency's programs and activities. The fund-raising activities, in turn, have not only brought in funds to support the organization's work, but were very effective in publicly representing and promoting the programs the agency offers that are directly linked to its organizational mission. In other words, the mission has never been very far from the very visible and successful fund-raising activities the office had been organizing all along. Media attention to the two big fund-raising events, Hustle and CowaLUNGa, as well as all the other creative approaches that have come and gone, has served the organization well.

In the final analysis, what is now known as the Respiratory Health Association of Metropolitan Chicago has plainly determined its primary loyalty is to participants who are members of the local community, and operating as a stand-alone organization will allow it to serve its primary stakeholders and fulfill its mission better than it could have done as a member of a regional office.

Chapter Nine

Needs of People with a Significant Physical Impairment

In this chapter, we will encounter two organizations: one deals with problems affecting people with visual impairment, the Chicago Lighthouse; and another deals with problems faced by people with hearing impairment, the Chicago Hearing Society.

CHICAGO LIGHTHOUSE

Organizational mission

An earlier mission statement put it this way: Chicago Lighthouse strives to improve the quality of life for individuals who are blind or visually impaired and open doors to opportunities, jobs, and choices that lead to enhanced dignity and increased independence.

The revised 2011 statement says: Chicago Lighthouse Industries' mission is to provide adjustment to blindness, training, job placement opportunities, and continuous employment for visually impaired individuals, including those with additional disabilities, that will lead to achieving their maximum potential through the development, production, and marketing of products and services that meet the highest quality standards using modern production methods and technology.

It also says of itself that it is a not-for-profit agency committed to providing the highest quality of educational, clinical, vocational, and rehabilitation services for children, youth, and adults who are blind or visually impaired, including deaf-blind and multi-disabled. Through its comprehensive range of programs and services, the Chicago Lighthouse respects personal dignity and partners with individuals to enhance independent living and self-sufficiency. The Chicago Lighthouse is a leader, innovator, and advocate for people who are blind or visually impaired, enhancing the quality of life for all individuals involved and for the community.

Organizational history

The Chicago Lighthouse was founded by a group of women, both blind and sighted, in 1906. The women first met in the home of Mrs. Winona Hood, the wife of a prominent doctor. They were motivated to help blind persons who, in those days, were forced to beg on the streets in order to support themselves. It seems astonishing now, but in those days, discrimination against the blind and visually impaired people was the norm. They were considered unemployable and could not support themselves, which made their situation all the more difficult.

Initially the women who joined together to help blind persons were primarily interested in providing food and clothing for those who were so afflicted. They solicited assistance in this effort from the members of various women's clubs. As they collected enough, they made up baskets and delivered them to the homes of blind persons using Mrs. Hood's electric car. By the end of the first year of such efforts, the women decided they would form an organization to be called the Improvement Association for Blind People. They also expanded their agenda to focus on finding work for the blind. In 1908, Mr. Joseph Sloan, the husband of one of the founders, donated a weaving machine, which allowed the association to establish a workshop to teach blind people to weave baskets.

By 1910, the association was well-enough established to seek a state charter. The objective was to help with the fund-raising efforts the group was now pursuing. The women held their first Tag Day fund-raiser in 1915, which brought in $6,524. This sum allowed the association to purchase a building, which it named the Chicago Lighthouse. The publicity surrounding this event helped the organization get wider notice and acclaim for its work. Donations started to increase. Some gifts were unusual for the time and received wider attention; for example, Mr. Thorpe, who ran a steamship between Chicago and Milwaukee, donated tickets allowing forty-seven blind persons to take the steamship trip.

Treating blind people with dignity and allowing them to experience the kinds of things that sighted people were enjoying was a primary objective; however, even more important was the goal of finding employment for blind people. The agency took great pride in its ability to place eighty people in factory jobs in 1915. This really was a tremendous accomplishment. It is also true that recognition of the amount of time and energy required to find employment opportunities for participants led the association to create a full-time position rather than relying on volunteers to carry out this responsibility. Edith Swift, daughter of former mayor George Bell Smith, accepted the job of director on a part-time basis around this time. The job turned into a full-time position not long after. She served as director of the agency until 1946.

Over her tenure, the organization promoted both work training and a variety of social activities for the people the organization was serving. Commitment to finding jobs for blind people led to the creation of a separate placement department. The training for factory jobs offered by the Lighthouse was so successful that companies began asking the agency to accept production contracts to have the work done onsite at the Lighthouse. One of its first major contracts required the production of one-half million sockets for Christmas lights. The need to check to make sure the sockets worked led to the development of an early "adaptive technology." In order to test the lights, which the workers could not see lighting up, the workers created a buzzer that would buzz when lights went on. That led to other adaptive technologies that worked with other manufacturing jobs.

In 1930, the organization changed its name to the Chicago Lighthouse for the Blind. It continued to grow and expand during the 1930s, the depression years. During the 1940s, when both clients and staff were eager to contribute to the war effort, the agency accepted a contract to produce munitions that resulted in employment of 250 men. The postwar years required the organization to shift its training programs to preparing people for peacetime jobs, which it did at three different workshop sites. Recognizing the need for more workshop and training space, the leadership of the organization launched a major fund-raising campaign with the aim of constructing a new building.

The board president broke ground for the new building in February 1955. The building, which had sixty thousand square feet of space, opened in November of the same year. Helen Keller was the featured speaker that day. (Helen Keller, who was both blind and deaf, became an important symbol of what is possible. She authored a dozen books, many articles, and traveled to make presentations.) The following year, on the occasion of the fiftieth anniversary of its founding, the Chicago Lighthouse celebrated by showing off the newly installed garden in the front yard of its new building. The Chicago Horticultural Society installed the garden as a celebratory gift to the Lighthouse. The event helped to make the point that blind and visually disabled people could enjoy what gardens had to offer even if they did not see the flowers.

The organization began developing programs other than workshop training preparatory to employment to assist its clients. For example, Dr. Alfred Rosenblum, who was an active member of the board, established a low-vision rehabilitation clinic in 1954. It was the first of its kind in the Midwest. It is now the oldest low-vision clinic in the country since the first one, opened in New York, is no longer functioning.

Milt Samuelson, who became the second executive director of the agency, took an interest in the needs of children who had various disabilities in addition to blindness. He was instrumental in creating a school for blind children in addition to a number of other programs aimed at helping visually handicapped children.

The single biggest breakthrough in assistive technology used by the visually handicapped was achieved during Mr. Samuelson's era, namely, development of the CCTV (closed-circuit television), which enlarges print so that people with visual disabilities can read ordinary text. That occurred in 1980. The story behind the invention starts in San Francisco. A flight attendant for United Airlines who was losing her vision was fired. She appealed to the U.S. Department of Rehabilitation to help her get an office job as a reservationist with the company, which United was reluctant to do. United Airlines agreed to hire her after she showed that access to a very early version of the CCTV would allow her to do the job. Eventually the company nominated her for an award in recognition of her diligence in her new job. CCTVs are far more sophisticated now and are considered to be one of the most common pieces of equipment used by persons with visual disabilities.

By the mid-1980s, the organization was again running out of space. Dan Lee, board chairman at the time, launched a campaign to construct an addition to the Lighthouse building to increase it by an additional 40,000 feet, which would provide 100,000 square feet of space. This was no easy task because the land the current building stood on was part of the Illinois Medical District on the University of Illinois campus. The university opposed the Chicago Lighthouse building plan, arguing that the agency did not provide medical care and, therefore, the university did not consider it to be a medical facility that deserved to be accommodated on the university's campus. The University of Illinois wanted to use the space to expand its own operations. The Chicago Lighthouse prevailed, and the new addition was completed in 1993. Dan Lee, who is himself visually handicapped, has been pleased to observe the continued work of the Lighthouse at close range since that time. He was singularly responsible for tracking the organization's history in preparation for its hundred-year anniversary in 2006. He not only researched the organization's history, he made a series of videos that document that history and describe current activities.

After a half century of association with the organization, James Kesteloot, the president and executive director, announced during a 2007 board meeting that he would be retiring in January 2009. Kesteloot's history with the organization began when he enrolled in the low-vision clinic at the age of thirteen and was followed by nearly forty years of employment at the organization during which time it grew and flourished. He was the agency's third executive director. His replacement, Dr. Janet Szlyk, accepted the position in 2008.

Organizational structure

The Chicago Lighthouse is a stand-alone agency. There is no national organization to which it could be connected. There are Lighthouses in a number of other cities; however, they do not have ties with one another. The Chicago Lighthouse operations are largely, but not entirely, concentrated in one location.

Its 2006 annual report, the hundred-year anniversary report, states that the organization served 56,473 people directly and a grand total of 71,145 people when the services provided by the Information and Referral program are included. This is compared to a total of 18,290 persons served only five years previous to that. The 2008 annual report, the latest one that is publicly available, indicates the number of persons served had increased to 89,335 persons.

The Chicago Lighthouse operates twenty-three clearly defined programs in addition to a wide range of more general services. The Placement Department, one of the earliest services, expanded to become the Chase Placement Office. Chase Bank has made space available to the Lighthouse in its downtown offices to assist people in finding jobs with large corporations that have offices in the center of the city.

The Industrial Program, which grew out of the early training programs the Lighthouse created to provide employment for its members, is basically a factory operation that employs people to make products the organization contracts to produce. It has had a contract with the federal government to produce clocks for many years. The current contract requires the Lighthouse to produce 160,000 clocks per year to be used in various government offices. Since the contract was signed, it has produced more than 3.5 million clocks. According to staff members, it is the single largest clock producing operation in the country. Virtually all the other clocks sold in the United States now come from China. When the government expressed reservations about renewing the contract a few years ago, saying the Lighthouse clock design had become outdated, the agency quickly retooled and came up with one hundred variations on the design. The federal government renewed the contract. The Industrial Program is located on the second floor of the agency's main building. People work on a number of contracts, in addition to the government clock contract, that involve light assembly work. The jobs offer a living wage plus fringe benefits.

The Lighthouse continues to operate a number of programs devoted to the needs of children. One well-established program, the Children's Development Center, experienced its largest enrollment in twelve years in 2008. It is currently serving thirty-five children. It graduated three children from high school and accepted twelve new students who were referred by the Chicago Public Schools as a result of school closings. Another is the Birth-to-Three Family Intervention program that helps parents teach valuable skills to their visually disabled or blind children. One of the growing programs it operates is the Illinois Instructional Materials Center, which provides books to blind and visually disabled children in the state. The children use and return the books so they can be recycled and used by other children. The facility houses more than eleven thousand book titles.

Programs focusing on adults include the Adult Living Skills program, which teaches independence skills. The Strickfaden Assistive Devices Center provides non-prescriptive devices such as talking watches and calculators. The agency operates a store where people can try out the new devices before buying them. It operates a Deaf-Blind program as well as a Seniors Initiative program. The Adaptive Technology program continues to develop new approaches to the challenges faced by the organization's members.

Three new programs were added in 2005. The Help Desk was launched with a grant from the Boeing Company. The Help Desk, which is housed in the agency's Adaptive Technology Center, was created to help visually impaired people understand and solve computer problems. In 2006, it was able to help visually impaired people in forty-seven states and four Canadian provinces. The Chicago Lighthouse established a Legal Clinic to provide free assistance for people who encounter employment discrimination, have tax issues, and other legal matters. The clinic operates under the leadership of a retired Cook County judge and dozens of volunteers from the University of Chicago Law School. In its first year of operation, it assisted nearly two hundred people.

The agency also created a radio station in 2005, CRIS Radio (Chicagoland Radio Information Service), which offers readings of local, state, national, and global news. To better serve audiences, the station added innovative programming in community affairs, law, health care, and other areas. It expanded to a worldwide audience by introducing live Internet radio streaming, providing anyone who wishes to use this service with access to information as it unfolds. The 2008 annual report states that the CRIS audience now includes more than forty thousand listeners.

According to the 2007 annual report, the organization was pleased to report that it was the recipient of many accolades in recognition of its achievements that year. For example, it was awarded the Golden Trumpet Award from the Publicity Club of Chicago for outstanding achievement in public relations, having received coverage in a range of media outlets across the country for the third consecutive year.

Organizational funding

The Chicago Lighthouse reported revenue of $18 million in 2010. This in contrast to the $8 million it reported in 2009. The significantly improved 2010 financial picture is due to a substantial increase in revenue in most categories, including a higher level of income from donations and a lower level of loss in return on investments. The 2010 financial record indicates revenue came from the following sources: about 24 percent from public contributions and bequests; 26 percent from industries and sales of products; about 41 percent from program revenues; and the remaining 9 percent from investment income and miscellaneous sources.

The agency receives some funds from corporations for dedicated purposes from year to year; for example, the agency's Office Skills program received $383,399 in software, plus the time and skills of experts, from Microsoft Corporation in 2006. In 2007, the agency received unrestricted donations from foundations including $500,000 from the Community Trust and $350,000 from the Polk Brothers Foundation. Because the agency owns land, a building, and equipment, its assets stand at around $41.7 million.

Having celebrated its first hundred years, the Chicago Lighthouse launched a $17-million campaign called "Bold Visions" in 2006. By November 1, 2007, it had attained 83 percent of that objective. The funds will be used to support current operations, enhance emerging programming, fund urgently needed capital improvements, strengthen the investment fund, establish a new venture fund, and, finally, construct much needed new space on the main campus.

Organizational evaluation

The Chicago Lighthouse is pleased to count more than four thousand persons as contributors whose continued support it considers to be a major indicator of the value of the services the organization offers. It is proud of the public recognition it has received from the media. It evaluates its performance based on informal indicators of satisfaction registered by those it serves and more specific indicators those who provide the financial support the agency depends on want to see. It carries out formal evaluations when they are mandated by funding agencies.

The agency is proud of the informal but highly lauded assessment made by the former mayor of Chicago, Richard M. Daley, who pronounced it the most comprehensive social service agency in the United States in 2010.

THE CHICAGO HEARING SOCIETY

Let us now turn to another organization, as a comparative case, mentioned at the beginning of this chapter, one that deals with another clear-cut disability—hearing impairment or deafness. The organization is the Chicago Hearing Society.

The Chicago Hearing Society story is based on material that is publicly available rather than on direct contact with organizational representatives. Representatives of the organization were not willing to discuss the organization's operations with me. I have chosen to include this case for a couple of reasons: first, because it offers an interesting contrast to the Chicago Lighthouse case; and, second, because we will encounter it again in the following chapter.

Organizational mission

The mission of the Chicago Hearing Society, when it was established, was:

- promotion of social intercourse among the membership
- assistance for the deaf and hard of hearing in the matter of procuring and retaining employment
- promotion of an interest in lipreading
- aiding and furthering in each and every way possible for any helpful work among the deaf and hard of hearing

Organizational history

The organization was founded in 1916. Twenty people met to discuss forming an organization to address the needs of those who were hard of hearing. The organization was to be called the Chicago League for the Hard of Hearing. The president, Gertrude Torry, and four other female officers were elected. An entertainment committee chair was appointed during this meeting as well. In fact, the first order of business was establishing a room for social purposes to be made available three afternoons a week. Three years later, the organization reported having 124 members. The annual meeting that year ended with the election of a new president plus three new members, all males, to the board of directors.

Consistent with its mission, one of the earliest programs the League decided to create was the employment service. It succeeded in placing fourteen of the twenty-three people seeking employment in 1919. Another major focus, promotion of lipreading, led to the creation of lip-reading classes. By 1920 the organization reported having enrolled one hundred students in classes presented by five or six teachers.

The same year, the Chicago League for the Hard of Hearing became the third chapter of the newly established American Federation of Organizations for the Hard of Hearing. When that organization changed its name to the National Society for the Hard of Hearing in 1941, the Chicago chapter changed its name to the Chicago Society for the Hard of Hearing. In 1947, when the national organization changed its name to the American Hearing Society, the Chicago chapter made the shift as well, becoming the Chicago Hearing Society (CHS).

The first program the organization began operating off-premises was hearing testing in the Chicago public schools. The early tests were based on tuning forks, whisper, and watch tests. The only assistive device available at the time was an ear trumpet, which according to the League's literature was "as big as a bread box" and not used by many. However, some progress was being made in development of assistive devices. The League exhibited those devices at the third annual Woman's World Fair held at the Chicago Coliseum in May 1927.

The League established what would become the present-day Hearing Aid Bank in 1930. It asked people to donate secondhand hearing aids, which it sold at a reduced rate or gave for free to those who could not afford to buy them. In 1941, the League opened a Hearing Aid Bureau where people could test the hearing aids that were on the market at that time.

The agency hired its first executive secretary, Mary Thompson, in 1941, as well as a number of full-time social workers. Mary Thompson continued to head the organization until 1970, when Dr. William Plotkin succeeded her in the renamed position of executive director.

CHS was very active over the next few decades, presenting a variety of programs designed to educate the public about deafness and the effects of noise, sign language classes, and counseling services for the deaf. It developed TV programming for deaf and hard-of-hearing children. The organization did experience some fiscal insecurity during the 1970s, but it seemed to have recovered during the 1980s. Its operating budget topped $1 million for the first time in 1989. The fact that the agency reported nearly the same figure, $1.3 million, as its operating budget about twenty years later in 1997 is a point worth noting and one to which we will return shortly.

The organization continued to create new programs during the 1980s. It created a six-week summer day camp for deaf and hard-of-hearing youngsters in collaboration with the Chicago Park District, which started in 1981 and continued until 2000. It began a screening service for preschoolers during the late 1980s, which the Chicago Department of Public Health took over in 2001. It sponsored several conferences dealing with disability issues and was actively involved in advocacy and legislative activity, which led to the formation of the Illinois Alliance for the Hearing Impaired. It promoted a variety of changes to help the hearing impaired such as a service providing sign language translations, captioning for videos and movies, hearing impaired aids for telephone users, and so on.

Organizational structure

While all this was happening, however, the organization was experiencing a great deal of administrative turbulence. Dr. Plotkin resigned as executive director in 1979 after serving in that position for nearly ten years. Between 1980 and 1995 the organization experienced executive turnover six times. New executive directors arrived as follows: Paul Krouse (1980), Janet Venable (1981), Richard Gelula (1984), Pamela Ransom (1985), Susan Kidder (1991), and Jill Sahakian in 1995. Jill Sahakian's position was eliminated in 2008; however, she was welcomed back about a year later and continues to serve as director.

In July 1997, the Chicago Hearing Society merged with the Anixter Center, which is dedicated to addressing a wide range of disabilities. (The Anixter Center story will be presented in the following chapter.) As we noted earlier, the CHS reported an annual operating budget of $1.3 million at the time of the merger in 1997. The CHS board president announced the merger, saying: "We believe our merger with Anixter Center will enable the Chicago Hearing Society to grow and to offer more comprehensive service to the community than would have been possible had we continued to operate on our own." The organization now operates under the Anixter Center umbrella, but it maintains a fair amount of independence in determining the programs it will provide. It collaborates with the staff at Anixter Center to provide services to Anixter Center clients who are deaf or hard of hearing.

Organizational funding

The CHS reported that it was working with a budget of more than $2 million for the first time in its history in 2002. The following year brought a number of changes—it became a founding member of CHOICES for Parents, which provides support to parents who have a child with a recently identified hearing loss. This effort was launched in anticipation of the effects of legislation passed in 2002 when all Illinois hospitals were to be required to begin screening the hearing of newborns. CHS also joined with Hearing Loss Link to better serve late-deafened adults. The same year, it closed its preschool hearing and vision screening program.

In 2003, it expanded its sign language interpreter services for video relay. It closed its sign language program (teaching of sign language) at the same time, after thirty-four years of operation.

The current mission of the Chicago Hearing Society is: To empower deaf, hard of hearing, and hearing people to communicate with each other.

WHAT WE CAN LEARN FROM THESE TWO CASES

Both the Chicago Lighthouse for the Blind and the Chicago Hearing Society grew from the bottom up. Although the CHS was a member of the national organization devoted to the needs of the hard of hearing, it was not dependent on it for direction. In the case of the Lighthouse, there has never been a national association to join. Thus both organizations largely operated as stand-alone organizations not linked to a national, headquarters organization. Yet the CHS was reporting a flat fund-raising record for about ten years before it announced that it would merge with another stand-alone nonprofit organization, one that focuses on services required by persons with a variety of disabilities. The CHS took this step after operating as an independent organization for more than eight decades. By contrast, the Lighthouse, which reported revenues of more than $18 million in the latest year of operation for which we have information, has been expanding its operations.

What does the Chicago Hearing Society's decision to merge tell us? It says that the stakeholders associated with this nonprofit organization acted in what they believed to be the best interests of the organization and the mission to which the organization is dedicated. It is interesting to consider that these two organizations, which might seem at first glance to have been quite similar to begin with—they have been in existence for a long time; they have comparable priorities, if not programs; and they seem to have faced similar challenges—ended up with very different growth records and organizational futures.

Both organizations have been offering various services and goods for which they charge a fee. These products account for a substantial portion of the budget in the case of the Lighthouse, but not a sufficient amount in the case of the CHS. Both organizations rely on public contributions to cover a large part of their operating costs. Although the interactional field in these two instances—the stakeholders, the beneficiaries, those who provide resources, and the communities in which they both operate—seem to be comparable, their fund-raising outcomes are obviously very different. The result is that their respective developmental trajectories also look very different.

The category of stakeholders that has played a significantly different role in the two organizations' fortunes is executive staff. The Chicago Lighthouse has had only four executive directors over the course of its lifetime. The CHS had one director from 1941 to 1970 and a second one over the next decade. After that, the agency had six new directors over the following fifteen years. Why this occurred is not something we can explain based on the information that is publicly available.

The difference in how outside parties in the two organizations' interactional fields have responded is worth noting. The contrast between the public faces of the Chicago Hearing Society and the Chicago Lighthouse is apparent in the amount of positive public attention the Lighthouse has received in recent years. Indeed, the Lighthouse received an award for the way it handles publicity in 2007 from media representatives. In sum, we can see that the two organizations had been operating in largely different interactional fields, which resulted in an impressive record of growth in one case and somehow missed producing anywhere near the same organizational pattern of development in the other case.

Chapter Ten

Helping People with Various Disabilities

In this chapter we will examine the workings of Anixter Center, which is dedicated to assisting people who have disabilities. The organization was created with a very circumscribed purpose during the second decade of the twentieth century. After several decades of pursuing its original purpose, it suddenly changed and began to expand, increasing both the number and types of programs it was prepared to offer. By 2004, it had become Chicago's thirteenth-largest charitable organization according to Chicago's major business publication, Crain's *Chicago Business*.

ORGANIZATIONAL MISSION

The mission of Anixter Center is to provide an array of services and supports for people with disabilities to live, learn, work, and play in the community.

ORGANIZATIONAL HISTORY

The agency came into existence in 1919 with the aim of providing services to deal with the needs of children who lost one or both parents to the influenza pandemic of 1918. It was incorporated as the Douglas Park Jewish Day Nursery, but the name was changed by the end of that year to reflect the fact that more extensive services were found to be necessary and were already being provided. It became the Douglas Park Jewish Day and Night Nursery.

After several decades operating as a full-time children's nursery, the organization made a significant change. The turning point came in 1956, when the board of directors decided to begin serving the needs of retarded children.

(Such children are now identified as developmentally disabled.) That produced another name change, to the Douglas Park Nursery and Training Center for Retarded Children. This change in focus inaugurated the dynamic growth that would follow from this time forward. The following year, the organization determined that it needed a school building, so it constructed a schoolhouse and renamed itself to reflect that change—the Chicago School for Retarded Children. Shortly thereafter, the organization began offering educational and training programs for developmentally disabled adults as well as children. By 1961, it was serving forty children and forty adults.

It did not take long for the leadership of the agency to see that the adult population it was serving would benefit from having paid employment. It launched a packaging business in 1961. The continuing expansion of the number of adults the organization was serving led to the purchase of a building that year to house the adult vocational training program. By 1969, the organization was providing employment services in addition to a number of other services for one hundred adult enrollees. It became informally known as the Chicago Workshop for the Retarded. It also took steps to move the six workshops that it had created during the 1960s into one of two locations. In 1974, the agency created the Transitional Employment Program, the first program in the nation to provide job training in industrial settings for people with developmental disabilities. It also opened a residential facility for adults with developmental disabilities the same year.

The school the organization had been operating at the Byron Center was shut down in 1978 in response to federal legislation passed that year requiring children with various disabilities to be mainstreamed into public schools. The school was reopened in 1982 when it became clear that some students could not be successfully served by public schools. Sixty-nine children were admitted that year.

The agency continued to initiate additional programs as it identified the need for particular kinds of services. The Literacy Program was established to provide individually designed literacy training to help adults with disabilities obtain and maintain good jobs. The Rehabilitation Aide Training program was initiated in response to the shortage of trained aides prepared to work with people with disabilities. The agency created an office skills program in collaboration with Wright College, which provided classes on the college's campus bringing together individuals with disabilities and nondisabled students. It created the North Suburban Employment Services agency, which was designed to help students with developmental disabilities make a successful transition from high school to employment. It launched a Professional Job Placement Program for People with Severe Disabilities in partnership with the Department of Human Services/Office of Rehabilitation Services.

By 1978, the agency was serving five hundred adults, which prompted it to change its name to Chicago Services for Work and Rehabilitation to reflect the services it was offering more accurately. It changed its name again in 1983 to the Center for the Rehabilitation and Training of the Disabled.

During the early 1980s, it established a for-profit division offering to provide office maintenance to major Chicagoland businesses. It also started the Supported Living Arrangements program with fifty scattered site apartments and added the Supported Group Living program to provide housing for people with mental illness. It developed the CILA (Community Integrated Living Arrangements) program, which aims to move people with developmental disabilities and mental illnesses from institutional settings into the agency's community-based residential facilities. It inaugurated the Factory Program to help special education students referred by the juvenile justice system in making the transition from school to work. And, it gained authority to grant continuing education unit credits for its in-house staff training program.

The agency went on to create a number of other for-profit ventures in order to provide employment or to help people develop skills that would lead to employment elsewhere. It opened the Janitorial Service in 1980; the Microfilm Services in 1983; and, the Southwest Suburban Micrographic Services in 1989. The latter two businesses merged in 1995, becoming The Imaging Service. It purchased Pen Prints, Inc., to provide factory work for students and created JobWorks to help individuals with hearing impairments find employment. In 1997, the agency began operating the Center Court Grill, a food service training program that serves as the cafeteria for the Illinois Department of Transportation's administration building.

It entered into a joint venture with a major rehabilitation institution in the area in 1990, the Schwab Rehabilitation Hospital and Care Network, now known as Access Healthcare Systems, to create a health-care facility dedicated exclusively to programs designed to serve people with disabilities. The enterprise was renamed Access at Anixter in 1995. The joint venture produced another program, New Focus, a community reintegration program for persons with brain injuries. Over the next few years the agency initiated a number of new health-oriented programs, including the Outpatient Substance Abuse Treatment program and the Addiction Recovery of the Deaf program.

The organization became the Lester and Rosalie Anixter Center in 1993. Over the next decade, the agency took steps that are atypical in nonprofit organizational circles deciding to merge with three established organizations. In 1997, it merged with CALOR, an agency specializing in services offered to members of the Latino community living with HIV/AIDS; and, with the Chicago Hearing Society, an organization that had been providing services since 1916 to people who are deaf or hard of hearing. In 2002, Anixter

Center merged with a third organization, the National Lekotek Center, a source for information on toys and therapeutic play for children who are hearing impaired.

The agency celebrated its ninetieth anniversary in 2009. In May 2010, Anixter Center launched a "new brand and tagline"—"The Ability to Soar"—at Chicago's first summer festival hosted by the Mayor's Office of Special Events. The historical account presented here does not touch on all the awards and other forms of recognition achieved by Anixter Center over the course of its life, of which there are many. That should not be surprising given how many innovative programs it offers.

Anixter Center named a new CEO in 2010. Within the first year of his tenure, he was faced with a drastic cut in funding that caused the agency to make plans to close down two homes. The state argued that the agency was not authorized to close down the homes. That led Anixter Center to initiate a lawsuit naming the secretary of the Department of Human Services and the director of the division of developmental disabilities as defendants. The case has not been settled at this writing.

ORGANIZATIONAL STRUCTURE

The 2011 Anixter Center annual report indicates that it is serving 5,500 people with disabilities through a variety of programs. It offers seventy services or programs at thirty-five locations across greater Chicago, including the following:

- education, training, and employment;
- housing and residential services;
- life skills and case management services;
- communication and socialization services;
- rehabilitation and recreation activities;
- health-care and prevention services;
- counseling and support services; and
- it is a leading advocate—statewide and nationally—for the rights of people with disabilities to be full and equal members of society.

  1. It operates fifteen (24-hour staffed) residences for adults with disabilities; four community-based residences through the Community Integrated Living Arrangements Program that offer case coordination services; and six apartment buildings supported by HUD (the U.S. Housing and Urban Development program).

2. It has a number of employment-oriented programs. Employment Opportunities, which assists people with disabilities to find and maintain jobs; JobWorks, which focuses on pre-and post-placement services for people who are deaf or hard of hearing; Anixter Center North represents job seekers, provides job readiness training, and on-the-job assessments; The Roberta Bachman Lewis Factory Program combines high school education, counseling, paid work, and job placement services for students who are referred through the juvenile justice system; CALOR, the bilingual employment operation for Latino people with disabilities due to HIV/AIDS; and Center Court Grille, the food service, on-the-job evaluation program that functions as a cafeteria for the Illinois Department of Transportation.

3. The Community Services category includes Independent Living, Community Resources and Support, Alternatives for the Developmentally Disabled, and CALOR. Each offers a wide range of services designed to help disabled persons live independently including case management services, meals-on-wheels through the Mayor's Office for People with Disabilities, vocational training, social activities, life planning, and so on. Community Services operates a Community Respite program providing relief services to primary caregivers of people with disabilities. It operates several programs focusing on the needs of those who are deaf or hard of hearing, under the auspices of the Chicago Hearing Society and National Lekotek Center. It also operates the Mental Health Services program, which is a member-driven service for people with mental illness that falls under Community Life Skills programming.

4. Health services are provided by ACCESS at Anixter Center, which is a primary care facility that offers outpatient services; plus a number of programs, some with titles that are self-explanatory—Substance Abuse Treatment for people with disabilities and Addiction Recovery of the Deaf; and New Focus, which is a community reintegration program for adults with acquired traumatic brain injuries.

5. Education. The agency operates the Stuart G. Ferst School, which provides both academic instruction and vocational training for students three to twenty-one years of age with behavioral disorders, autism, brain injuries, or developmental disabilities.

6. Training. The Training Institute offers education and training to employees of Anixter Center and other agencies; the Literacy program offers individualized instruction primarily through volunteer tutors.

7. Prevention. The Prevention program promotes healthy lifestyles.

8. Businesses. These include Imaging, Janitorial, and Packaging, all of which provide paid vocational training to people with disabilities and contract services to local businesses; a community interpreter business; and a Video Relay Service.

The decision to merge with three established organizations over the past two decades was motivated by the idea that the organizations would provide "added value." From the perspective of the Anixter Center, it was already involved in providing similar kinds of services. The mergers enhanced Anixter's ability to provide greater in-depth, targeted experience and expertise.

Those in leadership positions at Anixter Center express pride in the organization's accomplishments. Nevertheless, everyone involved recognizes that an organization that has so many programs and so many sites presents a major coordination and management challenge. The organization is very attentive to this issue and strives to address this challenge by employing a number of different mechanisms. A major effort toward this end was launched a few years ago. A change in leadership provided the occasion for a review of organizational accomplishments and future activities.

The CEO who oversaw much of the organization's expansion over the preceding thirty-five years retired in 2004. The new CEO started his tenure by spending some time getting to know individuals on the staff of the organization and working on board development and leadership. After he had been there for about a year, he asked board members, staff, and other interested stakeholders to participate in planning the agency's work for the next ten years—to develop a strategic plan.

The board of directors invited members of two standing board committees to take a leading role, the Planning and Quality Improvement Committee and the Branding Committee. Employees were represented by the Quality Coordination Council Committee, the VP Group, and a number of other ad hoc committees. The comprehensive strategic planning process was facilitated by Grant Thornton International Company and funded in part by the Chicago Community Trust. The preparatory planning process took several months. Participants were asked to present the results of their work during a two-day conference. In November 2006, the Anixter Center board of directors was ready to announce the goal that the strategic planning process produced—to become the premier provider of services and supports for people living with or at risk of disabilities; to provide services and supports for this population that promote community inclusion and are comprehensive, individualized, choice driven, and culturally sensitive.

Before we go on, it is interesting to consider the mandate given to the Branding Committee. It was asked to take on a very demanding task—to give the wide array of services offered by Anixter Center a shared identity by bringing all the organizations and the services they provide together under the Anixter Center umbrella and to do so without detracting from the respective unique identities and contributions of each unit or operation. Why this task is so challenging becomes clear when you consider the stance some of the participants took; for example, those involved in Chicago Hearing Society (CHS) activities. People who are deaf and hard of hearing do not necessarily see themselves as having a disability, certainly not in the same way that many of the other participants served by Anixter Center are disabled. Thus, CHS is a part of the larger umbrella organization, yet stands somewhat apart from it—clearly a difficult balance to maintain.

Having merged or partnered with the new organizations and the added participants to whose needs each respective organization responds, Anixter Center employees are already looking forward to new challenges. They are becoming aware of the rapidly growing number of people who are at risk of developing "secondary disabilities." That refers in part to the growing number of people who are part of an aging population and who are developing disabilities that they had not been confronting earlier in their lives.

One of the reasons the agency has begun to take an interest in this phenomenon is that federal government granting agencies are beginning to emphasize prevention of conditions that lead to disability. Accordingly, Anixter Center has begun evaluating how it can contribute to the development of programs targeting risk prevention. Services for this clientele are still in the planning stages.

ORGANIZATIONAL FUNDING

Anixter Center's 2008–2009 annual report states that it is working with an operating budget of just under $30 million. More than half (56 percent) of its income comes from government grants through the state of Illinois; 22 percent comes through other grants; another 18 percent comes from earned income and contract revenue; and 4 percent from contributions. Contract income refers to the gross revenue brought in through the for-profit businesses that Anixter Center operates. The Center Court Grille grossed about $105,000. The Imaging Service grossed about $307,000. The Packing Service, which employs about eighty program participants, brought in $589,000. The Janitorial Service grossed more than $2 million. The Chicago Hearing Society, which charges a fee for audiology and interpreting services, generated revenue of more than $2 million as well.

Anixter Center intentionally pursues different funding streams to prevent dependence on any one source of funding that might shift its priorities and not deliver essential funds at some future time. This was the thinking behind a new fund-raising event, an annual golf outing that brought in $237,000 in 2007, the first year it was held.

ORGANIZATIONAL EVALUATION

Many of the services the organization offers must be evaluated as a matter of contractual agreement with the government agencies and other bodies that provide funding to support the long list of specific programs outlined above. Each funding organization specifies its own evaluation criteria, which makes program evaluation a complicated task that requires a lot of time and effort. Anixter Center is evaluated by the Department of Human Services for services funded by the Division of Developmental Disabilities, the Division of Mental Health, the Division of Alcohol and Substance Abuse, and the Division of Rehabilitation Services. Additionally, the organization is monitored by the Chicago Department of Public Health, the Mayor's Office for People with Disabilities, the Department of Public Aid, and quite a few other government agencies that focus on more specific issues; housing regulations, for example.

The most comprehensive outcome evaluation process is that of the Commission on Accreditation of Rehabilitation Facilities (CARF), which requires the agencies it evaluates to document their 1) efficiency, 2) effectiveness, 3) satisfaction (on the part of participants), and 4) program access. CARF does not specify the indicators to be used in gathering these data. Each organization is expected to set its own benchmarks grounded in its organizational history. This is especially challenging in those instances in which national benchmarks are not available.

Confronted with the problem of gathering facts and figures in an effort to capture the outcome measures and indicators specified by evaluating organizations, Anixter Center could simply treat evaluation requirements as a major headache and just get it over with. The alternative is to see the process as a valuable feedback tool and use it in the service of program development in the short run and organizational planning in the long run. The agency has clearly embraced the latter option.

The director of the Quality Improvement and Strategic Design (QISD) department is primarily responsible for developing the measures that serve as performance indicators. She says the agency is trying to avoid a "data heavy, information poor" data collection result. There is no question that the organization is "data heavy" as the following statement presented in Anixter Center literature describing its perspective on outcome research indicates. The organizational literature says of the Outcome Management System:

> [It was created] to measure and analyze aspects of all direct service programs including efficiency, effectiveness, and satisfaction and to be responsive to the information needs of stakeholders. The Outcome Management System also allows the agency to build historical information surrounding each program.

The information gathered and generated through outcomes management is used for regulatory and reporting purposes, strategic positioning, and quality improvements.

The organization established a formalized process for assessing organizational performance in the early 1990s. The results have been compiled regularly since then. The director of QISD explains that the agency relies heavily on the trend data it compiles to indicate how the effects of its programs may be changing over time. The results are analyzed to determine the extent to which programs are producing increased benefit and to assess which programmatic aspects might benefit from additional attention. The trend data analyses also help the staff to determine which evaluation tools and measures are most useful.

The QISD director notes that many evaluation instruments are available, but she and her staff believe the instruments do not necessarily provide information of practical value for the organization collecting the information. In other words, such instruments result in the "data rich, information poor" condition that the organization wishes to avoid. Furthermore, she points out, Anixter Center does not rely on standardized, especially self-administered, evaluation instruments because so many agency participants are unable to read well enough to fill out the surveys.

The leadership of Anixter Center has determined that using "best practices" (the treatments that experts agree are most effective) as the standard against which to compare its performance produces the greatest return. The agency does not use a clinical research model to evaluate programs and interventions, because this model is based on the use of control groups. Agency staff members believe this carries too much risk of damage to its participants. (The clinical research model requires that one group receives a particular treatment that is withheld from a "control" group. The effects of treatment on each group are then assessed after a specified period of time.)

The Anixter Center employs three research tools to get feedback from the individuals and families receiving services—focus groups, written surveys, and direct mail surveys. According to the QISD department, the agency has been increasing its reliance on the information gathered through the focus group data-gathering method to obtain information on the impact of its programs. The QISD director has increasingly come to believe that measures of program success should not be limited to technical indicators, but should measure the common things we all want. That is, we all want to be safe, be satisfied with our living arrangements, our interactions, and so on. The ultimate measure of success, in her view, is the perception of choice and control over one's life, which is best expressed by the individuals involved in their own words.

This approach reflects a growing trend in the field—to move toward measurements that are rooted in the quality of "everyday lives." This is in addition to more traditional ways of measuring quality in health-care settings (e.g., staffing ratios, numbers of serious incidents, accomplishments of service plan goals, etc.). The expectation is that agencies that serve disabled clients are increasingly likely to be called upon to measure fulfillment of core life goals such as work, friends, relationships, wellness, and community participation. For many services at Anixter Center, this will build on what the agency has been doing for many years.

Accordingly, the director of QISD and her colleagues have been working on evaluation approaches that are centered on the individual. QISD volunteered to be audited by the Human Services Research Institute out of Boston; as a result, it began to investigate new ways of measuring outcomes partially based on National Core Indicators created by the National Core Indicators (NCI) Project, which is a collaboration between the Human Services Research Institute (HSRI) and the National Association of State Directors of Developmental Disabilities Services (NASDDDS). Participating states, twenty-one at present, work with HSRI and NASDDDS to identify common performance indicators, design a performance monitoring system, and document the relevant data collection strategies.

Anixter has also been developing its own self-perception survey and series of focus group questions that allow participants to assess their own state of physical health, mental health, and overall satisfaction with life in addition to evaluating the services and supports provided by the organization. The objective is to move from the results obtained through this step to the next step, which is to help the individual to create a life plan that outlines the targets the person wishes to set for himself or herself. This process allows staff to develop a person-centered service plan that meets the needs and expectations of the individual participant rather than imposing a standardized plan required by the funding source in which the person has no say. This may lead to the program participant saying that he or she is satisfied with the current state of his or her physical and mental health. Program staff must then accept a treatment plan that aims to maintain stability rather than seeking a change in status. Program evaluation has to reflect this objective, which then becomes the outcome against which program effectiveness is measured. This represents a very new way of thinking about what constitutes a desirable program outcome.

Obviously such individual person-oriented assessment requires a great deal of staff time. The organization hopes to train volunteers who come from outside of the agency and peer volunteers who are members of the agency to carry out some of this work. This would provide the added benefit of allowing participants to express points of dissatisfaction with their care without having to express dissatisfaction to the very persons with whom they are "partnered" for their care.

Having staff members involved in participant assessments focusing on self-assessed health and forming a person-centered plan has had an interesting and largely unanticipated effect. Staff members have reacted by saying they do not perceive themselves to have the kind of choice and control over their lives they are advocating for participants. Confronted with this reality, the organizational leadership has been making extensive efforts to include employees in the strategic positioning process.

Employee input is reflected in the value statement developed during the strategic planning process. The result is reaffirmation of the agency's commitment to its staff, making sure staff members know the work they do is highly valued by the organizational leadership. Anixter Center is pleased to report its direct service employee turnover rate is 27 percent, which is far below the industry average of 70 percent. Staff members are represented by the Service Employees International Union (SEIU). The union is generally acknowledged to be very forceful in its representation of employee interests, so the employees know they can raise concerns about working conditions and be effectively represented if need be.

The strategic positioning process

The strategic positioning process was initiated in 2005 by the newly appointed CEO. It was grounded in a lengthy and extensive organizational self-evaluation. The Boston-based Grant Thornton firm was invited to facilitate this process. Both employees and board members participated in the process of carefully reexamining the organization's mission, values, and organizational strengths. They did so with the understanding that results would be used to develop strategic positioning statements that would guide the organization's work over the next ten years. Participants were asked to work in small teams to produce one-page "future scan sheets" documenting facts and trends related to assigned topics, such as "best practices," population trends, competitors, labor, and so on. The groups were asked to reflect on the facts and figures and identify the implications for Anixter Center. The process took several months, culminating in a two-day conference with board members and employees.

The outcome was a revised mission statement together with a set of values to guide the organization in all of its future endeavors. Specific short-term objectives that reflect the organization's primary mission were identified in this process.

The tagline to the mission statement was reaffirmed: "We see the ability in everyone." Additionally, the following list of values was identified.

Person Centered

- We affirm the worth, capacity, and gifts of all people; and treat everyone with dignity and respect.
- We promote self-advocacy and advocate for full human rights and participation in the community.
- We promote healthy lifestyles and work together using our diverse talents and experiences to support individuals in leading a self-directed and full life.

Commitment to Employees

- We value our employees and provide a supportive, culturally sensitive work environment with opportunities for professional development and growth.
- We support healthy lifestyles for employees and promote well-being.

Open and Honest Communication

- We foster an accessible environment in which respectful communication and the exchange of ideas can occur.

Informed Action

- We strive to exceed expectations by basing our practice on the best available research and operational experience.
- With a vision toward being the best, we actively seek ways to improve and innovate through ongoing customer and employee feedback and by promoting a continuous learning environment.

Collaboration

- We achieve our mission and inspire communities through teamwork with people living with or at risk of disabilities, families, donors, volunteers, community members, our employees, and other professional partners.

Excellence

- We maintain a disciplined, results-oriented organization and operate within the highest ethical standards in all of our working relationships and business practices.

WHAT WE CAN LEARN FROM THE ANIXTER CENTER CASE

This organization is a very large, stand-alone entity. There is no national-level organization involved. Anixter Center clearly evolved from the bottom up. After operating as a home for orphaned children for more than three decades, it began offering services to children with developmental disabilities. After that, it expanded steadily over the following five decades. It made another significant leap at the turn of the twenty-first century when it decided to merge with three other nonprofit service organizations. That produced a very sudden increase in size and complexity. Dealing with the complexity involved in managing a large number of programs and organizations, some with separate identities of their own, requires a great deal of coordination, cooperation, and communication among board members, administrative staff, direct service personnel, and all other interested stakeholders—that is, virtually everyone in its interactional field.

Persons in managerial staff positions at Anixter Center are very aware of the fact that the agency's organizational leadership has a firmly established tradition of flexibility and openness to change. That makes working there interesting and not likely to become routine and boring. The pace of change does, however, require readiness to accept the need for continuing adjustment in dealing with the differences in the demands presented by all the programs the agency operates—how to organize them, how to ensure that both participants and staff are satisfied, how to evaluate outcomes to identify the benefits that are forthcoming, and so forth. The name changes the agency embraced over the course of its existence make clear its sensitivity to its identity or "brand" and how its work is perceived by those both inside and outside of the organization. In other words, the agency knows it must respond to a large number of interested stakeholders who bring a wide range of interests to the table.

The list of stakeholders interested in the programs offered by Anixter Center is extensive, starting with participants who present a long and varied list of disabilities. We know the organization strives to be responsive to the special interests of participants. We also know the organization has given explicit recognition to the importance of the role of staff. Additionally, the organization cannot ignore the views of representatives of the geographic community in which its facilities are located. The organization must be careful to avoid the risk of a NIMBY (not in my back yard) backlash. That is to say, members of some communities might not welcome as neighbors Anixter facilities and the people they serve. It must respond to the requirements of granting agencies, regulatory agencies, the organizations with which Anixter Center contracts to provide services. And, of course, donors must be cultivated.

The main mechanism Anixter Center relies on to manage the disparate demands of all its stakeholders is vigilance to evaluation of its performance and impact on beneficiaries as well as other stakeholders. Evaluation is, of course, required by fund-granting agencies. Not surprisingly, funders wish to know that the money they have awarded was used effectively. That is not, however, necessarily the same thing as providing clear evidence that the programs the organization operates are making a difference in the lives of the people who are being served. In other words, evaluation grounded in the perspective that the recipients bring to the process may not be the same as the perspective of funders. The agency is committed to carrying out outcome research, which is obviously a very complicated undertaking—more so when one takes into account the outcome criteria that various stakeholders are interested in seeing. Indeed, no one who does evaluation research—in the field, in academia, or in the funding community—has come up with indicators of program impact that everyone can agree on. There are established evaluation instruments that Anixter Center agency staff could use, which would save them a great deal of time and energy. The director of the QSID prefers not to use evaluation instruments developed for general use. She does not rely on such instruments, because that could turn the evaluation process into a pro forma exercise rather than a source of useful information.

The attention that Anixter Center devotes to evaluation clearly goes well beyond any requirements imposed by any of its stakeholders. The agency is committed to using the results of its program evaluations to provide feedback. The findings are available to all interested stakeholders. Of greater significance to the agency's record of accomplishment, staff members affiliated with specific programs are given the opportunity to weigh in on whether those programs could be improved, or whether they are successful and not to be altered. Program evaluation serves a very central function at Anixter Center. It provides the source material for informing its planning process that, in turn, reaffirms its mission, values, and concrete objectives.

Chapter Eleven

Battling the Spread of HIV/AIDS

The appearance of AIDS (acquired immunodeficiency syndrome) in this country dates back to the early 1980s. It did not take experts in the public health community long to realize that it was being spread through sexual contact. However, although it is hard to imagine now, it was initially thought to be a disease that was somehow limited to the population of white gay men. It took another few years before it became clear that the HIV (human immunodeficiency virus) infection came first and that this is what led to AIDS. Moreover, it did not take much longer to find that both men and women of all races and ethnicities are susceptible. Once the Centers for Disease Control and Prevention started tracking the spread of the disease, another unanticipated trend became apparent, namely, that the disease was spreading more rapidly in minority populations in this country. Some observers have been saying that mainstream efforts to deal with the spread of the disease developed far too slowly. Thus, there is good reason to believe that, were it not for activists across the country who pressed anyone who would listen to have the disease investigated and to insist that intervention programs be established, it would have taken even longer. What is most noteworthy about their efforts, for purposes of this discussion, is that the activists approached this challenge by establishing nonprofit organizations.

In this chapter we will examine the growth, development, and impact of two organizations: the Howard Brown Health Center (HBHC), which provides a variety of services, including direct care services, to members of the LGBT (lesbian, gay, bisexual, and transgender) community; and the AIDS Foundation of Chicago, which, as the title suggests, provides other organizations with funds to deliver needed services and individuals with funds to obtain the care they need. Both organizations must raise money; it is what they do with that money that differs.

THE HOWARD BROWN HEALTH CENTER

Organizational mission

The mission of Howard Brown is to promote the well-being of gay, lesbian, bisexual, and transgender persons through the provision of health-care and wellness programs, including clinical, educational, social service, and research activities. Howard Brown designed these programs to serve gay, lesbian, bisexual, and transgender persons in a confidential, supportive, and nurturing environment. Howard Brown is committed to working in cooperation with other community-based organizations serving and contributing to the gay, lesbian, bisexual, and transgender community.

Organizational history

The Howard Brown Health Center grew out of a clinic established in 1974 by four medical students who were concerned about the existence of untreated disease among gay men. More specifically, the clinic founders were motivated by what they considered to be the absence of culturally competent treatment of sexually transmitted diseases (STDs) afflicting gay men. When the AIDS epidemic first hit, the clinic had already developed a considerable amount of experience identifying and diagnosing HIV infection. By 1980, it had become the most reliable source of HIV education in the area, which it was prepared to offer to patients in person at its clinic or via the area's first information hotline.

The Center established its identity as a community-based research site shortly after it opened its doors, well before it started dealing with the HIV infection, by accepting the challenge of testing the hepatitis B vaccine. The Center's findings helped lead to approval of the vaccine. The success of this endeavor became the foundation on which the Center built its reputation as a facility dedicated to both the provision of community health services and to community-based research that would produce new treatments for the clients the Center sought to serve. We return to this topic when we consider program evaluation later in this discussion.

It took a few years for the clinic to become firmly established and to be renamed. It was named The Howard Brown Health Center in honor of Dr. Howard Brown, the nation's first openly gay health official working in New York City, for his work as an agent of change in the delivery of health-care services. Dr. Brown was actively involved in advocating for increased attention to the needs of poor and underserved minorities. He argued that all patients deserve to be treated with dignity and respect. He gained special recognition for his commitment to highlighting the need for cultural understanding, sensitivity, and appropriate care for gay, lesbian, bisexual, and transgender (LGBT) individuals.

The clinic was already well established when the country first began to acknowledge that the rising incidence of AIDS indicated it was taking on the characteristics of an epidemic. Accordingly, the Howard Brown Health Center began to expand its offerings in order to provide a more extensive range of health services. It moved quickly to be the first facility in the area to translate scientific information into applied information on HIV. It added primary care services, mental health services, behavioral health services, HIV/STD prevention care, and lesbian health services. It continues to add new programs and bring in new patients and clients.

The 2010 annual report includes a letter from the new president and CEO. It reveals a new auditing firm confirmed the suspicion among some members that the organization was suffering from financial mismanagement. The new president announced the addition of eight new board members and the need to launch an emergency fund-raising campaign with the aim of raising $500,000 in fifty days. Furthermore, it announced the goal of raising $1 million by the end of the fiscal year. The letter from the new president that accompanies the annual report states that the HBHC is also proud to announce what it accomplished over the previous year, which includes:

- Serving more than 7,000 patients through nearly 15,000 clinical visits and an additional 3,000 homeless or at-risk youth
- Conducting nearly 9,000 HIV/STI (sexually transmitted illnesses) screenings
- Carrying out nearly a dozen active research studies and nearly a dozen clinical trials

Organizational structure

The Howard Brown Health Center has moved well beyond its initial mission, which focused on the health needs of gay men, to provide services designed to meet the needs of a number of other population groups, namely, women, youth, and most recently older adults.

The Center provides primary care health services at several locations. The main clinic is housed in its headquarters building. The Center also operates the Triad Clinic, located at a community hospital in the area. The HBHC representatives make clear that the organization takes pride in providing a comprehensive approach to the delivery of care. It employs a multiphased, coordinated approach to patient care that includes medical, behavioral, and substance abuse screening and treatment, and coordination of support services. It places special emphasis on preventive health-care services.

The HIV/STD Prevention Department is at the forefront of these efforts. The services are provided by experienced health educators who are members of the communities they serve. This permits them to provide culturally sensitive outreach services, lead group interventions, and provide HIV/STD counseling.

HBHC provides more comprehensive needs assessment, service planning, and advocacy for clients and their families through the case management program. Case managers assist with the necessities of daily life such as transportation, help in finding stable housing, financial assistance, and coordination of physical and mental health care. Psychotherapy is available through the Behavioral Health Services (BHS) unit, which was established in response to the recognition of the tremendous need for culturally sensitive psychotherapy and support. The fastest-growing program associated with the BHS unit is the Crystal Clear Project that targets LGBT crystal methamphetamine users and is funded through a grant from the City of Chicago Department of Public Health.

HBHC is pleased to report that the organization's recent emphasis on serving specifically targeted populations is producing positive results. The number of visits to the Center by women has increased over recent years. Howard Brown credits two programs for this: Stand Against Cancer and the Women's Patient Navigation Program, which use innovative approaches designed to meets the special needs of lesbian, bisexual, and transgender women. A portion of the funding for cancer screening exams for low-income, uninsured, and underinsured women comes from the Lesbian Community Cancer Project. It is worth noting, however, that only 40 percent of the women who sought care for any of the services being provided over the past few years self-identified themselves as lesbian or bisexual.

The most active program the organization manages is one that focuses on the population under age twenty-four. Recognition of the special concerns that young people bring when they seek health-care services caused the Howard Brown Health Center to create a separate facility, the Broadway Youth Center (BYC). BYC opened its doors in 2004. It began by offering a set of core services including a drop-in center, case management, therapy, medical care, HIV testing, mentor programming, and support groups. It has added new programs as it identified the need for particular kinds of services over the next few years.

HBHC initiated two additional programs at BYC to address the HIV prevention needs of young transgender women. First is Transgender Women Informing Sista Trans-women on AIDS (TWISTA), a group intervention program funded by the Centers for Disease Control and Prevention (CDC). TWISTA is designed to educate young transgender women of color on HIV prevention. The second is Life Skills, another CDC-funded program. This is a research project aimed at helping young transgender women to increase their self-esteem, self-reliance, and ultimately develop HIV prevention skills.

In 2006 BYC launched the Education and Vocation program in recognition of the fact that lesbian, gay, bisexual, and transsexual youth are three times more likely to drop out of high school than their peers of the same age. The program provides individualized tutoring to help enrolled youth pass the GED exam and receive a high school diploma. Beyond that, this program provides career training and placement in collaboration with Inspiration Corporation, which is dedicated to helping youth who are experiencing or are at-risk of homelessness.

HBHC continually strives to find innovative approaches to the delivery of core health services. For example, it increased the availability of rapid HIV testing and return of results rates. The Center began offering off-site HIV testing in bars and clubs. The fact that the test can provide results in twenty minutes was very well received by members of the LGBT community. Doing this, the Center was able to achieve a rate that is double the national average for the number of clients returning to receive the results. Another innovative program recently instituted is the "edgy" smoking cessation program called Bitch to Quit! This is a statewide LGBT-focused peer support and assistance program created in response to the statewide smoking ban inside of most buildings. Additional funding for smoking cessation comes from the American Legacy Foundation, which supports the Put It Out! program.

The Elder Services Community Initiative, added in 2006, is designed to address the needs of isolated, vulnerable adults over the age of sixty. The program benefited from a $100,000 grant from the Baxter International Foundation, a $20,000 pledge from the Chicago Community Trust, plus the support of a number of community health-care delivery partners including Rush Medical Center, CJE-Senior Life, Heartland Alliance, and Midwest Palliative and Hospice CareCenter.

Another program, started in 2007, is the Latino Health Services program designed to provide culturally as well as linguistically appropriate services to gay Latino men. Minority health issues are further being addressed through the Technical Assistance/Capacity Development Project, funded by the Department of Health Human Services Office of Minority Health. The project provides training and capacity development to agencies dedicated to HIV prevention in the minority population.

Finally, one other very interesting unit, the Brown Elephant, a resale shop, serves a number of different functions. It is a fund-raising unit as well as a source of material goods for clients who need the things that are available at the Brown Elephant. We will get back to this branch shortly.

Organizational funding

According to the last fully comprehensive annual report in 2007, HBHC receives more than half of its funding, about 52 percent, from government agencies; 9 percent comes from patient fees. Additional funding comes from the following sources: Brown Elephant shop profits (23 percent); foundation, corporation, and organization support (6 percent); special events (4 percent); individual support and interest and donated service (less than 1 percent each).

A number of foundations and organizations provide funds to back the festive events Howard Brown likes to present every year. The two main special events are the Taste for Every Palate benefit and the fall Annual Gala. Why Howard Brown chooses to support an annual gala, which is a formal ball, whereas so many nonprofit organizations have done away with such events, is interesting to consider. According to the director of the Community Initiatives Department, Howard Brown does this because it allows the organization to recognize the special contributions made by some of the people associated with the organization. The Gala offers a festive and public setting to present awards to persons who have contributed something that deserves special recognition. Awards are given to three members of the community whose dedication to the goals espoused by the Center is considered to be especially noteworthy. Another award, the Spirit Award, is given to an employee whose efforts have been especially valuable.

Then there are the funds raised by the Brown Elephant. The Center operates four Brown Elephant resale shops, which together brought in 23 percent of the agency's funding in 2007—that translates into about $1 million.

The donations of clothes and furnishings that come into the Brown Elephant shops also provide household goods and clothing for the clients of the Broadway Youth Center who have had a falling out with their families and been forced to leave home. They are issued a voucher that allows them to get what they need to live on their own.

Organizational evaluation

The fact that 52 percent of the Center's revenue comes from government contracts and 6 percent comes from foundation and corporation support means Howard Brown must carry out evaluation studies required by funders. The Center keeps track of the number of people seen in the medical clinics who are then followed by case managers, seen at the drop-in centers, tested for HIV/STDs in bars, served by the smoking cessation programs, and so on. The statistics published in the 2007 annual report indicate the Center had 61,123 visits or contacts with 22,853 clients.

Although the annual report does not discuss the Center's research in detail, the fact that the Center has been engaged in a major study of HIV and AIDS since 1982 is known to everyone interested in AIDS research. This is when it was awarded a contract by the National Institutes of Health to participate in the largest study of the disease in the world. The Center has been following the health of and longitudinal progression of HIV in its HIV-positive subjects since then.

The Center regularly conducts surveys of clinical trial participants' views of the agency's work, which provides its clients with an opportunity to voice their opinions on how they are being treated. Patient satisfaction surveys of persons who use various other services offered by Howard Brown are conducted on a regular basis.

A few years ago the HBHC decided to see how well acquainted people in the community in which it is located are with the services the Center offers and to determine what other services they would be interested in having the Center offer. It launched a Community Needs Assessment study gathering one thousand responses, which indicated the Center was doing an excellent job. In order to have continuity in responding to community preferences, the Center created a Community Advisory Board at around the same time. This board is composed of a dozen or so current users of its services whose role it is to give the organizational leaders and staff a regular assessment of the consumers' perspective. This assessment is meant to go beyond the perspective offered by patients receiving medical services and the evaluation instruments they complete as required for government-funded projects.

AIDS FOUNDATION OF CHICAGO (AFC)

Organizational mission

AFC's mission is to lead the fight against HIV/AIDS and improve the lives of people affected by the epidemic. We pursue that mission through: Advocacy, Funding, and Collaboration.

Organizational history

The organization was founded in 1985 by four people who are identified in the AFC literature as "local visionaries." Their initial focus was on advocacy in Springfield and Washington, D.C. Current organizational literature states that the organization sees itself as "a catalyst for local, national, and international action on HIV/AIDS." Although the objectives the founders intended to pursue from the start continue to give the organization its primary focus, the organization has expanded its agenda to collaborate with government and community partners to pursue comprehensive strategies in the fight against

HIV/AIDS. It continues to focus on supporting and coordinating prevention, care, and advocacy projects. Furthermore, it continues to champion effective, compassionate policy and human rights to bring an end to the HIV/AIDS pandemic.

One of the earliest initiatives AFC pursued was the creation of the Service Providers Council to bring together community service agencies. The Council was established in 1986 in cooperation with fifteen local agencies that became Council members. By 1989, the Council had expanded to encompass seventy-five agencies. AFC established the Northeastern Illinois HIV/AIDS Case Management Cooperative that same year. This is a network of community agencies that provide case management services. Over the next five years AFC was able to extend its case management network of agencies to include those located in the "collar counties" around Cook County, where Chicago is located, including McHenry, DuPage, Lake, Kendall, DeKalb, Grundy, and Will Counties.

Another early initiative, grant making, was not necessarily something the founders had initially envisioned would become the activity for which the organization is now most widely recognized. By its third year of operation, 1988, AFC had raised enough money to distribute $200,000 in grant monies to local community organizations. The efforts of one of Chicago's best-known landmark stores, Marshall Field and Co., helped to launch this initiative, raising more than $500,000 in 1987 for the cause. By 1996, AFC was able to distribute more than $1 million in grant money to fifty-five agencies. In 1999, AFC was providing funds for a new case management initiative linking HIV-positive persons returning to the community from correctional settings with integrated health care and support services.

Consistent with its founding purpose, AFC recounts a long list of successes in advocacy efforts. The following are highlights. One of the earliest achievements occurred in 1992, when it was able to prevent the state of Illinois from closing a critical Medicaid program serving hundreds of people living with AIDS. In 1993, it reported that it succeeded in its efforts to lead an eight-month effort to increase the state of Illinois AIDS budget from $3.5 to $7 million. In 1997, it helped to save the Illinois AIDS Drug Assistance Program by convincing the governor to increase state funding. Another early initiative was AFC's focus on the need that people with HIV/AIDS have for assistance with housing. AFC created the first-ever AIDS housing strategic plan in 1995. It launched a three-year housing research project in 2002. It worked with the Chicago City Council to increase HIV prevention funding in the 2007 city budget by $500,000.

In recent years, AFC has been publishing a list of bills being debated by Illinois General Assembly that have an impact on HIV/AIDS prevention, health care, rights, social services, and related topics.

During the 2008 legislative session, AFC monitored forty bills. A report on the disposition of each appears on the organization's website. According to its 2009 annual report, one of the three goals AFC set for itself in 2008 was the creation of a Community Advisory Board, which is expected to work with its Housing Advisory Council. In addition, AFC planned to create a new Center for Housing and Health Partnerships to fund supportive housing options for low-income people with HIV and other chronic health conditions.

A third objective announced in 2008 was the creation of the Community/ Direct Fundraising initiative designed to empower agencies to enhance their ability to raise monies on their own. AFC states that 67 percent of the grants it awarded in 2008 went to community-based organizations serving African Americans and governed by African Americans.

Organizational structure

AFC is a stand-alone organization that has informal ties with organizations across the country that have similar missions. There is no umbrella organization. It has a very active board of directors, which operates through a number of ad hoc committees that focus on advocacy, grant making, fund-raising, and monitoring the agency's performance. The Services Providers Council is the oldest and most well established of these committees. It is led by an executive committee that has forty members.

When the organization opened its doors in 1985, it had a staff of four. The staff grew slowly but steadily, increasing to forty-five to fifty over the years since then. Ten years after it was established, AFC was already supporting the work being carried out by 150 service providers working at organizations serving HIV/AIDS patients in and around Chicago. Currently fifteen staff members are responsible for overseeing the provision of services to clients who seek assistance from facilities across the city. These staff members coordinate and oversee the work of case managers who work for the service provider organizations. AFC staff members work with physicians who provide care as well as a range of other service providers who are responsible for addressing a variety of basic needs beyond health-care services, such as housing. The funding for this facet of AFC's work comes from the Illinois Department of Public Health, the federal government, and a number of other foundations.

The 2010 annual report announced that the current president was leaving after twelve years of service to AFC to accept a position in a newly formed organization resulting from a merger between the National AIDS Fund and AIS Action located in Washington, D.C. The new president/CEO has been with AFC since 1991 and has been serving as vice president prior to his appointment. He is only the fourth person to hold this position since the organization was founded.

Organizational funding

The 2010 annual report indicates the organization had $22.1 million in revenue and an equal amount in expenses. The budget breakdown indicates AFC received 78 percent of its funds through government grants and 22 percent from private sources. The government agencies providing financial support include (starting with the agencies providing most funding) the Chicago Department of Public Health, Illinois Department of Public Health, U.S. Department of Housing and Urban Development, Chicago Department of Human Services, Illinois Department of Human Services, and U.S. Substance Abuse and Mental Health Services Administration.

It reports spending 92 cents out of every dollar on HIV/AIDS programs and services, distributed as follows:

- Grants to community agencies—64 percent
- Program and policies—24 percent
- Development—5 percent
- Administration—3 percent

It reports awarding $14.8 million in grants and contracts over the previous year. It funded 126 organizations and provided direct emergency assistance to hundreds of individuals through the case management service and housing network.

A committee established by the board of directors reviews funding request proposals submitted by organizations in the community. Those that seem promising receive a site visit from members of the committee as well as staff members. Many more requests come to AFC than can be funded. Accordingly only those that have an excellent chance of succeeding receive support. Staff members say many proposals are built on good intentions but are not sustainable.

In recognition of the fact that persons representing struggling community agencies come to their work with good intentions but relatively little training and experience, AFC offers organizational training for executive directors of such organizations. The purpose is to help them improve their chances of identifying funding for the programs and services they envision that promise to be sustainable over the long term. AFC offers its conference room to any group that wishes to hold its meetings there.

Recognizing that about half of the organization's discretionary income (in contrast to money associated with grants that are dedicated to carrying out specific activities) comes from the special events the organization hosts, let us take a closer look at what these are. The organization hosts three main fund-raising events: the AIDS Run and Walk, the World of Chocolate, and Dance for Life. The organization regularly receives offers to stage many more events. The director of public relations says he spends a good deal of time sifting through these to determine which to accept, because they invariably require both additional staff time and up-front outlay of funds to stage—some more than others.

The AIDS Run and Walk

AFC has sponsored this event since 2005. Before this time, a private organization was responsible. However, that organization did not manage its funds very well. It angered some of the agencies that were participating because they found they were receiving far less money in return than they expected. That organization gave up the run. The first year AFC took over, it made a slight change to the name of the run and offered to return 50 percent of the money to agencies that agreed to participate. The following year, it promised to return 75 percent. Participation improved, and fifty-nine agencies signed on. The third year, 2008, AFC registered seven thousand participants and raised more than $500,000. Because AFC is able to fund all the support services this kind of event requires, it has been able to return 100 percent of the monies raised to grantee agencies. In 2010, the event again attracted seven thousand participants and raised more than $450,000.

The World of Chocolate

The AFC considers this to be a very special event, which has been presented over the past six years. The event is held on December 1 in commemoration of World AIDS Day and is usually sold out well before it is scheduled to take place. In 2010, the event raised $175,000.

The AFC introduced a number of new features in 2007 that are described in some detail in the 2008 annual report; for example, entertainment presented by a jazz quartet and a well-known female impersonator named Larry Hot Chocolate Edwards. It also served as a platform for launching what the organization considers to be a "sensational cookbook" featuring recipes provided by nationally recognized drag queens whose photographs accompany their recipes. The cookbook was launched at parties in other cities and invited participants to select a recipe to receive the "people's choice" award for best recipe.

Another dimension of the World of Chocolate event is that AFC offers it as a "corporate team building opportunity." Corporations are each invited to send a team of managerial employees to the event early in the day. Those employees work together with responsibility for an unfamiliar challenge with a fixed deadline by the end of the afternoon. They set the stage for the event. Team members must work together under atypical conditions—without a set of instructions for accomplishing their assignment and without a leader identified by management. The members of the team simply have to work it out on the spot, under time pressure. They may schedule breakout sessions to see how well they are doing in accomplishing the task. At the end, many companies provide rooms for their employees so they and their families can enjoy the event and get a good rest. In short, a great deal of "synergy" surrounds the World of Chocolate event that does not end with the one-day event.

Dance for Life

This event, which was launched in 1992, involves all the major dance companies in Chicago. The performance fills one of the main performance centers in the city. The finale is spectacular—all the dance companies are on stage at the same time performing together.

According to the director of public relations, the three events attract very different but equally loyal audiences. The hope is that a number of new and somewhat experimental events launched over the past few years will become mainstays as well.

One such event is the fashion show that has been presented in May for the past four years. The show was the creation of the junior board. The junior board came into existence because the members of the board of directors, who have been with the organization since it was established and been very active and dedicated, began to feel the organization needed "new blood." An invitation to join a newly established junior board appeared in a variety of publications. The date set for the first meeting brought together forty people. The group decided to hold a fashion show, and it would revolve around a piece of red fabric that all the participating designers would have to use in whatever they would design. The AFC set forth the objective of $25,000 as the fund-raising goal. That year, 2006, the event brought in $16,000 and had $3,985 in expenses. The second year, 2007, the event raised $30,000 with $3,888 in expenses. It is now known by the following title: Make a Statement: Design for a Cure.

Finally, because 2010 marks the twenty-fifth anniversary of the Chicago AIDS Foundation's founding, the CAF hosted a celebratory gala. The gala had been a regular event until a few years ago, when board members decided it required too much effort and investment for the amount of money it brought in. However, board members consider the twenty-fifth anniversary celebration to be a sufficiently important occasion to justify putting on a gala ball. More than 1,000 guests attended, raising more than $500,000 dollars.

Organizational evaluation

AFC must evaluate its performance in response to the requirements called for by granting agencies. Because it continues to apply for and receive funds for new projects from government and corporate funders, this is an important ongoing activity. However, because AFC is itself a granting agency, an advocacy organization, and an umbrella organization that brings together the efforts of many small agencies, members of the AFC board recognize that the organization's multifaceted agenda requires particularly close monitoring. Accordingly, the staff has outlined the framework and understandings that govern how it carries out the work it is doing and how it proposes to evaluate its performance. All of this is stated in an extension of the mission statement, which articulates the organizational mandate, values, and strategic plan.

Mandate: AFC endeavors to inspire and unite individuals and institutions to achieve systemic changes. Our work is therefore multipronged and designed to impact:

• Individuals affected by and concerned about HIV/AIDS
• Agencies serving people with and at risk for HIV
• Service Systems, including the HIV service delivery sector
• Decision Makers and Opinion Leaders, including press and government officials

Values: Central to our unique model and approach are the guiding principles of inclusion, diversity, accountability, transparency, accuracy, efficiency, collaboration, and high performance. In addition, we rely on community input—especially from people living with HIV/AIDS and direct service providers—to guide and inform our work. The AFC board of directors and staff pursue these core values through each of our programs, services, and general operations.

Strategic Plan: In order to develop the strategic plan that is currently in effect, the members of the staff took on the task of gathering feedback from a variety of partners. They conducted a survey of four hundred community members and sought input from members of AFC's Service Providers Council, AFC board of directors, plus various other stakeholders. The result is a Strategic Plan titled "A Force for Change," which will give direction to AFC's activities during the 2008–2010 time period. In the words of the report announcing the plan, AFC made clear that the plan has three broad objectives designed to reduce HIV transmission and improve the lives of people with and at risk for HIV through advocacy, funding, and collaboration:

• Invest in leadership and advocacy
• Develop new prevention and care models
• Devise strategies to make organizations and the sector more effective and efficient

Another early initiative was AFC's focus on the need that people with HIV/ AIDS have for assistance with housing. AFC created the first-ever AIDS housing strategic plan in 1995. It launched a three-year housing research project in 2002.

It also identified a list of activities that would have priority status during 2008. In publishing the list, AFC made clear that participants in the policy development process selected these initiatives because they consider these activities to have the highest probability of resulting in measurable and immediate results. The AFC notes that the organization continues to be committed to other long-standing activities including promoting sterile syringe access, addressing discrimination and stigma, Medicaid and Medicare, and AIDS-related appropriations. However, it intends to give special attention to assessing its efforts in attaining the eight policy priorities identified to receive special attention in 2008. The list is split into prevention and care.

The four activities listed under prevention are:

1. expand condom access and widely promote condom use, including in prisons
2. fund and support comprehensive sexuality education
3. help individuals who inject drugs prevent death from overdose
4. enact the Microbicide Development Act, which would establish a branch within the National Institute of Allergies and Infectious Diseases (NIAID) devoted to coordinating microbicide research within the NIAID, Centers for Disease Control and Prevention (CDC), and the U.S. Agency for International Development (USAID)

The four activities listed under care are:

1. increase government funding for voluntary HIV testing services
2. expand housing options for people with HIV/AIDS
3. make good on promises to enact comprehensive health-care reform
4. permit and fund expedited partner therapy to reduce sexually transmitted diseases (STDs)

WHAT WE CAN LEARN IN COMPARING THESE TWO CASES

Both the Howard Brown Health Center and the AIDS Foundation of Chicago grew from the bottom up. What is remarkable is how quickly the two organizations grew, how rapidly they developed new programs, and how well recognized and respected they have become in such a short period of time, which, in turn, is surely what has led to the impressive amount of support they receive from contributors. They are viewed as successful regional organizations, although the stakeholder community interested in reducing the number of AIDS victims is so well organized that the two organizations have national reputations.

The HBHC comes closer to a mainstream health-care delivery organization than most of the other organizations we have encountered. Being in a position to collect fee-for-service payments from both public and private insurance companies to support the direct delivery of health services provides the HBHC with a steady flow of funds. The fact that it deals with a priority problem in the public-health community means it is also able to obtain a considerable amount of its budget from grant funding, again both from public and private sources. That circumstance permits the organization to provide services to persons who might otherwise be underserved: young people who have no insurance, for example; and others who may be reluctant to turn to mainstream providers. Thus, it can look to an array of stakeholders who are willing to provide the resources the organization needs to do the work it aims to do. Beyond that, the Howard Brown Health Center has been able to attract highly dedicated workers and volunteers for whom the services the organization offers have special meaning, in some cases, because someone they are related to or know well is or has been a victim of AIDS.

One of this organization's characteristics that makes it somewhat unusual is that it was started by physicians who were in a position to observe the progression of the disease, its side effects, and it social costs firsthand before the nature of the disease was clearly identified by the wider medical establishment. Their insights were critical to determining the services the organization would emphasize. Their interest, concern, and understanding in combination with the commitment of all the other people who came to work for this organization explains much about the rate at which it grew and developed. The fact that the professionals and laypersons who work in this organization or serve on the board share similar goals is not unusual. The fact that they seem to be able to work together so well to achieve their goals is atypical.

The AIDS Foundation of Chicago came into existence at about the same time as the HBHC. Its initial purpose was to help people understand the seriousness of the disease and understand how to prevent infection. The fact that it became so successful in attaining this objective so quickly shaped its fund-raising agenda.

The AFC is also a bottom-up organization founded by a small number of activists. It too was able to turn to persons who had reason to be interested in its work to help obtain resources (i.e., persons who came to the organization as committed stakeholders from the start). This helped to provide access both to other organizations in a position to provide funds and to individuals willing to offer time and money to help the organization become established.

The way this organization appeals to potential supporters is especially interesting because it offers such a variety of venues. The AIDS walk attracts the widest range of participants, who may not participate in the organization's work in any other way except by expressing their personal and financial support through the walk. The World of Chocolate event is, of course, designed to appeal to chocolate lovers. More recently, the addition of the cookbook is meant to appeal to those who appreciate the performance of drag queens. Finally, it is designed to offer something of value to persons who may have relatively little interest in chocolate or the drag queen cookbook (i.e., corporate executives who use the event as a corporate development and training opportunity). Similarly, the World of Dance event attracts a particular segment of society, but a segment that is clearly devoted to this artistic form of expression.

That the board chose to invite younger members of the community to create a junior board in order to bring fresh ideas, and that they were able to launch a new, innovative, and successful campaign, the Make a Statement: Design for a Cure, is an important new fund-raising mechanism. The fact that the organization receives many more proposals to help raise funds than it can accept is also important. As the public relations director points out, many people who contact the organization offering to hold fund-raising events come with good intentions but don't have enough experience to pull off all the parts required by their proposals. It is hard to miss the fact that this organization operates in an exceptionally generous atmosphere of goodwill and willingness to support the goals it espouses.

Chapter Twelve

Helping to Overcome Hunger

Feeding America is the largest domestic hunger-relief charity in the United States. Before the name change in September of 2008, it was known as America's Second Harvest or A2H for short.

Feeding America staff members point out that the United States has enough food to feed everyone in the country. That is not the problem. Making sure everyone has access to the food is the basic challenge, and that is the goal that the organization has set forth for itself.

Organizing a hunger relief effort is based on fulfilling two separate functions—food banking and food rescue. According to a publication put out by A2H in 2006, *Hunger in America 2006, Executive Summary*, food banking involves soliciting, receiving, inventorying, and distributing food and grocery products pursuant to grocery industry and appropriate regulatory standards. Food rescue involves collecting prepared and/or perishable foods from sites such as restaurants, hotels, and caterers pursuant to local health department and/or appropriated regulatory standards. (Food banks that are members of the Feeding America network generally carry out both functions.)

ORGANIZATIONAL MISSION

The organization defines its mission as follows: Our mission is to feed America's hungry through a nationwide network of member food banks and engage our country in the fight to end hunger.

One of the recent annual reports makes a special effort to identify the core values that govern the quality and nature of the interactions of the staff of Feeding America and network members with all its partners, donors, and clients. The values are: collaboration, respect, integrity, service, stewardship and accountability, urgency, and diversity.

ORGANIZATIONAL HISTORY

This organization traces its origins to the first food bank created by John van Hengel in Phoenix, Arizona, in 1967. Mr. van Hengel, a native of Wisconsin, held a series of largely unrelated jobs including sales manager for a manufacturer of archery gear, plastic rainwear designer, and driver of a beer truck before he sustained a back injury while working at a rock quarry. This left him partially paralyzed. When his personal life fell apart as well, his doctor advised him to move to a warmer, drier climate. He moved to Phoenix where he began volunteering at the soup kitchen at St. Mary's Church. He credited a woman he met there with the inspiration to salvage food. She came to the soup kitchen to supplement the food that she was getting from a grocery store dumpster. Her husband was on death row, and she had ten children to feed. She explained that the food discarded by the grocery store was fine, but she regretted it could not be stored for later use. When van Hengel spoke to the store manager about collecting the food that would otherwise go into the refuse bin, the manager agreed to let him take whatever he wanted. That encouraged van Hengel to ask managers of other local stores for permission to collect food from their bins. It did not take long before he got the managers to agree to donate the food before it went into the dumpsters. He recruited volunteers to help him gather the food from grocery stores and pick up fruit left unpicked in local fields and suburban gardens. For $150 he bought an old milk truck that he used to pick up the growing volume of food. Before long he needed to find more space to store the food he was collecting. The parish council of St. Mary's Church gave him a defunct bakery that someone had willed to the church and $3,000 to set up the operation.

The "banking" idea came from one of the people helping him collect the food. She drew a cartoon of a building with food being deposited and happy people making withdrawals—like a banking operation. He named the place where he was storing food the St. Mary's Food Bank. The food bank distributed 250,000 pounds of food that first year.

During his first decade at the food bank he took no salary. He wore secondhand clothes, got his weekly groceries at the food bank, and lived in a donated room above a garage. Fellow workers dubbed him the "Mother Teresa of celery," a title of which he was very proud. In 1976 he managed to get a $50,000 federal grant to establish a national food bank. That led to the creation of Second Harvest in 1979, which van Hengel crafted to serve as the clearinghouse for large donations from national corporations. The name comes from a biblical story of Ruth who gleaned grain left by reapers. Second Harvest continued to receive federal funding to assist in creating a network of food banks until 1982.

Mr. van Hengel left Second Harvest in 1983 to help found food banks in Canada and Europe. Three years later he set up a food bank consulting firm in order to help start food banks in South America and Africa. He died at the age of 83 in 2005.

Second Harvest moved its headquarters to Chicago in 1984. In 1999, the organization changed its name to America's Second Harvest and expanded its mission, adding the ultimate goal of ending hunger in America. In 2000, America's Second Harvest merged with Foodchain, which had become the largest food-rescue organization in the country. (As stated above, food rescue occurs when food that does not leave the kitchen in restaurants but would be discarded before the next day is collected for redistribution by food banks.) In 2005, the organization changed its name again to America's Second Harvest—The Nation's Food Bank Network.

The most recent name change occurred in 2008 in response to a study indicating that public awareness of the work being carried out by Second Harvest was far below that of other human services organizations. This is when a committee of member food banks and marketing directors was constituted to consider "rebranding" in order to increase recognition of the organization's mission and help the public to better understand the issue of hunger in America. The result was the newly identified Feeding America name or "brand." A number of initiatives were launched in order to advance its effort to become better known; for one, it formed an ad council to launch public service announcements in a campaign to raise awareness of hunger. Another initiative was the creation of the entertainment council, which includes forty well-known entertainers who have committed themselves to the cause of raising awareness of hunger. A third initiative, which had been employed previously but was now to receive greater attention, was engaging in "cause marketing" with various partners; for example, General Mills, NBC's *The Biggest Loser*, and Macy's—each of which created promotions designed to increase awareness and raise monies for the hunger relief.

ORGANIZATIONAL STRUCTURE

The 2010 Feeding America annual report indicates that the organization distributed 960 million pounds of food nationally, to a network of 200 food banks and 61,000 agencies, and countless volunteers who together helped to provide food assistance to more than 37 million hungry people. The Second Harvest annual report of 2007 stated that the organization employed about thirty-five people. This small number managed to coordinate the efforts of a network of more than two hundred member food banks and food-rescue organizations serving all fifty states, the District of Columbia, and Puerto Rico. The *Hunger in America 2010* study determined that the organization serves more than 5.7 million individuals per week.

Hunger in America 2006, Executive Summary describes the programs A2H had created to date in some detail. By then it could claim to have originated seven clearly identifiable programs operating through its member food banks.

Three programs focus on child hunger:

1. The Kids Café is the nation's largest meal service and nutrition education program. More than 1,600 sites were operating in forty-three states, mostly in urban areas, feeding children between ages five and ten. A2H estimated nearly 14 million children were in food insecure households; A2H was serving 9 million of these children.
2. The BackPack program was providing children with food for the weekend when they would not be getting school lunches. Food banks were distributing about 25,000 backpacks each weekend.
3. The Fresh Food Initiative

Two programs were established to increase the network's capacity to secure and distribute fresh, perishable foods:

1. The Seafood Initiative
2. The Community Kitchen was providing culinary job training to low-income adults to prepare them for careers in the food service industry. Many of the graduates had moved on to work in high-end restaurants. A few opened their own restaurants. There were thirty-six Community Kitchen programs in the country training more than one thousand students per year.

Two more programs were initiated to address special problems:

1. The Relief Fleet program was created to reduce the cost of transporting donated food to network members. Participating transportation companies contact A2H's national office when they have empty trailer space. Donation pickup and delivery are then matched with the companies' travel routes. In 2006, the Relief Fleet moved 24 million pounds of donated food, saving A2H $1.2 million in transportation costs.
2. The Disaster Relief program was established in 1989 in response to Hurricane Hugo, which hit South Carolina and other parts of the Southeastern United States; and the Loma Prieta earthquake, which struck San Francisco. Since then the organization has played an active

role in recovery efforts in the wake of disasters. In 2005, the year that Katrina, Rita, and Wilma hurricanes hit, the Red Cross and some other organizations were credited with distributing food to disaster victims. Most of this food came from A2H, which delivered 1,904 truckloads carrying nearly 59 million pounds of food and groceries that translated into nearly 46 million meals for victims.

One of the successes reported in the 2010 annual report explains the value of introducing the Athena Technology program, which is designed to permit all network food banks to use the same computer program platform. Food banks will no longer have to purchase or maintain separate software programs to carry out basic operating functions including accounting, inventory, fundraising, transportation, logistics, e-mail, and Internet. This is expected to result in $400 million in savings. PepsiCo, Inc., and Cisco, Inc., provided the funding to launch the program.

RELATIONSHIP TO NETWORK MEMBERS

Hunger in America 2006, Executive Summary provides a detailed outline of the nature of the contract between A2H and each member of its network of donors. The contract is issued in April of each year. It runs fifty-three pages. The purpose of the contract is to define benefits and obligations on both sides. It defines the compliance standards to which members are expected to adhere and spells out administrative requirements, operating policies, and noncompliance policies.

The contract lists ten benefits of partnership:

1. comprehensive liability protection (more on this below)
2. adherence to safe food-handling best practices
3. free product pickup from any location in the United States
4. complete product tracking and recall capabilities (more on this below)
5. centralization of product donations
6. national and local community impact and outreach
7. high warehouse operation standards established in cooperation with FMI (Food Marketing Institute) and GMA (Grocery Manufacturers Association)
8. reduction of fees associated with storage, transportation, and disposal
9. receipts for tax deductions
10. assistance to more than 25 million Americans each year

Liability protection is based on the Bill Emerson Good Samaritan Food Donation Act. The legislation was passed to give protection to food and grocery donors whose product may cross state lines. The law protects good-faith food and grocery donors from civil and criminal liability should the product later cause harm to its recipient. The Emerson Act provides protection for food and grocery products that meet all quality and labeling standards imposed by federal, state, and local laws and regulations but are for some reason unsalable. (Many unsalable products are now distributed through outlet stores for a reduced price. Grocery stores and manufacturers have to weigh the benefit of donating such products or distributing through discount outlets. We will get back to this point.) This includes products that may not be "readily marketable due to age, appearance, freshness, grade, size, surplus, or other conditions." The law protects all food and grocery donors including individuals, corporations, partnerships, associations, governmental entities, wholesalers, manufacturers, retailers, farmers, gleaners, and nonprofit feeding program administrators acting in good faith. Those whose operations can be charged with gross negligence are not protected by this law.

The contract describes what it calls the "product tracking and recall" feature as follows. It states that A2H monitors Network partners' practices on a biennial basis to make sure that the standards it sets forth in its annual contract, which encompasses the legal standards for liability protection, are being observed. Organizational literature makes clear that A2H distributes donated product only to certified member food banks and food-rescue programs, which, in turn, only distribute to registered and inspected 501(c)(3) charitable agencies. It uses a computerized distribution system, which allows it to track all product movement and provide recall capabilities to ensure product integrity. The Technology Department at A2H is responsible for designing the software and providing the hardware used by member food banks to track food coming in and going out. A2H has introduced a number of innovative, industry-matching technologies including AgencyExpress, which allows agencies to shop online; DonorExpress, which is used to receive donations from food and grocery companies; and Acorn, which is an online learning system that enables network members' staff to improve their skills. The corporations that donate food appreciate the technological sophistication and welcome the added liability protection it provides.

A couple of well-publicized food recalls in 2007 make clear how important the tracking and recall feature is. The February 2007 recall of peanut butter made by the company that produces Peter Pan peanut butter is a case in point. Peanut butter is a very basic food product in food pantries. It is shelf stable, nutritious, and popular with children. The U.S. Food and Drug Administration issued a warning in response to reports of 288 cases of foodborne illness in thirty-nine states linked to salmonella contamination found in the company's peanut butter, which is sold under a number of different labels. That led to a recall by the manufacturer of all of its peanut butter from every place that could possibly be distributing it throughout the country. The computerized record of products received by A2H food banks allowed each of them to track and recall all of the jars of peanut butter that went through their warehouses.

In April of 2007, the FDA announced that certain pet foods were found to be contaminated and had sickened and killed pets all over the country. A2H sent out a recall notice on pet food. The pet food was found to contain melamine, which has no approved use in human or animal food. Most disturbing about this story were reports that some people had eaten the pet food, because it is cheaper than food made for human consumption, and some had become sick. Although not all member food banks accept pet food donations and A2H did not expect that the people it was serving to resort to eating pet food, it wanted to avoid even the slightest possibility of that happening as well as avoiding the risk of sickness among pets.

ORGANIZATIONAL FUNDING

Organizational funding revolves around the organization's relationship to donors. The 2010 annual report indicates that the organization had revenue of $719 million. Total expenses including food procurement and member services costs amounted to $83,774. Donated goods and services amounted to $667,203.

Like all nonprofit, charitable organizations, Feeding America raises money by soliciting contributions from the public. Unlike the vast majority of nonprofit, charitable organizations, it holds no special events and sells no related products to the public. What is special about this organization is that it depends so heavily on donations of "gifts in kind"—the donation of products—to fulfill its mission.

Feeding America's annual report identifies three categories of donors who provide monetary donations. Leadership Partners are those who give $10 million or more. They include the following organizations: American Idol, ConAgra Food, Food Lion, General Mills, Kellogg's, Kraft Foods, Kroger, the Lincy Foundation, Nestle, PepsiCo Foundation, Procter and Gamble, Starr Foundation, SuperValu, and Walmart. Mission Partners are those who give $2 million or more or 20 million pounds of food or some combination. This category includes the following organizations: Bank of America, Big Lots, C&S Wholesale Grocers, Cargill, Chase Bank, Clorox, Coca-Cola, Daniels Fund, Google, The Kresge Foundation, Macy's, Morgan Stanley, Nielsen, The Pampered Chef, Safeway, Target, Tyson, Unilever, US Foodservice, Walgreens, Walton Family Foundation, and Welch's. The number of corporations in these two lists has been growing over the past few years. The third category of donors includes those who give $100,000 or more. That list, which appears in the annual report, is far more extensive.

The contributions a selected number of organizations made were described in more detail in the 2009 report. For example, the value of the contribution of twenty-five mobile pantries the Kraft Food Company donated is given special attention. The mobile food pantry trucks allow regional food banks to bring food to communities that are located too far from the food bank to permit clients to travel with any regularity to obtain food that will spoil within a short period of time. The mobile food pantries are greatly extending the reach of the food banks. The Lincy Foundation contributed fifty-two refrigerated trucks and did a considerable amount of work on raising awareness of the need to support hunger relief. The Daniels Fund contributed an information-sharing online system that allows food banks to compare prices on particular products, which permits them to negotiate better prices for certain staples (e.g., peanut butter).

The challenge of dealing with "in-kind" donations

An editorial in the online journal *Editor's Plate* captures A2H's relationship with its corporate donors: "It's a win-win-win. What better way to move unsalables, get a tax benefit and help hungry people?" (Fusaro 2005). The in-kind products A2H accepts includes products that are discontinued, mislabeled, unlabeled, promotional, bulk, seasonal, over-the-counter (drugs), prepared and perishable, test-product inventory, reformulations, overruns, health and beauty products, household cleaning products, boxes, and containers.

These are unsalable products from the perspective of retail outlets. Let's go back to the "unsalable" part of the win-win-win assessment to which the editorial refers. Food producers and distributors are not only interested in ensuring that their products are safe to eat or use. They are interested in ensuring that the public perceives their products to be of high quality. That means that the product must look exactly the same from one batch to the next. For example, we all know, at some level, that food coloring is used to enhance the appeal of many products—some cereals directed at the children's market, for instance. That means the color of the product is not natural and not an indicator of quality. However, when the color is not exactly what we have come to expect, we reject the product as being of poor quality—as if the added coloring is the best indicator of quality. Food producers know this and are quick to pull such products out of production so we do not lose confidence in that product and the mistake does not spill over to affect our view of all of the other products that carry the company's label.

Evidence of how important this issue is to the industry can be seen at the national "unsalables convention" the Food Manufacturers Institute sponsors each year in Las Vegas. Company representatives go there to discuss how to deal with products that do not meet company standards and must be discarded. Companies learn how to minimize the problems associated with unsalables, namely, the cost of hauling and dumping unsalable products. One of the topics that had been receiving attention a few years ago, that is, whether allowing outlets to sell the product at a reduced price risks producing a negative image of the product in the eyes of consumers, seems to have become less salient (i.e., less of a concern) over the past couple of years.

Managing the donation of gifts in kind requires a great deal of skill and sophistication. At the symbolic level, it requires shrewdness not only to understand the extent to which producers benefit from donating unsalables, but also to use that fact to advantage. At the practical level it requires knowledge of food handling to sort and distribute the volume of the products the organization collects. Staff members at both Feeding America and food production companies understand that contributing off-color products, as long as they are truly safe to eat, means the company can avoid the expense of storing and dumping products it will not be able to sell for a profit.

Feeding America, and Second Harvest long before, has exhibited a great deal of ingenuity managing the donation of gifts in kind by employing such creative mechanisms as "line rescue" and "value added." "Line rescue" is the collection of excess product at the production stage that would otherwise have to be discarded at a cost to the producer. This approach is used in cases when a product, such as cereal, is packaged in an automated assembly line operation. There is always spillage that ends up on the assembly line conveyor belt rather than in the cereal box. Feeding America accepts the leftover product, which is gathered into bulk containers. Feeding America picks up bulk packages of the product that is "rescued" from the assembly line and delivers it to food banks, which repackage the cereal into smaller bags suitable for distribution to families. (That operation is discussed later, when we focus on the operations of the Greater Chicago Food Depository.)

Feeding America also has "value added" processing arrangements with some producers. For example, fish that are caught accidentally by fisheries that aim to catch particular kinds of fish would have to be discarded. This must be done after the fish are sorted. Discarding the unwanted fish would mean having to pay to have it hauled away. Feeding America has arranged to pay the fisheries to process and bag the unwanted fish. It pays for the bags and processing, but not for the fish. The fishery treats the fish it bags as its donation. A number of years ago, A2H led the effort to amend fishery management regulations in Alaska to allow the retention of the "by-catch fish" to prevent it from being discarded as required by prevailing regulations.

Nonfood donations

Feeding America accepts a variety of nonfood products such as tissue, toilet paper, paper towels, shampoo, and household cleaning products. The companies that donate food may also donate a range of additional items that are essential to food banking operations. As mentioned already, companies may donate refrigerated trucks, refrigerators, freezers, boxes, serving dishes, and so on. All such donations qualify for a tax deduction.

Raising the money to deal with "in-kind" donations

The department responsible for raising money to deal with processing donated products was reorganized some years ago. It was called the development department, but its name was changed to the food sourcing and philanthropy department. The reorganization was completed to ensure that staff members who call upon corporations for monetary contributions are in close contact with staff members who are involved in gathering the in-kind donations from the same corporations. One of the food sourcing and philanthropy department's primary assignments is to obtain corporate and foundation grants. Some of the grants it obtains are earmarked for special purposes; for example, for purchasing additional trucks to expand transportation capabilities. Some are dedicated to "capacity building." An example of this is the grant from Ronald McDonald House Charities to A2H to support the expansion of Kids Cafés. Member food banks were invited to compete for these funds by submitting proposals to A2H. The Ronald McDonald House monies were then regranted to the food banks that presented the best proposals.

The department added a "cause-related marketing" function to its more traditional fund-raising activities a number of years ago. A particularly successful venture with the Barilla pasta company is a case in point. Second Harvest arranged to have prominent chefs contribute their favorite pasta recipes, which the Barilla company assembled and put on its website. The idea was that anyone who was interested could download the recipes for free with the understanding that for every click on this site, Barilla would contribute one dollar to A2H. One thousand clicks were projected for the first month. The target was achieved within one week. The department has been increasing its efforts to encourage other companies who may be willing to launch similar promotions, especially around holidays.

Although the nature of the relationship between donors and Feeding America or A2H during past years should be very clear at this point, let me make it even more explicit. The interactions that transpire between donor companies and Feeding America are businesslike transactions between highly successful organizations that result in benefits for both. That is not to dismiss the generosity on the part of corporate donors; it is to recognize that donors gain significant benefits. This includes recognition for corporate generosity; savings that would otherwise go toward storage, hauling, and dumping unwanted products; and, of course, a significant tax deduction.

The tax benefit

The 1976 Tax Reform Act made donating to charities more advantageous by increasing the income tax deduction and allowing the donor to determine the "fair market value" of the donation, not to exceed two times the cost. A2H provided an illustration to companies of how this works in its *Hunger in America 2006, Executive Summary* publication, which states:
Your company may take . . .

a. The sum of one-half of the unrealized appreciation (market value minus cost = appreciation) plus the taxpayer's cost, but
b. Not in excess of twice the cost of the contributed property.

Example:

Selling Price	$4.00
Cost	$1.00

Gross Profit equals $3.00
One-half of $3.00 equals $1.50
The maximum deduction can never exceed two times the cost ($2.00) in this case.

Those with even the most basic understanding of accounting will quickly realize that although the company is charging $4, the actual cost of the product is $1, but the company receives a $2 tax deduction. In other words, the government is giving companies an extra $1 of benefit to reduce their tax burden. This is not to say that the government should not offer this tax deduction. (It offers a lot of tax deductions to individuals that one could criticize if one were so inclined. There is the tax benefit that goes to home owners, which no one is interested in altering. It allows home owners to take a tax deduction on the "depreciation" of the value of the house, because it is no longer new, over a twenty-year period, even if it skyrocketed in value during that time. Moreover, each time the house is resold the twenty-year depreciation schedule begins anew.) This is simply to note that companies that donate products get an important benefit that the government is in a position to grant when they donate goods.

The government's food contribution

Feeding America solicits and receives both food and nonfood products from the government in addition to the products it receives from the corporate sector. The organization's government relations and public policy department procures food made available by the federal government through The Emergency Food Assistance Program (TEFAP) operated by the U.S. Department of Agriculture (USDA). Feeding America reports that its effort to promote passage of a major farm bill in 2008 promises to have a major impact on food insecurity in this country. We will have more to say about this legislation in a moment.

Over the years, A2H has periodically been the beneficiary of food distributed through another USDA entity, the Bonus Commodities program. This program is set up to respond to food growers who find their product is in oversupply—for example, cranberries, as occurred a few years ago. The government bought a portion of the cranberries, which reduced the supply and kept the price of cranberries at a level that allowed the producers to make a reasonable profit. A2H was invited to advise the government on the best way to process the product for distribution to food banks. The Agriculture Department then issued a request for proposal (RFP) for processors to bid on. The food that was ultimately produced through this mechanism went to the hungry. Although the product benefited the hungry, it is worth noting the government cash subsidy went to both the growers and processors.

Feeding America's government relations and public policy department is also involved in efforts to increase public awareness and education through congressional testimony, advocacy, and speaking engagements. It proposes and drafts legislation, analyzes policies and programs, and works collaboratively with other advocacy organizations on issues of shared interest. It represents its member food banks in advocating for effective public-sector assistance to low-income people.

In order to maintain the benefits that accrue to 501(c)(3) organizations, the charitable, nonprofit organizations that are so chartered may not spend any substantial proportion of their resources on lobbying. Feeding America's government relations department does, however, issue a weekly report on bills that are coming before Congress, lists committee members to let member food banks know if a local senator or congressman from the area is serving on a particular committee, outlines how members may best affect policy and interact with their representatives. Although there is no prohibition against advocating for or against particular government policies, the organization is careful to avoid any activities that could be construed as actually lobbying for passage of legislation, especially any legislation that might be seen as benefiting the organization.

An illustration of the distinction between advocating and lobbying can be found in a controversial proposal that was scheduled to come up regarding the Food Stamp program in 2006. The administration proposed to eliminate one of the main ways people qualify for Food Stamps because, it argued, people are receiving enough financial support through other programs. In advocating for increased rather than decreased funding for the Food Stamp program, the government relations department's objective was to make sure those in a position to affect the program's future understood the Food Stamp program does more than serve the needs of poor people. It emphasized the fact that food stamps represent money that ends up in the hands of food stores and all the other companies in the food production and distribution chain. Accordingly, any reduction in the food stamp program would not only hurt the recipients but would hurt all the commercial enterprises that provide food and other products to those people. A2H received some help in this cause from congresspersons who announced publicly they would try to live on the food that food stamps will buy for a specific period of time and have the news media report on what they were eating. Their reports left no doubt that the food stamps they received meant they would be getting very little protein and virtually no fresh produce and would instead have to survive on a regimen of rice, beans, and pasta. According to A2H's 2007 annual report, the U.S. House of Representatives ended up funding the program "at $118.3—a $10 million increase over 2006—and the U.S. Senate is providing $108 million for the program."

Another achievement related to food stamps came that year when, working in cooperation with the USDA and the state of Illinois, A2H managed to author and institute a pilot program to help people apply for food stamps at a local food pantry. The staff at the pantry was given the authority to help qualify people for food stamps on a temporary basis until they could go through the formal application process or no longer needed the stamps.

Food stamps received a good deal of congressional attention again in the autumn of 2008 when Congress was told that the number of people using food stamps had risen to 31,586,934—the highest participation on record. The rise in participation was attributed in part to the latest hurricanes to hit Louisiana and Texas, Gustav and Ike, and to the decline of the economy. (The statistics come from the Food Research and Action Center, a Washington, D.C., antihunger policy organization.) It was in this environment that Congress decided to rename the Food Stamp program. It is now known as the Supplemental Nutrition Assistance Program (SNAP).

Congress went on to pass a major farm bill by the end of the same year. The bill introduces three significant changes: 1) the government has increased its support of TEFAP (The Emergency Food Assistance Program) by 73 percent; 2) the minimum benefit provided through SNAP (i.e., food stamps) was increased for the first time in thirty years; and, 3) Feeding

America benefited directly as the recipient of a $15-million grant to improve its transportation capacity. All of this came at a critical time, given that the Department of Agriculture announced that as of November 2008, one of every six Americans was food insecure. This is the highest proportion reported to be confronting the problem since the Agriculture Department began tracking food insecurity in 1995.

A gift from the Bank of America Charitable Foundation and other donors helped Feeding America to distribute $2 million in grants to implement a SNAP outreach program. This allows food banks to assist applicants in applying to the SNAP program. Feeding America provided help to 130,000 clients to receive what translates into $200 million in benefits or nearly 78 million meals in 2010.

Revenue

In addition to cash contributions by donors, Feeding America receives cash payments from network fees collected by network members. The agencies that request food pay food banks for both the food and the services involved in food "banking." The work of collecting and distributing the huge volume of gifts-in-kind donations cannot be entirely supported through public contributions. The fees help to defray some, but not all, of the costs associated with transporting, receiving, storing, and distributing dry, refrigerated, and frozen foods. Fees are structured on a per-pound basis with an average of 14 cents per pound with an 18-cent cap. Some food banks are consistently well funded and able to charge a much smaller fee. In some cases the maintenance fee allows the food banks to deliver food and grocery items directly to member charities. In all cases, the food bank saves individual charities the high costs of transportation, storage, and personnel required to access and receive large volumes of food. The Salvation Army, for example, has traditionally relied on Feeding America food banks in most cities for the food that it distributes, paying a fee based on the volume of food it uses.

The revenue that Feeding America receives goes into a fund that is then available for redistribution. To illustrate, the organization awarded $26 million in grants to its members to hire staff to help increase their sourcing abilities. This, together with helping to support technological improvements such as linked data banks, is expected to increase the amount of food available for distribution.

ORGANIZATIONAL EVALUATION

Evaluating how well any organization is doing in fulfilling its mission is challenging, but it is even more challenging in this case. One obvious measure of performance has to do with financial efficiency. In order to judge its impact on the problem of food insecurity, the organization has been interested in establishing the baseline of need. In 2005 the A2H Board commissioned a study designed to determine the level of hunger in America. Similar studies were carried out in 1997 and 2001. The specific purpose of the 2005 study was to provide a comprehensive profile of the incidence and nature of hunger in the United States; extensive demographic profiles of emergency food clients; and information about domestic hunger and the charitable response. In other words, A2H's objective was to determine how it could best address the problem of hunger and to assess the impact it was having on reducing hunger in America.

This was the most comprehensive study of hunger in the United States conducted to date. A2H described it this way:

> *Hunger in America 2006* chronicles the nature and incidence of demand for emergency food assistance which, in turn, helps charitable feeding organizations better address the burgeoning need through program development and refinement. The results also better inform the public policy discourse so that federal nutrition programs can better serve those in need.

A2H established a technical advisory group to collect data that resulted in a comprehensive report on the extent of hunger in America. It contracted with Mathematica Policy Research, Inc., a leading policy research firm based in Princeton, New Jersey, to gather two kinds of data. It worked with 156 network member participants who agreed to collect data in their communities. Client data were gathered through face-to-face interviews with 52,000 people at feeding sites across the country. There were 156 local reports; 30 state reports; and 22 county level reports. The cost of carrying out the project was about $1.8 million. The full title of the resulting report is *The Almanac of Hunger and Poverty in America, 2006*. Altria, the parent company of Kraft Foods, and the Tyson Company were major supporters of the study.

A2H made clear that the results were "discomforting." A brief review of the findings makes clear that this is an understatement. As the *Almanac* reports, A2H food banks provided emergency hunger relief to 25.3 million low-income people, or 9 percent of all Americans, in 2005, which is an increase of 8 percent since 2001 and a 18-percent increase since 1997. Of all households served, 66 percent had incomes below the poverty level and 10 percent had no income at all. The average household income among all client households that year was $11,210.

What may be particularly surprising to those who have never needed assistance getting enough to eat were the following statistics on the employment status of those who were seeking help at that time: about 15 percent were working full time and 13 percent working part time. Of those who were unemployed, 8 percent had lost their jobs within the past three months and fewer than 12 percent had been without a job for one or two years. Only 4 percent reported that a traditional "welfare" program (TANF and General Assistance) was their primary source of income.

The most familiar federal nutrition programs are SNAP, WIC (Special Supplemental Nutrition Program for Women, Infants, and Children), and National School Meals Programs. Of households with children, ages birth to three years, that use Feeding America emergency food, 51 percent were also participating in the WIC program, 62 percent were participating in the school program, 51 percent participating in school breakfast programs, and 13 percent participating in the Summer Food program.

Only 35 percent of the people A2H was assisting at that time were participating in the Food Stamp program; only 56 percent of those who were eligible were participating because they did not realize they were eligible. (Eligibility is generally met if the household income is below 130 percent of poverty.) For eight out of ten of those who receive food stamps, the food obtained through the program lasts for three weeks or less rather than the four weeks for which they are allotted.

The *Hunger in America 2006* report concluded that 70 percent of all the households A2H serves were "food insecure" based on a standard established by the government. The U.S. Census Bureau and USDA Economic Research Service define food insecurity as "not always having access to enough food to meet basic needs." Some still charge that the "lure of free food" is bringing people who are not really in need. A2H took the position that few people would resort to standing in long lines and eating in soup kitchens if they did not have to do so.

Because of the downturn in the economy that occurred started in early 2008, the number of people who are "food insecure" has been rising. An update of the 2006 report carried out by the Greater Chicago Food Depository, Hunger in America 2010, indicates a 46-percent increase between 2006 and 2008 in the number of Americans who are food insecure.

Returning to the basic question we are addressing in this portion of our discussion—how Feeding America assesses its performance—we can see that the organization has done so by commissioning a very thorough analysis in 2005 of the need for the services it provides. It used the results of this analysis, first, to track the extent to which the need for food assistance was increasing; and, second, to identify the geographic areas and population characteristics of those in need in order to determine where the need for the food programs it was offering was increasing the most.

Since then, the organization has found that the need for food has been increasing across the nation and across all the programs it operates. The 2007 annual report stated that the organization recognized that the "ending hunger in America" mission holds out a clearly idealized and unattainable goal.

Accordingly, in developing the 2007 strategic plan, the board of directors identified two specific objectives, which made the steps to be used to attain the organizational mission far more concrete:

1. increase the number of people being served from 25 million to 30 million by 2012, that is, by 1 million per year over the next five years
2. advocate for federal nutrition programs, especially the Food Stamp program

Two years later, Feeding America reported it had achieved the second of the two goals and was doing everything it could to achieve the first. It has been striving to increase the number of persons served by focusing on the rising rate of hunger in this country. The hope is that this will increase the resources the organization requires to attain that objective. Increasing resources in the face of a major economic recession is not making this task any easier.

THE GREATER CHICAGO FOOD DEPOSITORY

In order to appreciate better the scope of the work that the hunger-relief mission requires, let us take a brief look at one of Feeding America's network partners—the Greater Chicago Food Depository (GCFD). GCFD was established in 1978. Twenty-six years later, it moved into a 268,073-square-foot state-of-the-art facility built to its specifications. That came about because it attained its $30 million fund-raising campaign objective in 2005. The facility has the capacity to store 10.3 million pounds of food. According to its 2009 annual report, it provided food to 678,000 people through the six hundred qualified, nonprofit member agencies (i.e., food pantries and soup kitchens) affiliated with it. This is not a typical food bank. Of course, none is typical. What makes it unique is the fact that GCFD is located in Chicago, which offers some unique food-sourcing opportunities.

Among the many factors that make GCFD special are the two major food conventions that come to town every May. When the conventions end, the exhibitors donate everything they bring to display to the GCFD. According to the director of food resources, the 2008 Restaurant Show produced eighteen 18-wheeler truckloads of food. Then there is the Taste of Chicago, which produces a bounty of food from stands set up to provide samples of their offerings for a week or so in early July. The food bank picks up all the leftover food, sorts it, and distributes it within a couple of days.

Because the GCFD is located in such a big city with many food-producing operations and a generous independent funding base, it is in a position to distribute bread and fresh produce without charging anything and charges only 7 cents a pound for everything else. It also operates a number of special programs that other food banks may not have. For example, it designed a training program, Pantry University, on food safety, nutrition, budgeting, and fund-raising for staff and volunteers of food pantries and soup kitchens. It is one of the first food banks to use Producemobiles, which it describes as "farmers' markets on wheels." The mobile food pantries, contributed by Kraft, allow it to bring food to twenty new locations. The Charter One Foundation contributed a new food rescue truck, which is a great help in collecting food that would otherwise go to waste.

GCFD has created a number of special partnerships with organizations in Chicago that are not available to food banks located in other regions. For example, it partners with the University of Chicago, which periodically carries out the Gap Track Survey. The survey tracks change to identify neighborhoods that would benefit from greater food availability and neighborhoods that no longer require food assistance. Anyone familiar with Chicago is well aware of the change in the Cabrini Green neighborhood. This was the site of a large number of high-rise public housing buildings that were demolished over the past decade to make room for expensive town houses. The community was completely transformed and clearly no longer needs a pantry.

The Greater Chicago Food Depository was able to support a study of food insecurity in the area, which it published as an update of the *Hunger in America 2006* study. It is titled *Hunger in America 2010 Executive Summary: A Report on Emergency Food Distribution in Cook County.* The document indicates that, as of October 2009, 37 million Americans were receiving food stamps, 17 million of whom were children; and 11.1 percent of all households were food insecure. This report contains a great deal of information. For example, food stamps provided under the SNAP program are currently lasting for 2.7 weeks out of the month; 34 percent of all food insecure households have at least one employed adult; and 29 percent of all food banks turned away people that year because they did not have sufficient food to distribute.

Visiting the GCFD facility and seeing the work that goes on there is startling. Imagine a clear plastic baggy, tied at the top, filled with cornflakes. Now imagine that the circumference of the baggy is about the size of a barn silo and that it is about twelve feet high. A group of volunteers, teenagers in this case, are standing at a trough into which someone has poured some of the cereal from the huge baggy. They are scooping up the cereal with great big scoops and putting it into two-pound plastic bags. They seem to be having a great time doing it.

In another room, other volunteers are packing cans into boxes. The director of food resources explains that the cans are called "brights" because they have no labels. Suddenly, he notices that the volunteers are putting labels on the boxes, not the cans. He says he will have to straighten that out. Each can needs a label if the cans will go into boxes of food meant for a family rather than the whole box going to a place where the whole box of cans will be used to prepare a meal for many people at once. You have to know what is in each "bright" can.

The facility is huge, so it does not look like many people are working, but quite a few people are around. According to the director of food resources, "everything has to be touched by a human being," which explains why the organizational literature states that the organization is committed to volunteerism. One of its brochures states: "Last year, more than 8,000 volunteers contributed over 80,000 hours of personal time. . . ." This is the equivalent of thirty-nine full-time employees.

WHAT WE CAN LEARN FROM THESE CASES

Feeding America illustrates an extraordinary organizational growth trajectory that began in a side room of St. Mary's Church more than forty years ago and evolved into the single most important hunger relief organization in the country. It moved from being a voluntary activity on the part of a few people to its current status as the largest organization of its kind in the nation. This is certainly a story of the transition from a bottom-up organization to what is unquestionably a highly successful entity that now clearly operates from the top down. In the process, it significantly altered the interactional field in which it operates.

What makes Feeding America so different from other charitable organizations is that it has virtually no interaction with the people who get the food that it gathers—the ultimate beneficiaries. They constitute the most important set of stakeholders, but stakeholders who are far divorced from the source of support that Feeding America depends on and therefore have virtually no voice in how the organization operates. Feeding America interacts almost exclusively with the executive staff at member food banks; with donors, largely corporate donors, both those who donate gifts in kind and those who provide funds to support particular programs; and with high-level government bureaucrats. In other words, the interactional field in which Feeding America operates is unlike that of most charities. Rather, it is more comparable to the interactional field in which large, successful for-profit organizations operate.

This has a dramatic effect on how the Feeding America staff members see themselves. They see themselves as participants in an effective and mutually rewarding relationship where everyone they interact with benefits from the transaction. They are definitely not coming to the donors hat in hand asking for charity. Instead, they are there to help corporations deal with their production problems, and help them to present themselves as worthy public citizens and generous corporate actors who deserve the tax benefits they receive. The organizational representatives they interact with reciprocate in kind—by all appearances their interactions with Feeding America indicate they see it as a highly effective and efficient operation with which they are pleased to be associated.

Part of the explanation for why staff members can assume this stance is that many come to Feeding America with years of experience in for-profit food companies. They are simply not intimidated by corporate jargon and managerial buzzwords. They are also not intimated by arguments presented by corporate spokesmen, who typically dismiss the performance of nonprofits as inefficient. Such an attitude is not likely to be displayed by any of Feeding America's partners.

Beyond its relationship with corporate entities, Feeding America not only has its activities monitored and regulated by government agencies but has a very strong working relationship with government agencies (e.g., the USDA). Its record of performance confirms its presentation of itself as a trustworthy and competent entity that any other organizational entity would be pleased to interact with.

The organization has a strong community of interest in its network of member food banks and a variety of other entities that are devoted to helping persons whose basic needs are not being fulfilled, starting with food. Given that the organization monitors hunger-related trends at the national level, its community of orientation is also nationwide in scope. We can see that Feeding America has an array of stakeholders from both the private sector and public sector who donate goods and funds, plus network members, and finally the public at large. All are influential stakeholders, but no one set of stakeholders is more influential than any other.

The Greater Chicago Food Depository has a somewhat different history but a similarly positive sense of its own performance at the regional level. Staff members make a point of saying that this organization started as a bottom-up operation during a period of social activism. People across the country had begun to think about the health and welfare of persons who were less well off during the decade of the 1960s. Moreover, Americans were suddenly becoming aware of diminishing natural resources. Admittedly not everyone is convinced of that assessment even now, decades later. However, it is clear that many people did start recycling cans, bottles, and newspapers during the 1960s and 1970s. The thought that conserving food might not be a bad idea also began to take hold at the same time. Local efforts to create and support food pantries and soup kitchens that began appearing across the country really evolved during this era. GCFD came into being in the wake of this period of social awakening.

What makes the GCFD special is that it operates in a particular geographic community that is characterized by a highly unequal, both economically and socially, community of interest. It interacts directly with both the moneyed donors and the needy beneficiaries in its geographic community. Its presentation of self is that of a highly efficient organization fully comfortable in dealing both with the corporate sector representatives and representatives of agencies that serve underprivileged people who have little power to affect how GCFD operates. It interacts with members of local regulatory agencies and local media. One of the important challenges it has taken on is helping the representatives of the agencies that serve the poor do the best job they can in operating food pantries. For that reason, GCFD has devoted some of its resources to designing and presenting training courses to help administrators of local pantries and other food distribution operations learn what they need to know to do a better job. Staff members at the Food Bank make clear they are sensitive to the plight of those who come to its door. They make sure they treat with respect the people who are struggling with the circumstances they find themselves in that require them to depend on a food bank.

Chapter Thirteen

Addressing the Need for Affordable Housing

This chapter presents the stories of three organizations that focus on the need for affordable housing. Two are faith-based, Bethel New Life and Catholic Charities; the third, LUCHA, is not. We will discuss the case of Bethel New Life in detail. The second two cases serve to provide points of comparison.

BETHEL NEW LIFE

Bethel New Life is a faith-based organization that focuses on "sustainable development" of the West Garfield community in Chicago where it is located. It describes itself as an organization that is committed to developing "initiatives that deal with the causes of problems in ways that build on the strengths of the people and the community."

Organizational mission

The organization states that its mission is to: Realize God's vision of a restored society by empowering individuals, strengthening families, and building neighborhoods through community-driven, solution-oriented, and value-centered approaches.

The organizational literature goes on to articulate the organization's vision using a biblical quote:

> If you put an end to oppression, to every gesture of contempt, and to every evil word; if you give food to the hungry and satisfy those who are in need, then darkness around you will turn to the brightness of noon. And I will always guide and satisfy you with good things. I will keep you strong and well. You

will be like a garden that has plenty of water, like a spring of water that never goes dry. Your people will rebuild what has long been in ruins, building again on the old foundations. You will be known as the people who rebuilt the wall, who restored the ruined houses. (Isaiah 58:9–12)

Organization history

Bethel New Life (BNL) came into existence when the small congregation at Bethel Lutheran Church determined it needed to do something about the declining housing stock in the community. One Sunday in 1979, the members of the congregation decided to establish a housing ministry. They voted to start a $5,000 fund-raising campaign with $5-contributions from all church members toward that goal. They incorporated the venture as Bethel Housing, Inc. The first step in making this venture a reality was buying an abandoned 1903 three flat located across from a junkyard. The house was being auctioned off by the U.S. Department of Housing and Urban Development (HUD), which set the minimum bid at $250. The Bethel Lutheran Church group's bid of $275 got them the title to the house. They knew the house needed a tremendous amount of work, which would require a lot more money. Where the money came from is recorded in a nostalgic account presented in the ten-year celebratory publication documenting the organization's early years. It seems that church members "borrowed on their credit cards, asked architect friends to draw up plans, and gave over evenings and weekends to skin their knuckles as rookie rehabbers." They gained encouragement from the two hundred or so curious people who came by to ask if they could rent the new apartments.

By the end of the year, the organization was proud to announce that it had a budget of $9,600 and two employees. The cofounders, Mary Nelson and Kate Lane, are credited with the organization's initial growth and development. Mary Nelson, the sister of the pastor of Bethel Lutheran Church, became president of the organization. Kate Lane, a church member and local resident, became director of housing services. It did not take long for the leadership to realize that the organization would have to do more than provide places for people to live. The people they were trying to help had to have the money to buy the houses, pay the mortgage, maintain the houses, pay real estate taxes, and so on. In recognition of that fact, the organization changed its name to Bethel New Life, Inc., in 1982 and expanded its vision of what the organization's mission would encompass. It catalogs an impressive list of accomplishments for an organization that started with lofty ambitions but a very small budget.

Senior housing was an early priority. The organization took on the construction of a forty-unit senior housing building, Anathoth Gardens, in 1982. It also managed to acquire ten town-house units at the same time. It helped to establish Habitat for Humanity in Chicago that year, which led to a visit by Jimmy and Rosalynn Carter two years later. That visit brought national attention to BNL at a very opportune time. It had just purchased the nine-story, 159-unit Guyon Hotel building for $25,000. Although the first estimate of $2.5 million to rehabilitate the building was challenging enough, finding the money to finance the project was far more difficult than anticipated because the building had stores on the ground floor. Chicago banks were not prepared to finance the rehabilitation of a mixed-use building in this neighborhood. The fact that Jimmy and Rosalynn Carter were willing to stay in the building for a short time attracted enough attention to produce the funds needed to proceed with the project, which was completed three and a half years later.

In 1989, BNL purchased St. Anne's Hospital, which reported having 427 beds at the time. The property stands on a 9.2-acre site. The facility is now known as the Beth-Anne Foundation Campus and is home to Beth-Anne Residences, a six-story building that provides 125 units of HUD-subsidized senior housing, adult day services, and Bethel's administrative offices. The campus also houses Beth-Anne Place, which consists of eighty-five units of senior supportive housing subsidized by HUD and the Illinois Supportive Living program. In addition, the campus houses the following programs: Molade Child Development Center, which has the capacity to serve eighty children; a Head Start program operates there; the Small Business Center, which also houses a large meeting, banquet, and performance space; a cultural and performing arts center; a professional office building, which was sold to a community group; The Villa, which is a two-story building housing outpatient mental health services provided by Loretto Hospital; and The Kasper Building, which is operated in conjunction with other community groups.

In 2005 BNL completed construction of the Bethel Center building. The building is located at the corner of Lake and Pulaski Streets. The location is significant for a number of reasons, but two are especially noteworthy. First, the elevated/subway station at this site was scheduled to be closed down. BNL organized protests because closure would have deprived the residents of the neighborhood of public transportation, which would have caused serious hardship. The organization not only succeeded in having the decision reversed, it managed to secure commitment from the city to invest $350 million to rehabilitate the station and bring commercial development into the community.

The second point of significance of the site is that the Bethel Center is a "green" building. The site was a "brownfield," which BNL cleaned up. The special features that make it a green building are as follows: a green roof; super-insulated walls, photovoltaic cells, and other specialized electrical features; at least 25 percent of building materials contain recycled content; 20 percent of the materials were shipped from within five hundred miles of

Chicago; 50 percent of the wood originated from forests grown and harvested using environmentally sensitive methods; all paint, carpet, adhesives, and wood were selected to ensure that they do not emit potentially toxic fumes; all rooms have an outside view, which is achieved through having skylights, light wells, and interior windows. All of this combines to produce the potential of 50 percent energy cost savings compared with the average commercial building. Clearly the organization has developed building expertise. Let us now turn to some of the other programs the organization has launched.

Going back to 1979, when Bethel Housing, Inc., was first established, it did not take long for the founders to recognize they would have to establish nonhousing-oriented services alongside the housing ministry. According to Mary Nelson, "We came to realize that just providing affordable housing wasn't enough—that you couldn't pay your rent if you didn't have a job, and that you couldn't hold a job if you were sick or had a sick mother or father at home." Another way of putting it, according to the BNL's own ten-year retrospective is—"attacking just a single problem is like fixing a flat on a car with no engine." BNL says of itself that it takes a more comprehensive approach. It further characterizes itself as follows: as rooted in faith and faith-based; as community-directed; as "asset-based" (building on the strengths and capacities of the people and the place); as seeking justice for all; and working in partnership with churches, corporations, government, and other groups to create a healthier, sustainable community.

Some of the organization's early initiatives, which served the organization so well during its initial developmental stage, were discontinued as the organization determined other programs would be more effective in helping the organization fulfill its mission. One such program was a food co-op, which served seventy-five families at its peak. It required a great deal of organizing effort and did not attract enough local residents to make it a successful enterprise; it was suspended. It is worth noting that a Greater Chicago Food Depository produce-mobile has been coming to the community regularly once a month since 2007.

The second project, Stitches Unlimited, provided sewing jobs for twelve individuals for a while but could not produce enough contracts to continue. It too was suspended. In deciding to drop these programs, the organization found that it learned a valuable lesson: "Don't be afraid to cut programs that don't work." By contrast, the senior programs the organization established continued to grow. BNL not only built the senior housing units, which provided jobs for local residents, but also it obtained a state contract to reimburse housekeeping services for the seniors, which provided more jobs. By 1985, Bethel was serving 500 neighborhood seniors and employing 230 service providers working both part- and full-time. In 1989, BNL created a model comprehensive care system for frail elderly, PACE, allowing them to stay in their homes. The program started with a budget of $5 million and provided employment for another two hundred people. BNL went on to establish a day-care center for seniors at the site, which created even more jobs.

Other early programs included a recycling center, which provided employment for twenty people. The center was paying out $1,500 a day in 1984 allowing residents "to turn trash into cash." It created a health clinic for seniors in the Anathoth Gardens facility. It is proud of its efforts to pioneer a community-based approach to reducing infant mortality through the Families with a Future program focusing on health education, coordination with thirty local health agencies, and celebration of babies through community baby showers. It established an anticrime and drug problem initiative, created a cultural arts program, developed a range of training programs, and on and on.

Its focus on education led to creation of the Freedom School for children and the Al Raby School for Community and Environment for adult training in community development. (Al Raby was a well-known 1960s civil rights activist in Chicago.)

None of this would have happened without the energy and commitment provided by Bethel Lutheran Church, which has been an anchor for residents in the community since 1890. Pastor Nelson says church activities provided the framework for weaving together a "fabric of trust" in the community. According to the director of external relations, relying on scriptures as a handbook or tool allows BNL to be the vehicle for community change for which the church provides fuel and serves as the direction setter.

The story behind the origins of the Bethel Christian School serves as a powerful illustration. When parents in the community came to the pastor to propose building the school, the pastor arranged a $200,000 loan from the Lutheran Church of America. When more money was needed, he frantically called around until he found another pastor who was willing to mortgage his house to loan Bethel the $13,000 needed to finish the job.

Bethel New Life is pleased to report that, as of 2011, it can take credit for creating one thousand new housing units, finding employment for seven thousand residents, and initiating an array of asset-building strategies. It says of itself that it "strives to turn problems into possibilities through community efforts that arise out of commitment to self help and self determination with community-based, value-centered, solution-oriented initiatives."

Organizational structure

Clearly BNL evolved into an organization that goes far beyond its original "housing mission"; it became a community-development corporation. It ultimately instituted four sets of programs:

1. At its core is the Housing and Economic Development initiative, which has evolved into three separate services: a) a financial services and products program that offers community residents practical help toward better financial management; b) office and retail leasing space for privately owned businesses in the community; and c) real estate development to assist residents to rent or buy a house.

2. Community of Elders Services. BNL now operates a) adult day services with emphasis on helping elders overcome physical and mental limitations, including Alzheimer's disease and dementia; b) the Elder Independent Housing unit in three residential buildings, which offers 24-hour on-site services; c) In-Home Care unit that allows elders to remain in familiar surroundings and avoid premature institutionalization; and d) the Supportive Living for Elders at the Beth-Anne Campus facility.

3. Family and Individual Support is the sector that has expanded most. It encompasses six programs: a) the Chicago Family Case Management unit, which provides assistance and medical care for women and infants; b) the Child Development Centers, which provide a comprehensive learning environment for young children; life skills, awareness, and esteem training; plus speech therapy and occupational therapy; c) the Emergency Fund to assist families and individuals during temporary financial crises; d) the Employment Services unit, which provides job search, training, and placement services; plus training in computer skills and career counseling; e) the RightStart Families unit, which targets pregnant women to make sure they receive appropriate care before and after pregnancy; assessment of the child at three months and twice yearly after that; and f) the Supportive Housing unit, which provides temporary, short-term housing (four months) for residency displaced persons plus training to obtain permanent housing.

4. Community Development, which is the critical dimension in everything the organization does in order to build a healthier, sustainable community. It is grounded in three programs: a) the Community-Building unit, which aims to gather community opinion about change; b) the Educational Advocacy unit, which is designed to support educational initiatives that bring together parents, students, teachers, and the community in order to develop quality schools of choice; and c) the Technology Access & Training unit to help bridge the digital divide by providing access to computer technologies.

A relatively new venture, the Community Savings Center (CSC), was established at the Bethel Center, which is the commercial facility built at the subway/elevated stop. The CSC is a collaboration among Bethel New Life, Inc., Park National Bank, and Trivent Financial for Lutherans. It aims to help people advance economically through sustainable asset building by bringing together financial education, accessible and affordable banking products, and a network of other local resources that support financial well-being.

The 2005 annual report, the last one that is publicly available, indicates the organization employs 352 people; relies on 525 volunteers, who put in 8,769 hours that year. It has 7,609 participants. The founding president, Mary Nelson, stepped down in 2005 after twenty-six years of service. The person who was chief operating officer of Bethel during the preceding four years became president. When he left to head a larger nonprofit organization in 2011, a national search led to the appointment of the third director in the organization's history.

Organizational funding

BNL's 2005 annual report indicates it was operating with a budget of $14.7 million. A little over half of that (53 percent) was funded by various government agencies through grants, contracts, and fee-for-service reimbursements; rental properties brought in 20 percent; 11 percent came from foundation and corporation grants; 2 percent came from contributions by individuals and churches; the remaining 14 percent came from a variety of other sources such as amortization, investment income, other fees and sales, and so on.

That is certainly a record of significant growth over three decades when it reported having a budget of $9,600, all from personal contributions and loans, in 1979. Five years later it was operating with a budget of $1.2 million and relying on funds from the government and foundations for 70 percent of its operating expenses. After ten years, in 1989, it had a budget of $4.5 million, tripling to $14.7 by 2005. The director of external relations at BNL attributes its ability to obtain funding for the projects it initiated during its early years of development to the fact that it came on the scene on the heels of the civil rights movement. She says there was a great deal more government money available to pursue community-development projects during the 1970s and early 1980s than there is now.

The money the government allocates for safety net services is not easily obtained. To illustrate this assessment, the director of external relations explained that it took five years to work out the funding arrangements to support the Beth-Anne Supportive Living facility. Money was available from HUD to rehabilitate the building for that purpose. However, the regulations governing HUD funds were not consistent with the regulations governing the Illinois Department of Public Aid funding, which was needed in order to cover some of the costs of providing services to the residents who would be living in the facility. The residents are able to function on their own, so this is not a nursing home. In order to pay their way, the residents must turn over their Social Security income to the facility. To be poor enough to qualify, they can have no savings and, of course, turning over their Social Security checks would leave them with no income. The facility provides them with food, housing, and medical care. However, if they wish to buy anything else—new shoes, for example—they are left with no funds to do so. BNL worked out an arrangement with the Illinois Department of Public Aid that would permit the residents to keep $100 per month to spend as they wish. Because the apartments have full kitchens, the residents may choose to have friends over and buy some treats for that occasion or they may spend the money on other necessities such as new shoes or a coat. When BNL does not succeed in working out such arrangements, it must seek extra funding from corporations and foundations to supplement the funds it receives through government contracts and fee-for-service reimbursements.

The extra money that its rental properties bring, which amounts to 20 percent of its budget, goes into facility maintenance, human resources expenses, and other administrative costs. It is spending about 4 percent of its budget for fund-raising, which is a much lower rate than most nonprofit organizations spend. It hosts one fund-raising event per year, the Gumbo Gala, which was held at Union Station for the first time in 2006. The fund-raiser was described as a great success even though it did not bring in as much as the organization had hoped.

Organizational evaluation

BNL recognizes that its initial aim—to improve the housing stock and the welfare of the community—led to programs aimed at addressing a much wider set of needs designed to help individuals in the community to help themselves. Its goals are so closely intertwined that evaluation of organizational performance rests on evaluating the impact the organization has had on the lives of individuals. Looking at its performance from that perspective makes it is easier to identify indicators. Bethel New Life says it considers the following to be the elements of a sustainable community: economic security, ecological integrity, high quality of life for all, and public participation in decision making. In a report of community change based on 1990 and 2000 census data, BLN presents the following profile of the changes that have taken place in the West Garfield Park community:

- Population Change: the community experienced a gain of 4.5 percent since 1985; since 1997, it gained 14 percent while Chicago as a whole gained only 6.45 percent
- Economic Security: 35.9 percent of the residents live in poverty (11.3 percent nationally); Bethel brought $120 million of new investment into the community and brought 500 new jobs to the community; it places 350 per year in full employment per year

- Ecological Integrity: development of the green Bethel Center building plus cleanup of the brownfield site on which it was built; it created three local parks; worked with Argonne National Laboratory to develop energy-efficient, sustainable initiatives; this helped to reduce the rate of elevated lead (in blood) found through screenings by half since 1994–1996
- Quality of Life (Safety): decline in the crime rate shifted the community from the rank of second to eleventh (out of twenty-five city police districts) since 1985
- Quality of Life (Education): all six elementary schools improved, according to No Child Left Behind federal standards; high school graduation rates in all three local high schools increased
- Quality of Life (Health): the WIC (Women, Infants, and Children) Program at five sites served almost two hundred families per month, reducing anemia in participating infants from 23 percent to 18 percent; the infant mortality rate dropped
- Quality of Life (Housing): dollar investment increased by 771.4 percent; more than $100 million of new housing developed; more than one thousand units of affordable housing developed; housing loans grew from 111 in 1990 to 433 in 2001; loans grew to $43.8 million, a 942.9 percent increase

The 2009 profile of the community, Key Indicators Report, June 2009, presents the most recent profile of the community BNL serves. It reports that more than 90 percent of the residents are African American, compared to the Chicago average of 36 percent. Only 34 percent of the forty-one elementary schools in the community met the state's definition of a "performing" school defined as 62.5 percent of students meeting or exceeding the minimum standardized test score. Of those who are over twenty-five years of age, 66.7 percent have a high school diploma compared to 87.2 percent in the rest of Chicago.

Median household income in 2007 was $30,490 compared to Chicago's median of $45,505. BNL's response is to provide extensive career development and financial counseling services. Its Smart Savers Program is, however, a very special feature. The aim of this program is to help participants save $2,000. Those who manage to do that are rewarded with a $4,000 match, which BNL encourages participants to apply toward a college education, starting a business, or down payment on a house.

BNL's position is that "the organization does not set up people to fail," which may be the best summary of the agency's impact on individuals. BNL reports only one foreclosure on a house that BNL made available to someone in the community before 2008 when foreclosures became common across the country. That is significant given that the organization proudly reports it has created more than one thousand units of affordable housing since it began its work.

Recognizing that BNL's organizational goals are so broad that evaluation of organizational performance is difficult to track or capture, board members and staff spent one Saturday a month from December 2005 through February 2006 developing a strategic plan that would articulate specific objectives the organization could strive to achieve. They determined that "Community of Choice" would be the concept guiding their efforts to give every resident the quality of life options that residents of every community would like to enjoy. They identified three priorities.

1. Quality Affordable Housing Options for All. They realized they wanted a mixed income community, in order to not leave people behind whose options are more limited. They determined that developing housing at lower than market cost is essential.
2. Education and Youth Development. Recognizing that every high school and elementary school in the area is underperforming, they determined to focus on educational improvement.
3. Wealth Creation. They resolved that increasing savings, investments, and home ownership rates is essential to developing indigenous stakeholders interested in the future of the community. They reaffirmed their commitment to emphasis on improving education and expanding affordable housing options as the avenues to rising collective wealth.

The board members and staff made the following pledge. They identified the values to which they were committed, to which they intended to hold themselves accountable, and for which they would be willing to risk everything. These are: Faith, Integrity, Family and Community, and Justice.

The strategic plan document puts it this way: "We also spoke about the organization's desired behaviors, which if everyone focused on would fundamentally change the way we do business as an organization:

• Being honest and open in our communications
• Doing things right the first time
• Being inclusive with staff, Board, volunteers, and other stakeholders
• Leading by example internally and externally
• Being fanatical about Bethel New Life, Inc. and the work we do"

Clearly the strategic plan has set forth an exceptionally demanding set of standards. At the same time, staff members say what they would most like to see happen is that there would be no need for the organization to exist.

However, no one thinks that is likely to happen any time in the near future. So the organization will simply have to continue stretching to reach the high bar it has set for itself.

CATHOLIC CHARITIES

Let us now turn to the second of the three organizations we are examining in this chapter—Catholic Charities of Chicago, which was established in 1917 by the Archdiocese of Chicago.

Organizational mission

Catholic Charities fulfills the church's role in the mission of charity to anyone in need by providing compassionate, competent, and professional services that strengthen and support individuals, families, and communities based on the value and dignity of human life.

Organizational programs and structure

Catholic Charities operates 159 programs from 156 locations. It relies on twenty-five hundred employees and eleven thousand volunteers to carry out its mission. It lists the following service categories: adoption, child development, counseling, domestic violence, emergency assistance, health care, homelessness, HIV/AIDS awareness, immigration/naturalization, legal, maternal/pregnancy, nutrition, refugee resettlement, senior services, substance abuse, and veterans' services.

Emergency aid is the newest program the agency developed. It came into existence when families displaced by the Katrina hurricane in 2005 began arriving in Chicago. Catholic Charities offered assistance to more than three hundred persons who found housing with relatives in the area but whose relatives did not have the funds to feed and clothe them. The agency provided housing for nineteen other families and case management services for more than 120 additional families.

Catholic Charities operates eleven Emergency Services Centers, which offer a variety of benefits to vulnerable persons, including those displaced by Katrina. The Service Centers serve dinner three nights per week; they provide clean clothing and food that can be stored and consumed without refrigeration. The agency provides transitional housing to more than five hundred people on any given night. Residents may stay for a period of three to twenty-four months while they work with counselors to return to self-sufficiency.

About 20 percent of the population the agency serves are veterans. The Catholic Charities estimates that about eighteen thousand homeless veterans are in the six-county Chicago metropolitan area. The organization devotes a significant share of its attention to the housing and related problems affecting veterans.

In 2006, Catholic Charities opened the Bishop Goedert Residence, which is a seventy-unit subsidized apartment complex located on the Veterans Administration campus in Hines, Illinois, developed to provide affordable housing for veterans. The organization also provides housing at Cooke's Manor, which is located on the Hines campus as well, for veterans who are struggling with addiction. The VA recently chose Catholic Charities to participate in a pilot project that will result in five new housing developments across the country to be built for homeless veterans. The site of the pilot project is the St. Leo Campus, located ten miles south of downtown Chicago. The development is projected to consist of 141 studio apartments plus space for services to address the needs of eight thousand vulnerable veterans in the area.

Another program focuses on low-income seniors who have difficulty caring for themselves. The 2009 annual report states that the agency provided independent living apartments for 1,500 seniors.

The agency has created a series of programs designed to strengthen families. In addition to the Emergency Assistance Centers, which are open to families, it operates a Family Shelter program; New Hope Apartments, which are scattered site apartments; and six regional offices where vulnerable persons can get a hot meal once a week. It is in the process of developing the St. Mary's Family Center in Berwyn, Illinois, which is projected to have the capacity to provide day-care services to 213 at-risk children. It established the Health Family Relationships and Marriages Initiative to help low-income mothers and fathers improve their relationships with each other. It operates the Lake County Family Self-Sufficiency program, which is intended to break the cycle of poverty and dependence. For women with addictions, it offers the Forever Free Recovery program.

Catholic Charities is the sole provider of the federally funded Women, Infants, and Children's (WIC) Program in the Chicago area. That program operates out of eighteen different locations in cooperation with other agencies and organizations that deliver health and social services in the area. A fact sheet, published in 2010, reports that Catholic Charities provided 5,655,329 meals to a total of 414,175 clients through a variety of programs aimed at reducing food insecurity over the past year.

Literature produced by the organization that focuses on the effects of poverty on the family outlines Catholic Charities' perspective on the issue:

Poverty threatens everything sacred to the family. It threatens life, it brings instability and it takes away safety and security. Poverty indiscriminately strikes out at adults, children and seniors, both as individuals and together as families. Unchecked, it spreads through a community like an infectious disease; it passes from one generation to another like a genetic trait; and it paralyzes and instills fear like inoperable cancer. Poverty also comes with its own mythology, including the primary myth that it is a disease of the lazy; that it can be overcome or avoided simply by hard work.

For a fuller discussion of the topic, the agency refers people to its seventh annual position paper on poverty released in the fall of 2005: *Overcoming Challenges, Transforming Lives: Women in Poverty*. The paper's main objective is pressing government agencies to streamline the processes that are supposed to provide services for poor women. A paper discussing Catholic Charities' work during a particularly stressful period in preparation for the 2009 annual meeting, titled *Promoting a Culture of Life for the Common Good*, outlines the Catholic Church's teachings on dealing with the challenges presented by poverty.

Organizational funding

Catholic Charities' 2009 annual report indicates an operating budget of $137,879,000. Its revenues come from the following sources: 87.8 percent from government grants, 9.5 percent from program fees, and 2.7 percent from contributions. It spends 1.6 percent on fund-raising and 7.3 percent on management and general expenses.

This financial picture may come as a surprise to many, that is, finding that Catholic Charities receives nearly 90 percent of the funds it uses from the government. From the organization's perspective, the fact that such a large proportion of its budget comes in the form of government grants is a mixed blessing. Although the level of funding it receives from government clearly indicates government agencies have developed confidence in the ability of Catholic Charities to deliver on the commitments it makes in how it spends those funds, there is no guarantee the money will be available from year to year. This means, according to the chief financial officer, the agency is operating at an uncomfortably high level of financial insecurity. Should the government discontinue any of the grants that support so many of its programs, the agency would be facing a crisis. The 2009 annual report makes this clear by stating that the agency ended the fiscal year with a deficit of nearly $20 million.

The lack of funds may become apparent under totally unanticipated circumstances. The press release Catholic Charities issued in April 2007 describes one particular crisis (the story and quotes come from a *Chicago Tribune* story reported by Casillas and Brachear 2007). The agency announced it would be discontinuing its foster care program after ninety years because the agency's insurer dropped its coverage. Catholic Charities had established the service in 1921, forty-three years before the state created the Department of Children and Family Services and mandated that the new agency assume responsibility for identifying children needing placement. However, Catholic Charities remained the oldest and the largest program in the state, caring for nine hundred children until 2007. It was forced to discontinue operations when it could not find another insurer willing to provide coverage.

The problem stemmed from a 1995 lawsuit that resulted in a $12-million payout. The suit was on behalf of three children ages one, two, and three, who were subjected to cigarette burns and forced by the foster parents to eat off the floor. Although this was an obviously regrettable situation, most commentators agreed such things can happen and are difficult to identify when children are too young to speak up for themselves. Comments by outside experts, for example, a University of Chicago faculty member, outline the significance of the agency being forced to discontinue services: "For them to be pulling out of the business in a major city like Chicago is a major challenge for the field. . . . It doesn't bode well for the public-private partnership that has existed in child welfare for 100 years. That's a big deal." The state is in the position of having to find other smaller and possibly less-experienced agencies to take over the care of the nine hundred children. It is rare that an agency with this kind of record and reputation would be unable to obtain insurance after one lawsuit, even if it was an especially costly lawsuit. Indeed, that is what was apparently especially troubling to many observers.

Foster care provides an excellent illustration of the complexities involved when one focuses on housing, because the need for housing involves people of varying ages and varying family situations. Simply supporting housing initiatives is not enough to address the needs of the people being housed, whether they are very young, very old, or incapacitated in any number of ways. Housing vulnerable clients quickly points to the need for all kinds of additional services.

LATIN UNITED COMMUNITY HOUSING ASSOCIATION (LUCHA)

Let us now turn to the third organization addressed in this chapter—LUCHA, which is a secular community-based nonprofit organization.

Organizational mission

The mission of the Latin United Community Housing Association (LUCHA) is to stabilize the Latino community and other residents of Humboldt Park, West Town, Hermosa, and Logan Square by developing decent and afford-able housing and providing housing services. LUCHA provides technical and community organizing assistance, housing advocacy, housing rehabilitation, and construction and home-ownership counseling. LUCHA uses a commu-nity-controlled approach through which home owners, tenants, and landlords enhance their pride in ownership. This requires their participation in the development, preservation, and control of the local housing stock.

Organizational history

LUCHA says of itself that it "was founded in 1981 by a group of citizens of West Town, Humboldt Park, and Logan Square who were concerned about the loss and deterioration of the affordable housing stock in the community as well as the lack of affordable housing for low-income residents. It has evolved to become a premier provider of affordable housing, including the first single room occupancy residence SRO constructed in the City of Chica-go since 1950. LUCHA has also effectively organized community members to advocate for better housing services from the government and the private sector. Finally, it has worked with community residents to access housing products and services and provided them with housing counseling and tech-nical assistance. Along the lines of our mission, LUCHA has accomplished improving the housing stock in order to make the community more attractive in the eyes of lenders and businesses."

During its first year of operations, 1981, the agency negotiated a $1 million reinvestment program with a local bank. By the end of the decade, it completed a $2.45 million rehabilitation project of one apartment building and initiated an $800,000 project aimed at providing additional housing for low-income residents in the community. Over the following decade, LUCHA implemented a $16 million loan program for first-time home buyers, recruit-ed more than six thousand Latino applicants to the Section 8 rental subsidy program, and developed a state-of-the-art office building at its current loca-tion. This is also when it succeeded in obtaining $3.3 million to build the first SRO (single resident occupancy) building developed in Chicago within the past fifty years, which now provides housing for sixty-eight single men and women.

In 1985, it helped establish twelve resident block clubs that could serve as the source of information about community needs. In 1987, it partnered with the city to assist 150 families to build new facades for their homes. By 2000, it had helped purchase homes by providing financial assistance to cover down payment and closing costs. In 2006, it completed development of thir-ty-six units of affordable rental housing by constructing eleven new apart-ment buildings in a $7.5 million development project.

Organizational structure

These accomplishments have largely come about in conjunction with LU-CHA's community development work. The executive director explains that the agency's position is that it is best to involve community members from the beginning.

Accordingly, the organization works toward this goal through five pro-gram areas. These are:

1. Community Organizing department—is primarily responsible for or-ganizing residents who are then asked to, first, identify the area's needs; and second, to participate in advocating for funding and financ-ing to rebuild the community
2. Homeownership Reinvestment department—offers financial assis-tance to help pay for down payment and closing costs
3. Housing Services department—helps with roof and porch repair, heat-ing unit repair and replacement; is responsible for the Senior Citizen Repair program, Emergency Housing Assistance program, and provi-sion of "forgivable" loans in some instances
4. Energy Conservation department—helps to connect residents with contractors who will seal cracks, insulate walls and ceilings, repair doors and windows free of charge for qualifying households; helps residents understand how to lessen costs of energy
5. Building department—is responsible for rehabbing dilapidated build-ings and turning empty lots into affordable housing

The first step LUCHA takes in considering a new project is to present com-munity residents with information about the status of their community. Those who express interest are then invited to learn more. Getting community members involved leads to discussions about the nature of the problems confronting the community. That leads, in turn, to identifying solutions to those problems. At that stage, the agency arranges to offer a range of work-shops on how to obtain funding to rehabilitate property, to get support for improvements that cut energy costs, to understand how to influence develop-ers who are building expensive town houses that local residents cannot af-ford, and so on.

A full understanding of the finances involved in operating rental property illustrates the problem very well. The average rent in the surrounding com-munity for a family-sized, three-bedroom apartment without heat in 2006 was about $1,800 per month. That is $21,600 per year just to rent the space, which is clearly unaffordable for a low-income family. When the agency announced it would be making thirty-five apartments available at an affordable rent in November 2006, it received eight hundred applications. Applicants had to have an income in the range of $28,000 to $30,000 to qualify. That event clearly indicates there is a critical shortage of affordable housing in the area.

The underlying issue is that so many residents of the neighborhood do not have sufficient income to rent, much less to buy a house. Accordingly, LUCHA sees its role not only as a developer of housing, but as a developer of job opportunities that will provide people with enough money to save for a house, and ultimately an increased rate of home ownership that will produce greater community stability and vitality.

Although the executive director is pleased to say the agency has not had any foreclosures on houses it helped residents buy before 2008, he has had other headaches. For example, the year before, the organization was losing renters because a drug dealer had set up business across the street from one of the LUCHA rental buildings. It seems that one of the tenants was giving the drug dealer access so he could contact residents in the building. The executive director explained that he had to hire a security company to monitor the comings and goings of the drug dealer, to identify any accomplices, and to initiate revocation of the rental contract of the offending resident, which finally led one evening to the arrest of four people engaged in the sale of drugs. In the meantime, LUCHA lost the rental income of the tenants who left and paid $5,000 or $6,000 to get rid of the drug dealer—not an insignificant sum to an agency that would prefer to use the money in other ways.

The agency is staffed by twenty to twenty-five people, some of whom are unpaid college student interns.

Organizational funding

The agency is a member of a 35-community development consortium, all competing for the same declining pool of dollars. The following is based on a 2006 report, which is the most recent report that is publicly available. HUD had cut its budget by 10 percent the previous year and 7.5 percent the year before that. In 2006, the agency had an operating budget of $1.5 million; 30 percent or $5 million of that is development and property management revenue; $400,000 from government grants; $600,000 to $700,000 from banks, corporations, and foundations.

Some of its funding comes from the city. It receives support through four separate contracts with the city: Chicago Housing Development, Housing Resource Center, Home Repair Program for Seniors, and Home Ownership Counseling Center. LUCHA also depends on funding from various corporate foundations and banks. However, some of its support comes from in-kind assistance rather than direct funding, as is the case of the People's Energy, the local supplier of electricity to the city, which negotiates a reduced rate for some of LUCHA's projects.

Organizational evaluation

LUCHA has been conducting annual community assessments, which it uses to inform residents of the status of the community. It has used the same information in advocating for additional resources in appealing to the city, foundations, and corporate donors. It has responded to its funders' expectation that it will evaluate its performance through information presented in its annual report. It presents detailed information to prospective funders regarding the loans, rental properties, and rehabilitation projects. It has not been conducting other types of systematic evaluations to date. Of course, the organization requests and receives regular feedback from members of the community.

However, it also recognizes this is not the same as a systematic evaluation. The result is that two senior members of the staff are attending monthly workshops designed to help them develop an evaluation instrument. The challenge is to develop measures that focus on tracking benefit to the community, to individual residents and families, to the city, and to society. This is obviously not an easy assignment. LUCHA recognizes it will have to invest more time and effort to do it right.

WHAT WE CAN LEARN FROM THESE THREE ORGANIZATIONS

Bethel Life and LUCHA are bottom-up organizations based in their respective communities and responsive to local residents. Catholic Charities is a division of a larger hierarchical organization, the Archdiocese of Chicago, which itself is part of a worldwide organization. The Archdiocese is primarily engaged in the church activities of parishes, which are largely concerned with operating grade schools throughout the city. Thus, Catholic Charities constitutes one part of a bigger and more complex enterprise. It is certainly not a bottom-up organization because it does answer to the Archdiocese, which provides some of its funding and is involved in setting its agenda. It is unlike the other two organizations in another respect—it is not based in a particular community. It aims to address the problems presented by certain groups of individuals across the entire city of Chicago. By contrast, Bethel New Life and LUCHA are highly regarded within their local communities but not well known outside of those communities. Another difference is that Catholic Charities has a much longer history in the city and has a presence in communities across the city. In other words, a broader range of stakeholders have reason to know about and be interested in the work of Catholic Charities than is true of the work being carried out by the other two organizations.

The three have in common direct dealings with the beneficiaries they aim to serve. None of the beneficiaries of the services the three agencies provide are in a position to pay for those services. Virtually all of the beneficiaries of the three organizations serve are divorced from the funders. All three receive a substantial portion of their funding through government grants—nearly 90 percent in the case of Catholic Charities, 70 percent in the case of Bethel New Life, and 30 percent in the case of LUCHA. It is worth noting that the two faith-based organizations receive a far larger share of their funding from the government. There is no question that the government is partnering with these organizations because they are committed to providing services to the most vulnerable populations. This observation illustrates the extent to which public-private partnerships have evolved to provide safety net services.

The more support these organizations can obtain on top of government funding, the greater their sense of financial security. The kind of government aid they receive also makes a difference. Bethel New Life obtains some of its funding by providing services other than housing; health care, for example, is paid for by both federal and state government agencies, namely Medicare and Medicaid. Reimbursements from these two agencies are fees-for-services rendered. Relying on this funding stream has generally been less risky than relying on government funding that comes in the form of grants.

Grants typically only partially cover the range of services the organizations we have encountered in this chapter offer. Housing grants generally do not include funds to assist with the costs of food, clothing, and a variety of other social services. The organizations must apply for additional funding for any of these additional services if and when they decide to offer them. Such services may or may not qualify for government grants, but may be essential in the case of some beneficiaries if they are to overcome the difficulties in their lives that have brought them to the doors of these organizations in the first place.

Developing affordable housing is an initiative for which the government is providing a decreasing amount of funding. The goal of making affordable housing available to beneficiaries who are not fully prepared to purchase a house presents a complex challenge. The challenge not only involves teaching the prospective buyers what they need to know to be home buyers. It involves getting local lending institutions to lend money to people who might not ordinarily qualify for a loan. Major banks are not much interested in dealing with individuals who require relatively small amounts of money to buy houses in struggling communities. On the other hand, major banks have apparently made enough loans to people who were not able to meet their payments that they are considered primarily responsible for the economic downturn that the country began experiencing in 2008.

Small local banks have more reason to be interested in the expectation that rising community fortunes will produce an increasing number of customers. However, local banks are also more vulnerable because they do not have vast monetary reserves to fall back on in case people default on their loans. Community banks must be certain the value of the houses for which they issue loans will not drop below the amount they lend. Should the homeowner default, the lending institution wants be sure it can get its money back by selling the house for at least as much as the money it has loaned to the buyer. Assurance that the lender is not taking too much risk depends on the prospects for future community stability and, with any luck, community improvement and rising value of housing stock. Rising housing value means homeowners may eventually be able to sell that house and buy a house of higher value, returning to the bank for an even bigger loan, hopefully in the same community. At the same time, rising housing values has the perverse effect of making an increasing number of houses unaffordable.

As an aside, the director of external affairs at Bethel New Life makes the point that the idea of moving up and out of the neighborhood is not something people in her neighborhood understand. She says it's a yuppie thing. In her community, once you manage to buy a house, you stay there. You become a stable member of the community, which is a real benefit to the community. At the same time, this is the source of an emergent problem. Retired persons on a fixed income, especially elderly women, living alone, have difficulty maintaining their homes. This threatens to cause housing values to fall. Neighbors have been willing to pitch in and help each other, but eventually that may not be enough.

As is clear, housing presents a much more complicated set of challenges than one might expect at first glance. However, housing is a basic need. Whether the aim is to provide housing for vulnerable populations with the expectation that the beneficiaries will become self-sufficient or whether the aim is to assist people so they are able to rent an apartment or buy a house, a housing mission involves providing a great many more services. None of the three organizations can count on a clearly identifiable set of stakeholders ready to support them based on a standing interest in their respective activities.

Who are the stakeholders in these cases depends on the set of beneficiaries we wish to focus on. Both Catholic Charities and Bethel New Life aim to help people who are totally dependent on the agencies, not only for housing, but for all other needs. Both depend on various government programs to carry out their work.

Bethel New Life and LUCHA are both committed to community development of the geographic communities in which they operate. This is not a goal to which Catholic Charities aspires. Bethel New Life and LUCHA strive to encourage members of their respective communities to become actively engaged in community affairs (i.e., to become stakeholders with an interest in community improvement). They also aim to convince lending institutions to become stakeholders. Both organizations make every effort to convince local political representatives to lend support and become vested stakeholders. Turning beneficiaries of the services these organizations offer, who are there because they cannot help themselves, into stakeholders with a voice in organizational programming is the ultimate goal.

In all three cases it is true that the wider the range of supportive stakeholders they can develop, the better. Coming closer to achieving that goal would not only help in securing the funds the organizations need to operate the programs they offer, but the need for certain programs would not be as pressing.

Chapter Fourteen

Conclusion

In the body of this book, we examined the workings of a selected number of nonprofit organizations. It is now time to see what we can learn by considering what the case studies in combination can tell us. In other words, we will now be looking for points of commonality and of contrast. If we had looked at the stories presented by more organizations, we might be dealing with even more insights—that is the nature of case analysis. However, we do have quite a few observations to work through as it is. Let's start with the broadest observations and work toward more specific linkages and interpretations.

As we saw in the early chapters of this volume, nonprofit organizations have been growing in size and scope in the recent past. This has brought broader attention to what nonprofit organizations do and how they do it. It has also provided critics with greater momentum to voice their complaints regarding aspects of what a particular nonprofit organization or nonprofits in general are doing. In short, the growth and development of this sector explains why the level of clamor regarding the role nonprofits play has been escalating in recent years.

Given that nonprofit organizations have been assuming an increasing responsibility, we should not be surprised to find them becoming more resolute in the effort to increase the resources at their disposal so they can better achieve the objectives they have identified. The upshot is that a greater number of nonprofit, charitable organizations have become widely known, not only for their causes, but for their fund-raising campaigns, special events, and the amount of money they are able to raise. Newer, smaller nonprofit organizations, which are materializing at an unprecedented rate, are undoubtedly surprised to find they must be very creative and determined in promoting themselves and their causes in order to attract recognition and support in what is now a crowded field.

As a result of all the publicity nonprofit organizations have been receiving, organizational representatives have been forced to be more cognizant of increasingly larger numbers of stakeholders, who come to the nonprofit sector with varying goals regarding what they expect the organizations to accomplish. Those who speak for nonprofit organizations are finding they must respond to the demands presented by previously uninvolved onlookers who suddenly see themselves as having a stake in what a particular or whole category of nonprofits are doing. The organizational officers and staff must treat the queries and suggestions coming from such onlookers with deference, because nonprofit organizations depend on the support of a mix of stakeholders for their survival. They must be careful to avoid the pitfalls that come from trying to please some by taking steps or making statements that result in the alienation of others.

It is important to keep in mind that the most assertive invested stakeholders are not necessarily supporting the work of nonprofits for the same reasons. In fact, as we found earlier, they may be lining up on opposite sides of the fence. Frumkin captures the difference well (2002, 17–19). He says that on one side we find those who see themselves as "a self-selected group of socially committed individuals dedicated to the idea of making a difference and initiating change." They tend to see nonprofit organizations as ideal and untainted partners to government, able to deliver services to the most disadvantaged, whose interests do not receive attention from mainstream organizations that are more responsive to supply and demand considerations. Furthermore, they are attracted to nonprofit political activity and the ability of such organizations to mobilize groups around issues in a distinctive way. They see the nonprofit sector as "a means to exert pressure for social change and justice" through programs that are basically funded by the government.

On the other side are those who are interested in backing the efforts of nonprofits precisely because they see them as "an appealing alternative to direct public expenditures on social programs." These people are convinced that publicly supported social programs produce poor results. They tend to believe nonprofits, especially faith-based nonprofits, can bring a moral or spiritual component to social programs that public entitlement programs lack. And they think nonprofits offer innovative local solutions, which they consider to be "a powerful alternative to the ongoing search for uniform national solutions" to society's problems.

This assessment of the differences in the underlying impetus for supporting the expansion of the nonprofit sector brings us back to the observations Alexis de Tocqueville and Robert Putnam made about American society. As you will recall, de Tocqueville documented the readiness of Americans to participate in voluntary organizations of all sorts during the first half of the nineteenth century; and a century and half later, Putnam declared that the rate of participation in voluntary organizations had declined dramatically.

One of the trends Putnam considered to be particularly lamentable was that people were increasingly substituting sending a check in place of finding the time to participate in voluntary organizations. Of course, this phenomenon is not difficult to understand. It is due, in part, to the fact that so many more women are working now than was true decades ago. The result is that others in the family must pitch in to accomplish all the tasks that were traditionally handled by stay-at-home wives. Thus everyone in the household is spending more time dealing with the demands of both work and home, leaving far less time to devote to outside activities. And as we all know, even when people are away from the workplace, many are electronically tied to it during what is supposed to be their free time.

There is no question that Putnam's observation, that sending a check produces a very different connection to nonprofit, voluntary organizations than actually volunteering one's time and doing so in person, is an important one. Sending a check is, however, better than not sending one. For now, as I see it, the nonprofit sector would not be expanding if the organizations involved were not receiving a steady stream of support—support coming in various forms (i.e., time and money, from a variety of sources).

Whether Americans are giving enough, participating enough, or volunteering enough are not easily answered questions. Enough for what? Putnam made the attention-grabbing and controversy-inspiring observation that participation in voluntary organizations is necessary to ensure the quality of civic life. Seven years after he made that pronouncement in *Bowling Alone*, he issued a revised assessment of America's future, indicating there might be reason to hope that Americans have not entirely abandoned their sense of community and all that it implies. This was in response to the findings presented in *Volunteering in America: 2007 State Trends and Rankings in Civic Life* issued by the Corporation for National and Community Service. That report stated that 61.2 million Americans volunteered in 2006, which, as the authors of the report point out, appears to be a historic high. In commenting on the report, Putnam puts it this way: "It tells all Americans how we are doing as citizens. Citizenship is not a spectator sport, and we can all do better. This report points the way."

Taking our cue from the latter observation, I would add that developing a better understanding of what particular nonprofits do and how they do it, as we have done here, should lead to greater appreciation of the extent to which their efforts produce a sense of social connectedness and community. It should help explain something that is basically intangible—that is, how nonprofits advance the quality of civic life, which Putnam says is the ultimate benefit nonprofit organizations can bestow. And it is worth recalling that this point of agreement is shared by all those folks standing on opposite sides of the fence we pointed to earlier—arguing for the superiority of private, for-profit versus public, government approaches for addressing social issues.

With that said, let us now embark on a more targeted comparative apprai-
sal of the organizations we have studied by returning to the insights found in
the two classic case studies on the National Foundation for Infantile Paralysis
by David Sills and the YMCA by Mayer Zald.

ANALYTICAL FRAMEWORK AND THE TWO CLASSIC CASES

According to David Sills, the founders of the National Foundation believed
the biggest threat to the organizational mission they set forth was goal displacement. This is still considered to be a crucial concern among nonprofit
organizations. However, it is currently more commonly referred to as "mission drift." Sills was among the first to make the point that vague, amorphous, and hard-to-measure organizational goals are at great risk of being
displaced. In the case of the National Foundation, the organizational purpose
it had set forth could have been displaced several ways.

To begin with, the increase in the amount of money raised each year
could have easily become the organization's primary performance indicator,
displacing the goal of finding a cure for polio. After all, it is far more
satisfying to know that one is making progress, as indicated by an increase in
the amount of money being raised, than it is to keep funding research to find
a cure for a disease, because research generally does not move at a steady and
predictable pace. That made the exact rate of the National Foundation's
organizational success difficult to assess even as there might have been good
reason to think that the research agenda was advancing. Scholars have traditionally referred to this as a challenge to the means-ends continuum. This
concept captures the idea that the "means" (i.e., mechanisms put in place to
attain particular goals) can displace the "ends" or goals if sufficient attention
is not devoted to keeping them separated. It is easy to see how a short-term
goal that is easy to measure might present an attractive alternative to a long-
term, hard-to-measure objective.

Sills spent some time outlining the risks to the mission presented by two
sets of participants or stakeholders. He made clear that the founders of the
National Foundation recognized that the activities members of local chapters
were engaged in—namely, caring for friends and neighbors afflicted with
polio—were so compelling they could easily have drained off all the resources that, in their view, should go toward finding a cure for polio, the
basic goal to which the founders of the parent organization were committed.

A related source of risk Sills identified stemmed from the risk that careerism posed. The founders of the National Foundation did not consider the
annual chairmen of the national campaign to present much of a risk of engaging in careerism or tolerating goal displacement. The fact that they were
selected because they were highly successful businessmen made it less likely

they would be interested in maintaining the position of chairman or working to shift organizational resources away from research so that more polio victims could be helped.

The founders thought the real risk of careerism would manifest in the case of administrators of local chapter offices. The founders believed chapter administrators might expand the programs the chapter was offering to benefit victims in the community in order to develop more support from local contributors. The administrators could then need to increase the staff answering to them, which would require expending more money on office space and supplies. This would require raising funds to maintain the local chapter's facility and staff salaries. The most ambitious local administrators could then recruit more influential supporters who they could mold into a forceful local constituency. All this would clearly drain resources from the parent organization's primary goal to find a cure for polio.

The founders' directive requiring the local chapters to rely on volunteers rather than a permanent staff functioned to avoid the risk of careerism and of goal displacement at the local level. Besides, recognition of and dread of polio was so widespread there was no concern about a shortage of volunteers interested in helping to care for their neighbors. A steady stream of new volunteers not only helped to keep enthusiasm high, it helped to prevent entrenchment of persons who could hoard information and prevent other volunteers from becoming recognized for their contributions.

Sills makes it clear the two categories of stakeholder did not overlap in most cases. The local volunteers and the national campaign administrators were not likely to be acquainted with each other, so the chance that they might join together to form a coalition in order to challenge the organization's goals was very small. Like the local chapter staff, the national campaign chairmen were volunteers; they served for a few months over one year and would not be invited to serve again in future years. The volunteers connected to the local chapters may have served for much longer periods, but there was turnover there as well. The two categories of volunteers had little opportunity to get together to plan any activities. The beneficiaries of the national campaign, the researchers, and the beneficiaries of the local chapters, persons afflicted with polio, did not share goals and would not have much reason to interact.

Consider the categories of stakeholders we identified originally: 1) recipients or beneficiaries; 2) funders; 3) persons in organizational leadership positions; 4) members of the community of interest; and 5) outside interested parties such as evaluators, regulatory agencies, and so on. Of these, the National Foundation founders, who constituted the organizational leadership, were unquestionably the single most influential category of stakeholders. The organizational structure they created allowed for little chance of overlap of interests, activities, and opportunities across stakeholders to pose a challenge to the founders' definition of the organizational mission or arrangements for attaining the goal set forth in the mission statement. They decided how fund-raising would be conducted, how the money they collected would be distributed, and took full responsibility for evaluating organizational performance.

The YMCA case Mayer Zald documented is a story in which neither mission drift nor goal displacement is of concern, because the organization put so much emphasis on "means" rather than "ends" from the start. The organizational goal was, and is, anything but concrete. How the organization goes about the task of achieving the organizational mission is wide open to interpretation and the influence of participants, who are also the major stakeholders. As you will recall, that is exactly the way the founders wanted it to be. According to Zald, the YMCA program recipients or beneficiaries were in an excellent position to determine the programs the local Y with which they were affiliated would offer because they were simultaneously the principal funders and members of the primary community of interest. Their collective readiness to pay a fee for a particular program served as the unmistakable indicator of the value of a program and was recognized to serve this purpose by all concerned. Thus they also served as program evaluators and source of the evidence on program success that informed those in the position of organizing programs. From the beginning, the overlap across the range of stakeholder categories was built into the organizational structure. The combination served to trump the role played by any one stakeholder category, including the leadership at the local level as well as the national headquarters.

These two classic case studies tell us a great deal about the relationship between the organizational mission and the other organizational features we focused on in each case study we discussed. The cases say a lot about how the organizational mission is defined and by whom; how the design of the organizational structure works to advance the mission; how funding arrangements affect programming; and, finally, the extent to which evaluation of the organization's performance is related to who is evaluating the organization's efforts to attain its basic mission.

Moving from the insights the two classic studies provided, let's see what insights we can come up with in reviewing the findings based on the case analyses we conducted using the four-factor framework—mission, structure, funding, and evaluation. It goes without saying that different categories of stakeholders can be seen playing a central role in each of the cases.

COMPARATIVE CASE ANALYSIS: *MISSION* AND *STRUCTURE*

Under ideal circumstances, the organizational structure functions as the bridge that allows the organization to translate its mission into programs and activities. It is important to understand, however, that the bridge operates as a two-way street—any structural changes an organization makes are likely to have a feedback effect on the mission. Decisions that involve structural changes, such as introduction of new programs, shifts in the needs or demands presented by new and different categories of recipients of services, an expanding number of beneficiaries, and so on, will almost certainly have an impact on the organizational mission. It is not that organizations should not be making such changes. It is that the implications of making changes need to be well thought out to prevent goal displacement, mission drift, or, put more simply, the need to redirect funds from planned programming. Unanticipated problems and complications could redirect the flow of resources, which could alter the organization's focus as well as its identity.

The organizations we considered vary a great deal in size; and that, in turn, told us something about the way they wish to present themselves to the public, the challenges they are willing to take on, constituencies they interact with, and so on. Organizational expansion may have substantial implications for organizational structure. Growth to serve a larger number of beneficiaries is, of course, an important objective. Growth that is based on expanding the kinds of clients the organization serves requires more deliberation. Growth for the sake of growth is not particularly advantageous.

In some of the cases we examined, the organizations established separate units that they created specifically to provide employment for beneficiaries. Where we have seen such entities operating, we found that they also provided the parent organization with control over a source of income it could use to support its mission. The Chicago Lighthouse for the Blind, Anixter Center, Howard Brown Health Center, and Bethel New Life are noteworthy in this regard.

Another thorny structural question that organizations may face is whether they should operate as members of a larger unit or go it alone. That is the question the Lung Association considered on more than one occasion, making different choices from time to time. Costs and benefits are involved, as we saw, which the organizational leadership had to consider each time the opportunity presented itself.

We also saw organizations finding themselves pressed by stakeholders to grow in new directions even when the organizational leadership had not planned to. Although the Salvation Army is not one of the organizations we studied in any detail, we did note that the unexpected gift from Mrs. Kroc requiring it to build what for the Salvation Army would be extravagant recreational facilities provides us with a graphic illustration of the struggles that can ensue when strings are attached to an exceptionally generous gift. The question that worried the leadership was whether the organization would change given that it could not operate the facilities she envisioned without charging beneficiaries a substantial fee, something it had not done in the past. However, the downturn in the economy made the problem less urgent when it became more difficult to collect enough additional money to establish as many facilities as the gift had specified.

COMPARATIVE CASE ANALYSIS: *MISSION, STRUCTURE,* AND *FUNDING*

There is little question that one of the biggest challenges facing nonprofit organizations is raising enough money to pursue the goals they have set for themselves. The objective in most cases is not so much developing an increasingly larger operating budget but ensuring the existence of a steady and reliable source of funding. Nonprofit scholars disagree somewhat on the best way to achieve that. Some argue that developing a good relationship with stable funding sources—for example, a small number of especially supportive foundations—provides the most secure funding base. A greater number argue for a diverse funding base, because it is far less risky—the "don't put all your eggs in one basket" approach. This is much the same advice personal investment counselors give to individuals. The idea is that if one kind of investment begins to lose value, you can balance the loss with other investments that have a better return. In the nonprofit funding arena, this means raising money from various sources, including the following: granting agencies, both government and private, individual contributions, fees for services, associated for-profit ventures, production of products that can be sold, and special events.

Virtually all the representatives of organizations that rely on government grants, and to a lesser extent foundation grants, for a substantial portion of their funding express concern about the stability of their funding arrangements. The problem, they point out, in relying on grant funding is that foundation and governmental priorities can and do change. In the case of government funding, even without an announced change in priorities, the government may simply reduce funding for programs when it decides to direct its focus and resources to a new overriding priority such as a war, as happened during the first decade of the twenty-first century. The level of both government and foundation funding may decline during downturns in the economy as happened several times over the past few decades, most acutely during the most recent decade. How concerned organizational representatives say they are about heavy reliance on grants varies depending on how secure their other sources of funding are. The Catholic Charities' story illustrates the risks involved in being very highly dependent on government funding, even more so if, as is true in this case, the government does not fund certain related expenses such as insurance to protect the agency against lawsuits.

In other cases the leadership expresses less concern because some portion of the funding comes in the form of fees-for-service in addition to grants. That is true of the Howard Brown Health Center, the Anixter Center, and Bethel New Life, all of which receive more than half of their funding from well-established government programs in the form of fees for services rendered rather than grants, programs that are so well entrenched they are very unlikely to be dropped. In each case, the organizations have also created entities over which they have complete control that bring in a steady stream of funding independent of government grant programs—the Brown Elephant in the case of Howard Brown, contract businesses in the case of Anixter Center, and rental properties in the case of Bethel New Life.

The VNA sustained steady financial loss over the last years of its existence in part because it had become increasingly more dependent on the fees-for-service it was receiving from newly established government programs. This happened because the VNA was suddenly faced with competition for reimbursable services it alone had been providing without this source of funding. The new organizations that came into existence in response to the fees the newly established government programs were paying had organizational goals that were quite different from those the VNA embraced. The VNA had been committed, and continued to be committed, to serving anyone who asked for its services, including persons who did not have health insurance coverage. This is, of course, in sharp contrast to the goals embraced by the newly established competitors, which were not interested in providing services that would not be reimbursed. How much free care, goods, and services a nonprofit can provide without sustaining irreversible financial loss is a critical question, one that is faced by the majority of nonprofits.

In short, the more control over the funding sources the organization has, the more likely it is to feel secure about its revenue, its future, and the viability of its mission. The Chicago Lighthouse, for example, has revenue coming from the industries it operates and sale of products it offers, program fees, public contributions, and investment income in addition to other miscellaneous sources such as special grants from corporations. Similarly, the AIDS Foundation counts on foundation and corporation grants for slightly more than half of its revenue, but balances that by sponsoring a number of highly successful public fund-raising events that account for nearly a third of its revenue.

It is interesting to find instances of organizations that depend largely on public contributions expressing less concern than those that rely on government and foundation funding, which one might assume to be a more reliable source. This is true of the Respiratory Health Association of Metropolitan

Chicago, which receives more than half of its funding from public contributions. It is worth noting, however, that it operates under very special conditions, allowing the leadership to feel reasonably confident that its high-profile fund-raising events, especially the Hustle Up the Hancock event, are so
well established they will continue to be successful, and the revenue coming
from such sources is not at much risk. This is not to say that staff of the
RHAMC expresses no concern about the impact an economic downturn
might have on their ability to support the programs they operate. However,
they do not expect their high-profile programs to result in crippling losses.

The Feeding America funding arrangements are unique, because the organization receives so much of its support through in-kind donations. The
Salvation Army and the Howard Brown Health Center accept in-kind donations as well, but donations of this kind are not their primary source of
revenue or support. In the case of Feeding America, nearly 90 percent of its
revenue comes in the form of donated goods and services, which goes a long
way in accomplishing its objectives. Additional funding comes from public
support, foundation grants, corporate promotions plus funds generated
through internal operations, including network membership fees, conference
fees, publications, and such. This combination of funding sources works for
Feeding America because the amount of money involved is so large. The
organization needs to set aside a very small percentage of its funds to cover
support services at about 2 percent of its total budget; of that, 0.62 percent
covers management and operating costs and 1.36 percent covers the cost of
fund-raising. That leaves 98 percent for the programs Feeding America operates.

Even though Feeding America's administrative expenses are low, the
staff is pleased to describe the new, creative approaches the organization has
instituted to raise more money that will reduce operating expenses even
further and leave more money for program expenses. The challenge, according to staff members, is not so much that the organization is at risk of
declining contributions, but that the economic downturn means the level of
need has risen at an unprecedented rate, more rapidly than the food banks
with which it partners and the pantries they support can address.

COMPARATIVE CASE ANALYSIS: *MISSION, STRUCTURE, FUNDING,* AND *EVALUATION*

At this point let us return to the topic of stakeholders, especially stakeholders
other than funders, who might influence organizational programs, which programs are advanced and which are altered as a result. They all have a role in
monitoring organization activities to ensure that the organizations are working to fulfill their objectives as well as they are able. We have established the

fact that the organizations we have encountered treat their respective missions as the driving force behind the activities and programs they institute. However, because organizational missions are invariably broad, we also know that organizations find it difficult to know how close they are coming to fulfilling their respective missions. As a result, many organizations devote considerable attention to addressing the challenge of identifying the mechanisms they will employ to track their efforts to fulfill their missions, in other words, to self-evaluate.

As the case analyses make clear, organizations that have clients who are in a position to make their needs and wishes known tend to employ very different evaluation mechanisms than those whose clients may be in a position to express their preferences but not in a position to make demands.

Organizations that rely heavily on grants from the government or from foundations know that they must present formal reports to these funding sources on how the money they receive is being used. The grantors want solid evidence that the organizations they fund are using the money effectively and, under the best of circumstances, achieving measurable positive results. Figuring out the best way to assess program effects is a major challenge and one that has inspired a great deal of attention from a variety of observers, particularly policy makers. In order to avoid charges of bias or ineptitude, many nonprofit organizations have turned to academics and various nonprofit consulting groups, who are assumed to be knowledgeable and unbiased, to come up with evaluation measures and instruments.

Some organizations rely more heavily on the evaluation process to provide feedback they can use in strategic planning and future development. The organizations that are most interested in evaluation results tend to be the ones that cannot readily rely on beneficiary satisfaction as an indicator of program effectiveness. The efforts the Anixter Center invested in evaluation illustrate the point. The beneficiaries of Anixter programs receive a great deal of attention because the Anixter Center is committed to measuring how well Anixter programs are serving them, but their satisfaction is not considered to be the best indicator of organizational success.

It is also interesting to consider the difference between evaluations that are designed to assess the impact on individuals and evaluations that report the impact on larger units, such as particular communities or society as a whole. In order to assess the impact on a whole community, the nonprofit organization may find it useful to establish a base of comparison. That is why Feeding America spends some of its resources on assessing the level of hunger that exists in separate communities as well as in the country as a whole. It uses these data to report trends and comment on what it is doing in response to those trends.

Similarly, Bethel New Life and LUCHA are interested in assessing a number of indicators of need for housing including the need for affordable housing in specific communities; the rate at which gentrification is proceeding in those communities, making housing more expensive; the lending practices of local banks; and so on. Both organizations aim to track housing trends and use these as a base of comparison to assess the impact they are having.

In the end we can see that all the attention devoted to improving the technical features of evaluation instruments is crucial. This is pretty much the only mechanism available to both the organizational leaders and all other stakeholders who have an interest in determining whether the people being served by nonprofit organizations are being well served, regardless of whether the money being directed to those organizations comes from the government, foundations, private companies, or individual contributors. For that reason evaluation results are likely to be distributed to all stakeholders to show how successful the organization is in addressing its mission.

Special challenges and how the organizations dealt with them

It is worth returning for a moment to the challenges that the organizations confronted and how they responded. The VNA confronted two challenges later in its life—one, technological change and the price tag attached; and two, competition from the for-profit sector. It chose to reorganize. A couple of organizations can be credited with achieving a very unusual outcome—they fulfilled their respective missions. This was unquestionably clear in the case of the National Foundation for Infantile Paralysis. It happened, but with much less certainty, with the coming of the TB vaccine in the case of the Respiratory Health Association of Metropolitan Chicago. The organizations dealt very differently with what is, on the surface, a similar outcome, in part because of their different organizing structures as well as the attention that existing cases or suspected cases of polio or TB required. The Respiratory Health Association of Metropolitan Chicago illustrates one other interesting characteristic—it has been highly innovative in coming up with unique fund-raising mechanisms. The problem here is that the organization could not patent those mechanisms, so it had to keep coming up with new ideas. The AIDS Foundation faces a related but slightly different problem. It is apparently being flooded with innovative fund-raising ideas—the problem is that the enthusiasm on the part of those with the ideas is not always accompanied by practical experience in carrying them out.

The Anixter Center, which has an impressive growth record over the past half century, has more recently agreed to bring several established nonprofits into the fold. The challenge here is not hard to comprehend—how does the parent organization achieve a balance that allows the merged organizations to maintain their special identity or purpose while sharing the advantages the Anixter name and successful operations offer? They must work that out, because no one has come up with a formula for doing it.

The Feeding America and Greater Chicago Food Depository cases illustrate the challenges involved in accepting in-kind gifts. There is no question both have succeeded in doing this. The problem they both face is that the need for food continues to escalate while the organizations that contribute are facing a downturn in the economy that poses a threat to their profitability and ability to increase their contribution levels.

The most revealing story all nonprofit organizations confront to some extent is captured by the need for affordable housing. The Bethel New Life story is especially poignant. Setting out to address the need for affordable housing quickly led to efforts to help community residents accumulate the funds needed to purchase those affordable houses. That meant Bethel New Life turned to developing employment opportunities for community members so they could establish savings accounts and qualify for bank loans. The next step was to convince the local bank that community members were a good risk. In the meantime, the organization's officers and staff found they had developed an extensive knowledge base related to housing that would help them negotiate advantageous deals with contractors and architects, and not be thrown by urban renewal regulations.

Of course, all of the organizations faced the day-to-day challenges including hiring the right staff, coordinating the work of the volunteers, keeping a close watch on organizational identity and public image, to name a few of those challenges.

Summing it all up, final thoughts, and the new questions they raise

In retrospect, what is most interesting to me in reviewing the case studies is, first, finding how varied the range of objectives and activities is that nonprofit organizations have chosen to embrace; and, second, how closely they come to realizing their objectives. There does not seem to be a single best approach. It is interesting to see that the organizations recognize they must make a serious effort to maintain their focus on the *ends* they are trying to attain rather than the *means* they will use to attain those ends. They must do this to prevent "mission drift." This is worth noting because of the tremendous variation in approaches the organizations we encountered are using to translate their invariably highly abstract and complex missions into practical programmatic agendas without succumbing to mission drift.

And as we have repeatedly observed, the means they employ in pursuing their respective missions have implications for organizational structure. For example, we encountered instances in which organizations had to consider such dilemmas as whether they would be better off discontinuing ties with the national umbrella organization and whether to accept a very generous donation with strings attached. In such cases, those in a position to make the decision did not proceed without engaging in a great deal of soul-searching regarding their missions and the consequences of making structural changes.

The pressing need for funding they all confront is especially interesting to consider, in my opinion, because it shows how much creativity characterizes the workings of these organizations. The cases make clear there is no single best approach. Given sufficient energy and effort, a wide variety of fund-raising approaches can be successful. Finally, we can see that the problems associated with the need to assess program outcomes requires greater attention on the part of some organizations than others, largely because funding agencies require this kind of information and the public does not.

If this discussion leads you to conclude that nonprofit, charitable organizations play a more significant role in our society than you initially realized because they deliver valuable services, then you are getting the primary lesson scholars in this field want you to come away with. However, if the discussion has caused you to consider the extent to which nonprofit organizations provide the venue for the emergence of social ties across members of society who would not otherwise be likely to interact, then you have developed what may be an even more important and more subtle insight, which some scholars believe is the most significant social impact nonprofit organizations can claim—that they have the ability to enhance social civility and create social capital.

In light of this conclusion, ask yourself what motivates the detractors who are so adamant in arguing that nonprofit organizations are not making a valuable social contribution; arguing that they are inefficient and ineffective; and, even more inexplicable, why they are so passionate about it. Is it possible these critics are motivated by a set of values and beliefs that generally go unstated, beliefs that have less to do with the organizations and their work and more to do with their view of individuals who are benefiting from what nonprofits do?

How society sees the people who seek help from nonprofit organizations opens up a set of policy questions to which we have not paid much attention throughout this discussion. Consider the victims of the recent recession. They are sometimes portrayed as blameless victims. The media have also reported that many of these people continue to have difficulty recovering after many months—indeed, a couple of years—have passed. Are the experts and other observers the media presents us with still willing to see them as blameless victims, or has too much time gone by? The policy issues such questions raise include the following: how much responsibility should society take for helping people with life's basic needs—health, food, shelter—when they are not managing to do that for themselves? Should we take the position that everyone in this country deserves basic health care, adequate food, and affordable housing? Does it matter that the country is rich enough to provide everyone with the basics, or is it more important to argue that some people do not look to be striving to achieve those things and are engaging in destructive behavior that is having a negative effect on them and on society? In other words, should we be distinguishing between those whom society deems to be "deserving" and those whom society sees as "undeserving"?

Of course, once one starts thinking about such matters, it is not long before someone might raise the question of whether it would be better to do something before the fact—so fewer people would need help and become "undeserving." Should we be asking if there is good reason to devote society's resources to finding out why some people do not seem to be able to help themselves and use more resources to address those factors? These are obviously not questions to which we will be devoting much more attention at this point in our discussion. However, they seem to me to be well worth reflecting on.

As becomes apparent at this point, only if we agree we should be providing everyone in this country with basic ingredients can we then debate whether we should be relying more extensively on nonprofit organizations or other entities to deliver those goods and services. I fear there is little likelihood that Americans will reach consensus on the answers to these questions soon. Therefore, the best we can hope for at the end of this discussion is that those who value the contribution nonprofit organizations are making might find ways to enhance the efforts of the organizations that are already doing so much to provide the goods and services that benefit the people who continue to need them.

References

Appelbaum, Binyamin, and Robert Gebeloff. 2012. "Americans Feel Conflicted as the Safety Net Expands." *New York Times* (February 12): 1, 24–25.

Badelt, Christopher. 1990. "Institutional Choice and the Nonprofit Sector." In Helmut Anheier and Wolfgang Seibel (eds.), *Third Sector Comparative Studies of Nonprofit Organizations.* Berlin: Walter deGruyter, 53–63.

Bethel New Life, Inc. 2009. "Key Indicators Report" (June).

Bryce, Herrington. 1992. *Financial & Strategic Management for Nonprofit Organizations*, 2nd ed. Englewood Cliffs, NJ: Prentice Hall.

"Buffett Still Has More Money to Give Away." 2006. Associated Press release (July 2).

Burk, Penelope. 2003. *Donor-Centered Fundraising.* Chicago: Cygnus Applied Research, Inc.

Butler, Amy. 2009. "Wages in the Nonprofit Sector: Management, Professional, and Administrative Support Occupations" (April 15). Bureau of Labor Statistics, http://www.bls.gov/opub/cwc/cm20081022ar01p1.htm

Capek, Mary Ellen, and Molly Mead. 2006. *Philanthropy.* Cambridge, MA: MIT Press.

Casillas, Ofelia, and Manya Brachear. 2007. "Catholic Charities Dropping Foster Care." *Chicago Tribune* (April 17): 1–2.

Center for Policy Alternatives. 2005. "Privatizing Prisons." Press release (February 28).

Cho, Sungsook, and David Gillespie. 2006. "A Conceptual Model Exploring the Dynamics of Government—Nonprofit Service Delivery." *Nonprofit and Voluntary Sector Quarterly* 35: 493–509.

"CMS's Special Focus Facility Methodology Should Better Target the Most Poorly Performing Homes Which Tend to Be Chain Affiliated and For-Profit." 2009. GAO-09-689. Washington, DC: United States Accountability Office (August).

Congressional Budget Office. 2011. Trends in the Distribution of Household Income Between 1979 and 2007. Washington, D.C. (October): 21.

de Tocqueville, Alexis. 1969. *Democracy in America*, trans. Lawrence Mayer. New York: Harper & Row.

DiMaggio, Paul. 2001. "Measuring the Impact of the Nonprofit Sector on Society Is Probably Impossible but Possibly Useful: A Sociological Perspective." In Patrice Flynn and Virginia Hodgkinson (eds.), *Measuring the Impact of the Nonprofit Sector.* New York: Kluber Academic/Plenum Publishers, 249–72.

DiMaggio, Paul, and Helmut Anheier. 1990. "The Sociology of Nonprofit Organizations and Sectors," W. Richard Scott and Judith Blake (eds.). *Annual Review of Sociology* 16: 137–59.

DiMento, Marie, and Nicole Lewis. 2007. "Record-Breaking Giving." *Chronicle of Philanthropy* (February 22): 2.

Eisenberg, Pablo (edited by Stacy Palmer). 2005. *Challenges for Nonprofits and Philanthropy: The Courage to Change—Three Decades of Reflections*. Lebanon, NH: Tufts University Press.

Finn, Peter. 1998. "State's First Private Prison Open in March." *Washington Post* (January 18).

Flynn, Patrice, and Virginia Hodgkinson (eds.). 2001. *Measuring the Impact of the Nonprofit Sector*. New York: Kluber Academic/Plenum Publishers.

"Food Stamp Program: FNS Could Improve Guidance and Monitoring to Ensure Appropriate Use of Categorical Eligibility." 2007. U.S. Government Accountability Office (GAO-07-465).

Froelich, Karen. 1999. "Diversification or Revenue Strategies: Evolving Resource Dependence in Nonprofit Organizations." *Nonprofit and Voluntary Sector Quarterly* 28: 246–68.

Frumkin, Peter. 2002. *On Being Nonprofit: A Conceptual and Policy Primer*. Cambridge, MA: Harvard University Press.

Fusaro, Dave. 2005. "Second Harvest . . . Now and Year-Round," *Editor's Plate* online. FoodProcessing.com (October 1).

Galaskiewicz, Joseph, and Wolfgang Bielefeld. 1998. *Nonprofit Organizations in an Age of Uncertainty*. New York: Aldine deGruyter.

Gray, Bradford. 2001. "Measuring the Impact of Nonprofit Health Care Organizations." In Patrice Flynn and Virginia Hodgkinson (eds.), *Measuring the Impact of the Nonprofit Sector*. New York: Kluber Academic/Plenum Publishers, 185–98.

Gronbjerg, Kristen. 1991. "Managing Grants and Contracts: The Case of Four Social Service Organizations." *Nonprofit and Voluntary Sector Quarterly* 20: 5–24.

Handel, Michael. 2003. *Sociology of Organizations: Classical, Contemporary and Critical Readings*. Thousand Oaks, CA: Sage.

Himmelstein, Jerome. 1997. *Looking Good and Doing Good: Corporate Philanthropy and Corporate Power*. Bloomington: Indiana University Press.

Hopkins, Bruce. 2005. *Starting and Managing a Nonprofit Organization: A Legal Guide*. 4th ed. Hoboken, NJ: Wiley.

Hutton, Stan, and Frances Phillips. 2005. *Nonprofit Kit for Dummies*. 2nd ed. New York: Wiley.

James, Estelle. 1990. "Economic Theories of the Nonprofit Sector: A Comparative Perspective." In Helmut Anheier and Wolfgang Seibel (eds.), *Third Sector Comparative Studies of Nonprofit Organizations*. Berlin: Walter deGruyter, 21–29.

Jensen, Brennen. 2007. "Lung Group's Stair Climb Has a Leg Up on Other Charity Races." *Chronicle of Philanthropy* (March 22).

Johnston, David. 2006. "The Ultra-Rich Give Differently from You and Me." *New York Times* (July 2): BW3.

Joslyn, Heather. 2002. "Nonprofit Employees Are More Satisfied Than Other Workers with Their Jobs, Says New Brooking Survey—But Problems Loom." *Chronicle of Philanthropy*'s Philanthropycareers online (October 10).

Kanter, Rosabeth Moss, and David Summers. 1987. "Doing Well While Doing Good: Dilemmas of Performance Measurement in Nonprofit Organizations and the Need for a Multiple-Constituency Approach." In Walter Powell (ed.), *The Nonprofit Sector: A Research Handbook*. New Haven, CT: Yale University Press, 154–66.

Kissane, Rebecca, and Jeff Gingerich. 2004. "Do You See What I See? Nonprofit and Resident Perceptions of Urban Neighborhood Problems." *Nonprofit and Voluntary Sector Quarterly* 33: 311–33.

Lewis, Nicole. 2007. "Wealthy Americans Increased Their Giving by 20% Last Year." *Chronicle of Philanthropy* (May 17): 17.

Light, Paul. 2002. *Pathways to Nonprofit Excellence*. New York: Aspen Institute, Brookings Institution Press.

Lipman, Harvey, and Ian Wilhelm. 2003. "Pressing Foundations to Give More." *Chronicle of Philanthropy* (May 29): 7–9.

Lynch, Marie, Jennifer Engle, and Jose Cruz. 2010. "Subprime Opportunity: The Unfulfilled Promise of For-Profit Colleges and Universities." Educational Trust.

Mahar, Maggie. 2006. *Money-Driven Medicine*. New York: HarperCollins.

Meyer, John, and Brian Rowan. 1977. "Institutionalized Organizations: Formal Structure as Myth and Ceremony." *American Journal of Sociology* 83: 340–63.

Oster, Sharon. 1995. *Strategic Management for Nonprofit Organizations: Theory and Cases.* New York: Oxford University Press.

Pew Research Center. 2010. *The People and the Government: Distrust, Discontent, Anger and Partisan Rancor.* Washington, DC (April 18): 1–142.

Picketty, Thomas, and Emmanuel Saez. 2010. "Income Inequality in the United States, 1913–1998." *Quarterly Journal of Economics* 118 (February 2003): 1–39. (Tables and figures updated to 2008 on the Emmanuel Saez website, July 2010, http//:elsa.Berkely.edu/ ~saez/.)

Pillar, Charles. 2007. "Money Clashes with Mission." *Los Angeles Times* (January 8).

Powell, Walter. 1987. *The Nonprofit Sector: A Research Handbook.* New Haven, CT: Yale University Press.

Powell, Walter, and Elisabeth Clemens. 1998. *Private Action and the Public Good.* New Haven, CT: Yale University Press.

Powell, Walter, and Rebecca Freidkin. 1987. "Organizational Change in Nonprofit Organizations." In Walter Powell (ed.), *The Nonprofit Sector: A Research Handbook.* New Haven, CT: Yale University Press, 180–94.

Powell, Walter, and Richard Steinberg (eds.). 2006. *The Nonprofit Sector: A Research Handbook.* 2nd ed. New Haven, CT: Yale University Press.

Putnam, Robert. 2000. *Bowling Alone: The Collapse and Revival of American Community.* New York: Simon & Schuster.

Ravitch, Diane. 2010. *The Death and Life of the Great American School System.* New York: Basic Books.

Reich, Robert. 2010. "Foreword." In Richard Wilkinson and Kate Pickett, *The Spirit Level: Why Greater Equality Makes Societies Stronger.* New York: Bloomsbury Press, vi.

Roeger, Katie, Amy Blackwood, and Sarah Pettijohn. 2011. "The Nonprofit Sector in Brief." *Nonprofit Almanac 2011.* National Center for Charitable Statistics at the Urban Institute.

Rosenberg, Joseph, Patrick Rooney, C. Eugene Steuerle, and Katherine Toran. 2011. "What's Been Happening to Charitable Giving Recently? A Look at the Data." Urban Institute Center on Nonprofits and Philanthropy and Urban Institute–Brookings Tax Policy Center (October).

Russo, Gina. 2002. "Winning the Talent War: New Brookings Survey Finds the Nonprofit Sector Has the Most Dedicated Workforce." The Brookings Institution press release (October 3).

Sack, Kevin. 2008. "Foundation Starts News Service to Cover Health Care Topics." *New York Times* (November 24): B4.

Salamon, Lester. 1987. "Partners in Public Service: The Scope and Theory of Government-Nonprofit Relations." In Walter Powell (ed.), *The Nonprofit Sector: A Research Handbook.* New Haven, CT: Yale University Press, 99–117.

———. 2003. *The Resilient Sector: The State of Nonprofit America.* Washington, DC: The Brookings Institution Press.

Salamon, Lester, and S. Wojciech Sokolowski. 2006. "Employment in America's Charities." The Johns Hopkins Center for Civil Society Studies (December).

Schemo, Diana Jean. 2006. "Study of Test Scores Finds Charter Schools Lagging." *New York Times* (August 23): A14.

Schlesinger, Mark, and Bradford Gray. 2006. "How Nonprofits Matter in American Medicine, and What to Do about It." *Health Affairs,* Web exclusive (June 20): W287–W303.

Schwinn, Elizabeth. 2003. "Survey of Human-Services Workers Predicts a Labor Exodus." *Chronicle of Philanthropy,* Managing online (April 3).

———. 2007. "Seven American Lung Association Affiliates Sever Ties with National Charity." *Chronicle of Philanthropy* (May 10).

Seefeldt, Kristin, Gordon Abner, Joe Bolinger, Lanlan Xu, and John Graham. 2012. *At Risk: American's Poor during and after the Great Recession.* Bloomington: School of Public and Environmental Affairs, Indiana University.

Sills, David. 1957. *The Volunteers.* New York: Free Press.

Smith, Steven Rathgeb, and Michael Lipsky. 1993. *Nonprofits for Hire: The Welfare State in the Age of Contracting.* Cambridge, MA: Harvard University Press.

Steinberg, Richard. 2006. "Economic Theories of Nonprofit Organizations." In Walter Powell and Richard Steinberg (eds.), *The Nonprofit Sector: A Research Handbook*, 2nd ed. New Haven, CT: Yale University Press, 117–39.

Storch, Charles. 2007. "ALA's Chicago Group Breaking Off on Its Own." *Chicago Tribune* (May 10): Section 5, 5.

Strom, Stephanie. 2006. "Bill Gates' Charity Races to Spend Buffett Billions." *New York Times* (August 13).

———. 2007. "Nonprofit Groups Draw a Line at Some Donors." *New York Times* (January 28): 17.

———. 2009. "Big Salvation Army Project Falls Short of Donor's Vision." *New York Times* (June 15): 13, 14.

Thomas, Landon. 2006. "A Bequest between Friends." *New York Times* (June 27): C1, C4.

Tuckman, Howard, and Cyril Chang. 2006. "Commercial Activity, Technological Change, and Nonprofit Mission." In Walter Powell and Richard Steinberg (eds.), *The Nonprofit Sector: A Research Handbook*, 2nd ed. New Haven, CT: Yale University Press, 629–44.

Weisbrod, Burton. 1988. *The Nonprofit Economy.* Cambridge, MA: Harvard University Press.

———. 2001. "An Agenda for Quantitative Evaluation of the Nonprofit Sector." In Patrice Flynn and Virginia Hodgkinson (eds.), *Measuring the Impact of the Nonprofit Sector.* New York: Kluber Academic/Plenum Publishers, 273–90.

Welytok, Jill Gilbert, and David Welytok. 2007. *Nonprofit Law and Governance for Dummies.* New York: Wiley.

Williams, Grant. 2010. "Number of Charities and Foundations Passes 1.2 Million." *Chronicle of Philanthropy* (March 15).

Young, Dennis. 2001. Social Enterprise in the United States: Alternative Identities and Forms. EMES Conference, Trento, Italy (December 13–15).

Zald, Mayer. 1970. *Organizational Change: The Political Economy of the YMCA.* Chicago: University of Chicago Press.

Index

About the Author

Grace Budrys is professor of sociology at DePaul University in Chicago. She is currently serving as director of the Master of Public Health Program at the university. Her scholarly work has focused on a wide range of health care topics including the health care delivery system, health policy, health disparities, and a number of specific challenges that health organizations and occupations have dealt with over time, such as local health planningorganizations and doctors' unions.